e for **Sonny Liston**
ry Behind the Ali ★ **Liston Fights**

★ Paul Gallender digs into the ring life and psyche of Sonny Liston, one of the most misunderstood athletes of his or any generation. He attempts to portray the real personality of one of boxing's greatest champions who had to fend off Gestapo-like tactics during his career, not only from the police forces of several major American cities, but also by bigoted sportswriters of his time. In all respects, Paul succeeds.
— *J Russell Peltz, boxing promoter, International Boxing Hall of Fame Class of 2004*

★ Nowhere else is there such a detailed account of the Liston-Ali bouts. I think Liston would have approved of Gallender's real story of his fights with Ali. The book is a credit to Sonny and the man he really was.
— *Willie Reddish Jr., Liston's friend and the son of his trainer*

★ Reading many of the pages brought back mixed emotions of my memories of Uncle Charles. I could vividly remember some of the stories Paul recalled in the book, which brought smiles to my face. He painted Sonny in a different light, as a gentle giant, and not, the angry man many proposed him to be.
— *Helen Long, Liston's niece*

★ This book is one of a kind! Gallender will open a lot of eyes about the sport of Boxing and show people what a bad deal my father got. Thanks a lot, Paulie. I know Sonny would have liked you. You could have called the book, THE TRUTH, PLAIN AND SIMPLE.
— *William Wingate, Liston's son*

★ This book is a bird's-eye view of a very, very special human being. Sonny could have been the Black Athlete of the Century.
— *Gary Bates, Liston's sparring partner*

★ I became spellbound by the amount of research Paul did. It was more research than was done on Abraham Lincoln.
— *Lem Banker, sports analyst and handicapper*

SONNY LISTON

SONNY LISTON

THE REAL STORY BEHIND THE
ALI ★ LISTON FIGHTS

PAUL GALLENDER

PARK PLACE PUBLICATIONS
PACIFIC GROVE, CALIFORNIA

SONNY LISTON

The Real Story Behind the Ali–Liston Fights

Paul Gallender

Copyright © 2012 Paul Gallender

All rights reserved under International and Pan-American copyright conventions. No part of this book may be used or reproduced in any manner whatsoever without written permission except in the case of brief quotations embodied in critical articles or reviews.

SOFTCOVER ISBN 978-14781851.85
HARDCOVER ISBN 978-1-935530-65-7

Front cover design by Gene Harris
Interior design by Patricia Hamilton

Published by Park Place Publications
Pacific Grove, California
www.parkplacepublications.com

Printed in U.S.A.

First U.S. Edition: July 2012

www.sonnyliston.net

To Sonny Liston
I got your back.
And so does Josie Roase.

CONTENTS

ACKNOWLEDGEMENTS XIII

INTRODUCTION XV

PART ONE
BEHOLD HIS MIGHTY HANDS 1

CHAPTER ONE
A SUFFICIENCY UNTO HIMSELF 3

CHAPTER TWO
ONE BITCH OF A TOWN 17

CHAPTER THREE
A VALUABLE PROPERTY 31

CHAPTER FOUR
GUILT BY ASSOCIATION 49

CHAPTER FIVE
THE CHAMP NOBODY WANTED 72

CHAPTER SIX
CHAMPION FOR LIFE 90

PHOTO GALLERY

PART TWO
IT WAS BEAUTY KILLED THE BEAST 115

CHAPTER SEVEN
A PERFECT SETUP 117

CHAPTER EIGHT
BOXING IS A SPORT FOR YOUNG MEN 138

CHAPTER NINE
A LOST-HEAD 158

CHAPTER TEN
IT WAS A VERY BAD YEAR 171

CHAPTER ELEVEN
CAUGHT IN THE CROSSFIRE 192

PART THREE
TO LIVE AND DIE IN VEGAS 219

CHAPTER TWELVE
HOME AT LAST 221

CHAPTER THIRTEEN
AND THAT'S THAT 235

EPILOGUE 247

NOTES 251

INDEX 267

ACKNOWLEDGEMENTS

Thirty-five years is a long time to spend writing a book and this biography is a large portion of my life's work. My passion for telling Sonny's story has grown over the years and it has never been greater than it is now.

I've asked everyone I've interviewed the same question: Apart from Ali, who could have beaten Liston? Almost everyone has responded in one of two ways; they've either said "that's a good question," or they said nothing at all. I spoke with very few sportswriters about Sonny because I decided that the time to debate them would be after the publication of this book, rather than before. I'll win those debates because the case I can make for Sonny Liston is as powerful as he had been, in and out of the ring.

Nevertheless, I must pay homage to several writers whose work I greatly admire. Jimmy Breslin, Marshall Smith and Bruce Jay Friedman wrote great pieces about Liston. And I would be remiss if I did not express my admiration for the superb work of several *Sports Illustrated* writers in the 1960s. The journalistic talents of Mark Kram, Jack Olsen, Gilbert Rogin and Barbara La Fontaine clearly outshine mine.

Some of my most important interviews occurred early on. Robert "Barney" Baker, Davey Pearl, Irving "Ash" Resnick and Morris Shenker generously helped me understand the heavyweight champ in a very personal way. Conversing with the great fight historian Jimmy Jacobs showed me that I could indeed hold my own in a discussion about the history of boxing's heavyweight division.

Former champs Floyd Patterson, Ernie Terrell, Joe Frazier, George Foreman, and Jose Torres were gracious in the time they gave me and forthright in their comments and recollections, as were promoters Don Chargin, Truman Gibson, Henry Winston, and Mickey Duff. Speaking with the great trainers Eddie Futch and George Gainford, for me was both informative and exhilarating.

I want to thank Philadelphian George Hansen Jr. for introducing me to Liston's son, William Wingate. William introduced me to Tommy Manning and Mitchell Allen, both of whom knew Sonny well. Getting to know Willie Reddish Jr., whose father trained Sonny, was an absolute pleasure. Thanks also to the Hon. Joseph Casciato and Paul Abdoo Jr. for sharing memories of their fathers with me.

In St. Louis, Jesse Bowdry's daughter, Kim, was responsible for my getting to know two of Sonny's nieces and one of his nephews: Helen Long, Fannie Mae Hopkins and Henry Page all basically welcomed me into their families by sharing their intimate stories, which helped me form an even more in-depth picture of this great man.

In Las Vegas, I came to know many fine people including Sonny's sparring partner, Ben Skelton. Tony Davi was a confidante of Liston's good friend, Johnny Tocco, and Lem Banker was one of the few people who could tell the ex-champ when he was out of line. Gary Bates sparred with Sonny and became one of his best friends, and if I had the inclination to write another biography, he would be my subject. Ali's former business manager, Gene Kilroy, told me some heartfelt stories about his boss. Former police officer Dennis Caputo was one of the few law enforcement officials who never had an ax to grind with Sonny.

By the time she was four years old, Dana Gentry was dear friends with Rocky Marciano, Joe Louis and Sonny. I'm grateful to the great Esquire photographer, Carl Fischer, for allowing me to use a photo he took of Dana and a Santa Claus-clad Liston. Dana's mother, Marilyn Resnick, was close to Geraldine and Sonny Liston, and Martha and Joe Louis, and Marilyn's memories of the Ali rematch in Lewiston were central to my being able to tell the real story about that bout.

Finally, I am indebted to Philadelphia promoter and boxing historian, J. Russell Peltz, for meticulously fact-checking my manuscript. Russell found several errors and for that, my hat is off to the man.

INTRODUCTION

If you were born after 1960, what I'm about to say will probably surprise you. No great athlete was ever more highly regarded by his peers than Charles "Sonny" Liston. Archie Moore was voted the best Light Heavyweight of the 20th Century and he described Sonny as "something extraordinary with a pair of Everlast gloves." Moore told that to *Sport Magazine* a few months *after* Liston lost his title to Muhammad Ali.

Most all-time rankings list the great Joe Louis either first or second best in his division. Moments after Sonny lost his title, Louis matter-of-factly said Cassius Clay had "just beaten the greatest heavyweight champion in history."

The Triple Crown of Compliments was completed when *Today's* Matt Lauer twice asked Muhammad Ali to name his most significant accomplishment in *or out* of the ring. Both times, the man known as the Greatest responded by saying, "beating Sonny Liston," and did so with no hesitation whatsoever.

Boxing's three best big men of all time were in awe of Sonny, as was the entire sports world. Gilbert Rogin's characterization of Liston as the nearest piece of talent to Godzilla was an accurate description both of his ability and the public's perception of him when he was champ. Veteran trainer Angelo Dundee said Liston stood over the division like a colossus. When Louis said, "Nobody's gonna beat Liston 'cept old age," there was no reason or indication to think otherwise. "The second Patterson fight was supposed to be the death knell of boxing because Sonny Liston was unbeatable," said Fred Brooks, the president of Sportsvision whose company provided the fight's closed-circuit telecast.

If you're a man or woman in your 60s or older, you probably remember being in awe of Sonny Liston yourself. From 1959 through 1963 he was the only perfect storm boxing has ever seen. He was to his sport what Babe Ruth was to baseball, what Tiger Woods has been to golf, and what Usain Bolt is to track. He was unbeatable and the best there ever was, but as Jack Olsen wrote in *Sports Illustrated*, "It seems like a hundred years ago...Now it takes almost an act of will to recall the time when Sonny Liston was the most awe-inspiring fighter on earth." Olsen wrote that in 1968.

Sonny took the biggest fall in the history of sports. It began when Liston lost to Ali, at the time a brash adolescent known more for his mouth than his fighting ability. When Liston was forced to lay down against Ali in their rematch 15 months later, his reputation, career and legacy went down with him.

Today, what's generally known about Sonny is an ad nauseam rehash of all of the negative and cruel things that have ever been written or spoken about him. Neil Leifer's famous photo of Liston lying on the canvas looking up at Ali in the first round of their second fight has defined him and his career for more than 45 years. "That Lewiston (Maine) picture has always bothered me," Sonny's niece Helen Long told me. "The memory of him should not be of him lying on the canvas like that." Unfortunately and unfairly, the Lewiston "fight" doomed no less than the second best heavyweight of all-time to a legacy of unrelenting scorn, contempt, and humiliation.

Less than two years after his only successful title defense, Sonny was barred from fighting anywhere in the United States. Just five-and-a-half years later, his wife, Geraldine, returned home to Las Vegas and found his body; he had been dead a week. Today, Liston's place in history is a mere footnote to Muhammad's career. But for Ali's Friday the 13th hernia three days before their scheduled rematch in 1964, it could and probably would have ended up the other way around.

With the exception of Doc Young's 1963 biography, those who have authored books about Liston or referenced him in books about others are dismissive of his talent and contemptuous of him as a human being. Their insults differ only in degree. Here's how bad it's gotten. In his 1992 book on Ali, Ferdie Pacheco wrote, "You have to understand what an unbeatable, tough, threatening, bestial champion Sonny Liston appeared to be." In a 1993 book on Ali, the author said this: "George Foreman is generally viewed as a second Sonny Liston, or, more precisely, as the man Liston had only appeared to be." In its Chronicle of 20th Century Sport, the *Sporting News* said Ali "methodically wiped away 'the ugly Bear's' aura of invincibility." Once mythical, the world's toughest man somehow became a myth!

Sonny Liston was an American giant who was never allowed to become an

American hero. Instead, he was treated even worse than Jack Johnson was, and this country hated Johnson. Remarkably, nothing has changed in the 41 years since Liston died and because of that, most of what you think you know about the man, in or out of the ring, has no basis in fact. A.S. "Doc" Young's 1963 biography, *The Champ Nobody Wanted*, is the only favorable book ever written about the man, respectfully known as the Bear. And, wouldn't you know it, the book is so scarce that it'll cost you at least $100 to buy a copy on Ebay, and most likely that one was stolen from a library.

More than anything else, you should know that Muhammad Ali never fought the real Sonny Liston, just as Larry Holmes never fought the real Muhammad Ali, Rocky Marciano never fought the real Joe Louis, and Jess Willard never fought the real Jack Johnson. The reputations of Ali, Louis, and Johnson are still intact and have actually grown, in spite of their humiliating losses—and believe me, those were very humiliating losses. In Liston's case, the Ali fights buried both his reputation and his legacy. Fortunately, I was able to exhume them intact.

SONNY LISTON

PART ONE

BEHOLD HIS MIGHTY HANDS

CHAPTER ONE

A SUFFICIENCY UNTO HIMSELF

Charles Liston's hands were so big at birth that the midwife who delivered him told his mother that her baby was going to be a boxer. As it turned out, Helen Liston's son grew up to become a six foot, one-half inch, 212-pound freak of nature with physical attributes that no other boxer, and perhaps no other person ever possessed. One writer suggested that a geneticist must have bred him in a test tube for the purpose of beating up other men. "Sonny Liston was a massive ball of muscle," said his Las Vegas sparring partner Gary Bates. "Nobody was ever built like that."

Sonny's hands, the muscles of which were as finely developed as all of his other muscles, would become the epicenter of professional boxing. His massive 15 ½ -inch fists were as big around as cantaloupes, and once people saw them, they never forgot them. "All they would talk about around camp was how this man's hands were the size of hams," said Muhammad's Ali's first wife, Sonji. Floyd Patterson's manager Cus D'Amato used to marvel at the "abnormality" of Liston's thumbs, which the Associated Press called sausage-sized. People compared his fingers to bananas and cucumbers. When *Esquire's* Robert Riger shook Liston's hand, he said it was like patting a mattress. "I couldn't feel the edge of his hand anywhere," said Riger.

"His hands were so large! I couldn't believe it. They always had trouble with his gloves, trouble getting them on when his hands were wrapped," said Father Alois Stevens, who became very close to Sonny during his incarceration at Missouri's Jefferson City Prison. Las Vegas Sheriff Ralph Lamb saw Sonny playing blackjack and thought the two cards he held in his hands looked like postage stamps. Bates remembers leaning over a jewelry counter when Sonny slapped his ass so hard he thought he had been hit by a paddle. As a backseat passenger Sonny would rap the side of the car so loudly that everyone within earshot thought the vehicle had been rammed.

Liston's fist delivered the greatest weapon in the long and storied history of professional prizefighting, his inescapable, pulverizing left jab. "I developed that jab myself," said the plain-spoken Liston. "I jab wherever his head is. I jab to hurt. That's all." Great fighters have great jabs and Sonny's was the absolute best. His sparring partners called it the cannon and its impact was fueled by his incredible 84-inch reach.

Sonny had learned on the streets and in jail that you couldn't survive without a good jab. "Man, you don't hit first there, you don't hit," he would say. "Keep poppin' that jab right to the middle of the forehead and the other guy can't punch right because he's never got the balance to punch right." In his book, *My Life Story*, Joe Louis counseled young boxers to jab through their target rather than at it. Sonny went Louis one better by attempting to impale people with it. When asked how he would have fought Sonny, Louis said he wouldn't have jabbed with him.

"His jab always lands around the temple," said sparring partner Ben Skelton, who worked with 11 heavyweight and light heavyweight champions. "I've never felt a punch to equal it, and that includes Joe Louis.'" Sonny's jab was so hard that Skelton was still taking pain pills a week after being hit with it. Trainer Angelo Dundee said he saw Liston knock people's teeth out with his jab and likened it to a battering ram. Rocky Marciano speculated that being hit with it was like running into a boxcar or a trailer truck. Trainer Johnny Tocco saw Sonny knock guys out with a single jab and described him as a killing machine in the ring.

"He knocked me out with a right but it was that left jab that did the original damage. The left jab numbed me," said hard-hitting Cleveland Williams. Chuck Wepner was Liston's final opponent and claimed he heard his bone shattering when Sonny's jab landed. Ray Schoeninger had sparred with Liston in Denver in the mid-1960s and said the stitching in his headgear came apart when Sonny hit him. "He shattered my teeth. He knocked my shoulder out of place. Hey, I lost three teeth when he hit me with a jab wearing 20-ounce gloves. He knocked me on my ass from a foot away," said Schoeninger.

Sonny's jab set the stage for his crushing left hook, which George Foreman said would blast your head off. Sonny could hook off the jab, meaning he didn't have to recock his left arm after throwing it. Liston's hook followed his jab with catlike quickness and his massive shoulders generated so much power that he needed only a few inches to deliver a debilitating blow. "It's a thing of beauty. If anything, it has become better with every fight," his trainer Willie Reddish said in 1963, Liston's only full year as champ.

After Liston stopped 10th–ranked Wayne Bethea 69 seconds into their 1958 fight, a dentist took 16 teeth out of Bethea's mouth, all of which had been either broken in half, cracked down the middle, or knocked loose by one of Sonny's left hooks. "There is nothing pretty about Sonny when he moves," wrote Jimmy Breslin in his coverage of that fight. "But he has that left hand out in front of him and that is all he needs." Reddish said his fighter sometimes delivered his blows so fast that you couldn't count them. "I may look slow but I'm pretty fast for a guy my size," said Sonny. "The big difference, actually, is not in the feet, it's in the hands. I have fast hands, like Louis. When I start throwing punches, they're plenty fast."

Liston destroyed heavy bags on a regular basis. Former Nevada state boxing commissioner Art Lurie saw Sonny drive a left hook into a sandfilled punching bag so forcefully that the s-hook holding the bag was wrenched open, straightened somewhat, and sent flying, taking the bag with it to the floor.

"Liston would step into the 200-pound bag and hook it straight up in the air where it would hang for one long and terrifying instant, before it fell back into place at the end of a one-inch logging chain with a vicious clang and a jerk that would shake the whole room," wrote Hunter S. Thompson. "Nobody hit those bags like Sonny," said Johnny Tocco. "He tore bags up. He could turn that hook, put everything behind it. Turn and snap. Bam!"

Liston's left hand was so devastating that it obscured his equally powerful right hand. "You can win with one hand, but it's always easier for you if you got two," Sonny said. "I got two." Angelo Dundee wrote that Sonny's uppercut was as good as any in the history of the division. "You ask Williams about my right hand," said Liston. "He thinks anybody's crazy if they say my right's not so good." When second-ranked Zora Folley regained his senses after being knocked out by Sonny in the third round he asked what had happened. "I knocked you out," said Liston. "Oh, now I remember," replied Folley. "And they told me not to worry about your right hand." Asked what it felt like to be hit by Liston, Folley paused and said, "I can't describe it. You would have to experience it for yourself."

Former top-rated heavyweight Nino Valdes of Cuba said being hit by Liston was like being kicked by a mule and later, numbed by morphine on his death bed, he compared his pain to that inflicted by Sonny's punches. Marty Marshall said two of Liston's punches hurt his ear and his side for the rest of his life. "He was ferocious. That's the only way to describe him," said Gary Bates. "He's mean in the ring. He can mess up your guts with one swipe," said Ben Skelton. Former middleweight champion Rocky Graziano said Liston could hit an opponent once and take all the fight out of him. When Bert Whitehurst faced Sonny in 1958, he fared much better when he fought inside, negating the power Sonny could generate with his arms extended. "It was like being in the eye of a hurricane. On the outside it was hell, but in close it was calm and I was safe."

Sonny's enormous punching power meant trading punches with him was not a viable option. "He hurts a man whenever and wherever he hits him," said Joe Louis. Jim Graham of the *Denver Post* said Sonny's punches sounded like a rifle slug tearing into the side of a deer. Veteran Philadelphia fight figure Joey Curtis said Liston could have killed a man in the ring if he wanted to. "I'd like to see anyone punch with him," marveled Zora Folley's manager Bill Swift. "If Sonny hit you and you didn't go down, you did a lot of funny things standing up," said Teamsters organizer Robert "Barney" Baker. "He was an animal. I'll tell you right now, he was an animal." For the record, Barney Baker was one rough son-of-a-bitch.

Johnny Tocco worked with Liston, Foreman, and Mike Tyson and said Sonny was clearly the hardest hitter of the three. That's saying something because George and Mike were great fighters who could hit very, very hard. "Sonny was just such a really powerful wrecking machine," said Tommy Hearn's trainer Emanuel Steward. "He had unbelievable brutal punching power. I remember the fights he had with Cleveland Williams—oh my god!"

Liston said he never tried for an early knockout but that he hit whenever the opportunity presented itself. Sonny always said that no fighter hit harder than he did, and many of the greatest heavyweights confirmed his belief. Ali said Liston could have banged a hole in Fort Knox if he wanted to. "I said he was ugly and he couldn't dance, but I never said he couldn't punch. It frightened me, just knowing how hard he hit," Muhammad admitted years after the two fought. Foreman was 19 years old when he first sparred with Sonny in 1968 and was in awe of the old man's punching power. "He was the only fighter who ever, *ever*, stopped me consistently in my tracks with one punch, backed me up like a sports car," said Foreman. Louis said Liston punched harder than anyone he'd ever seen. "He's a real strong man. I'm glad he wasn't around when I was fighting," he added. Joe's manager Julian Black said while his fighter used to jar an opponent with one hand and knock him out with the other, Sonny could flatten you with either hand.

In 2003, *Ring Magazine*'s crack team of boxing writers ranked Liston as the 15th greatest puncher of all time and rated seven heavyweights ahead of him. To rank the greatest heavyweight punchers of all time, you really need two lists: one for Sonny and the other for everyone else. In terms of sheer punching power, Liston was Louis squared. "He was super strong. Nobody was like him," said longtime promoter Don Chargin. Louis claimed Sonny was the strongest man he'd ever seen. *Newsweek* went Joe one better by saying Liston might be the strongest man in the world.

"Liston's the most powerful heavyweight I've ever seen," said veteran boxing referee Bernie Weissman, who worked three of Sonny's early-round knockouts. "He's a weightlifter with finesse, and you can't hurt him. When I grabbed his arm to break a clinch, it was like grabbing a beast." Foreman was bigger than Liston and many years his junior but he couldn't match the old man's strength. After doing roadwork in Las Vegas in the late 1960s, referee Davey Pearl put a wheelbarrow at the bottom of a ravine and filled it with rocks. Sonny moved it up and back down three times while George moved it up just once. "I'll tell you something," Pearl told me, "when it came to strength, Foreman was a kindergarten kid compared to Sonny, a kindergarten kid!"

One of Sonny's assistant trainers remembered the day in a steam room, during training for the first Patterson fight, when Liston picked up a 50-pound weight with his right hand, tossed it up over his head, and caught it with his left. His first manager, Monroe Harrison, said he once saw Liston pick up the front end of a Ford and hold it for a while. Monroe made Sonny promise never to do it again. "He was *strong*," famed Las Vegas casino executive Ash Resnick told me. "He used to put his arm around me in the casino and get me in a headlock and listen, I'm pretty strong too, but Sonny, he just handled me like a baby."

Tom McNeeley played football at Michigan State before fighting Floyd Patterson for the title in 1961 and had known hundreds of football players who weighed between 250 and 290 pounds. "They were all bigger than Liston, but not one of them created the same impression. When Liston walks into a room, he completely dominates the room." Norman Mailer declared Sonny to be a Presence, while sportswriter Shirley Povich described him as a sufficiency unto himself. "When you sat around, you knew you were around royalty, and he didn't have to do anything other than be himself," said Foreman.

Most people were stunned when they saw Liston up close for the first time. "Everything about him exhibited immensity and power," wrote *Look Magazine*'s Marshall Smith. Robert Lipsyte watched Sonny train and described him as a great machine on display. "His body is so awesome, it is reassuring to hear him speak and not utter some terrible atavistic growl," wrote *Sports Illustrated*'s Gilbert Rogin. "Surely he is one of the world's most terrifying humans," added Smith.

With his 48½ inch chest and 17½ biceps, Liston had the upper body of a much, much heavier man. "He was as big around in the shoulders as that soda machine over there," said Ray Schoeninger. Seattle reporter Phil Taylor thought Eddie Machen looked like a middleweight compared to Liston when they fought in 1960, even though, at 198 pounds, Eddie was only 13 pounds lighter than Sonny.

Mirroring Liston's great strength was his legendary ability to take a punch. A sparring partner remembered that Sonny's abdomen was so strong that his "shield of muscle" seemed to render him bulletproof. His chin appeared to be made of concrete, and the blows he absorbed in his two fights with Cleveland Williams left boxing people shaking their heads in amazement. "I been hit, but I never been close to being wobbled up," Sonny once said. "Nobody can hurt that man," marveled Jesse Bowdry, a top light heavyweight contender who sparred with Sonny for many years. "Sometimes I think he doesn't even feel my best punches, and I'm no little baby." One of Sonny's handlers insisted you could hit him with a baseball bat and he'd still come after you. "When I broke his jaw, he didn't even blink," remembered Marty Marshall. "You hit him with your Sunday punch but he don't grunt, groan, flinch, or blink. He don't do nothin'. He just keeps coming on. He's discouraging that way."

Looking at Liston was discouraging as well. His unforced and unchanging facial expression created a demeanor that perfectly complemented his fighting ability. "Sonny Liston occupies a position sui generis for the very truculence of his boxing persona—the air of unsmiling menace he presented to the Negro no less than the white world," wrote Joyce Carol Oates in *On Boxing*. With the exception of children and priests, Liston intimidated everyone, from boxers to writers to spectators. His glare was immortalized in the Animals' song *I'm Mad*.

Sonny even intimidated his friends, including boxing's first black promoter,

Henry (Champ) Winston. Winston affectionately described his friend as the equivalent of a 3,000-pound gorilla in any test of wills or staredown. "He could intimidate you very easily, and you'd be foolish to fight back because he's having fun psychologically beating you up. He's gonna win that one every time." The gorilla in Sonny Liston could be triggered by a look or a word or summoned at will.

"Sonny, you ought to smile more often. You scare a person to death with that look," said Father Edward Murphy, a Catholic priest who became close friends with him in Denver. Liston's championship photographer Paul Abdoo said the only way he could get him to smile during his photo shoots was to tell him to say the word shit. "Charles has his scorned look," conceded his wife, Geraldine. "He's got the look and he don't say much and that scares people. But it's just a look. He ain't as mean as he looks."

Sonny was universally seen as the baddest, roughest, toughest man on the planet and outside of his inner circle of friends, that's precisely what he wanted people to believe. He said he looked tough in the ring because he was trying to scare the other guy. At weigh-ins and during pre-fight instructions, Sonny's glare would make most of his opponents seriously question their choice of occupations. "His baleful, obsidian stare intimidates fighters, sportswriters and the occupants of the first 20 rows of any arena he enters," wrote SI's Morton Sharnik.

Clay commented on Liston's glare just prior to their first fight. "When I walk into a room where he is and see him staring at me with that mean, hateful look, I want to laugh, but then I think maybe it's not so funny. I'm pretty sure the way he acts is just a pose, the same way I have a pose, but that look of his still shakes me."

Bud Collins said looking into Liston's eyes gave you the feeling of "gazing into a hair-triggered, double-barreled shotgun. Veteran fight handler Al Braverman said Sonny "could give you a glare so baleful you'd just want to fold up." Liston's glare was so legendary that former middleweight contender Rubin "Hurricane" Carter would look at his opponents with what he proudly called his Sonny Liston smile. Angelo Dundee said Liston stared down a fighter as if he were a dead man. Eddie Machen said Sonny glared at him like he was going to eat him alive.

Norman Mailer said people held their breath when near Sonny. "Perhaps no fighter had ever brought to the ring so palpable an aura of menace," wrote SI's William Nack, who referred to Liston as the toughest guy on the planet. Novelist Gay Talese thought of Liston as the most menacing human being of his lifetime and a born destroyer of other people. He didn't think anyone could survive him.

"The public image of Sonny Liston verges on the indigestible," said Sharnik.

"Sonny Liston was a mean fucker," wrote famed publicity director Harold Conrad. "I mean, he had everybody scared stiff. People talk about Tyson before he got beat, but Liston, when he was champ, was more ferocious, more indestructible, and everyone thought, unbeatable." Tyson has said that the only heavyweight champion he would have been afraid of fighting was Liston.

If any of Dundee's fighters gave him trouble, he threatened to put them in with Sonny, who he referred to as a killer, a destroyer, a dreadnaught, and the Monster Man. "Nobody wants any part of that guy," Dundee said in 1960. "He could kill you." Sonny had to give his opponents the major share of the purse simply to get them to agree to fight him. As far as Sonny was concerned, the biggest mistake any fighter ever made was getting in the ring with him. "Fighters were scared to death of him," promoter Don Chargin said bluntly. "They were beat before they entered the ring." Not one of Liston's opponents ever scheduled a victory party.

Liston never had a sparring partner or opponent who wasn't in genuine awe of him, no matter how brave a man he was. "We always had a problem getting sparring partners. Nobody wanted to spar. Sonny was too tough," said Sonny's first manager, Frank Mitchell. "Everlast made 22 oz. gloves for Sonny Liston and his sparring partners had to get chest protectors because he broke ribs in the gym," said promoter Don Elbaum. "To spar with him was terrifying," said Gary Bates, who trained with Sonny late in the late '60s. "I figured any time I went down I was about to become a martyr. I thought it was my last day on earth." Ben Skelton nicknamed Liston the Bear. "It became sort of a grim, hurtful joke to us sparring partners," said Ben. "He just won't believe that anything or anybody can hurt him. And he fights the same way."

Former champ Ernie Terrell sparred with Sonny on many occasions and said his fighter's attitude separated him from every other fighter he knew. "Liston didn't spar," said Ernie. "He put his fight out there when he was sparring. He's in the ring to kill you, not to just beat you or knock you out—but to kill you. He goes outta the corner and tries from the bell to blast your brains out."

Carter once volunteered to spar with Liston in Philadelphia, when there were no other sparring partners around. Despite a 50-pound weight disadvantage, Carter survived the three-round session only to discover upon taking off his headgear that he was bleeding from both ears. Brave but not stupid, Carter immediately left town for Newark, New Jersey, knowing that if he had stayed in

Philly his pride would have compelled him to climb back in the ring with Liston again the next day.

Archie Moore belongs in any conversation about the best pound-for-pound boxer of all time. His career began 21 months before Louis beat Jimmy Braddock for the heavyweight title in 1937. Archie won the light heavyweight title three months after Marciano beat Jersey Joe Walcott in 1952 and he retired from the ring seven months after Liston beat Patterson in 1962. "It's a shame he wasn't fighting big time when he was in his prime," Ali once said of Moore. "It would have been like a young Satchel Paige in the big leagues." Moore had 218 bouts that we know of, lost only 23, and accumulated more knockouts, 131, than any fighter in history. This is what he said about fighting:

> "Fighting is as much a part of life as death is, because the fight begins from the moment the person is taken from the womb and lasts until he is put into the grave. When a newly born baby enters the world, he fights for his first breath, am I right? OK. And then before he's put into the ground he's fighting for that last breath, am I right? OK, well that's it. A man fights all his life to live happily, or no matter how he chooses to live he fights for his substance on earth, he fights for the better things in life. He fights physically, you know, because people do something to him that he doesn't think is right. This is why I say fighting is as much as living or death is."

Welcome to the life of Charles Liston. With his remarkable body, Charles was born to be a fighter and the son-of-a-bitch who was his father made sure he was raised that way. Sonny used to say he'd been fighting to stay alive from the day he was born. Little was ever known about Sonny's formative years and what was offered by him or anyone close to him was rarely questioned. That was fine with him since his childhood was anything but happy, and he hated being asked about his age. Liston said he was born in 1932 in a flimsy shack in Forrest City, Arkansas, the 24th of 25 children that Tobe Liston sired over a span of 44 years. "Yessir, my father was the champion in his field too," said Sonny.

At five-foot-two, Charles' mother, Helen, was a stout woman who, by her son's recollection, gave birth to 12 or 13 kids. He inherited her large head, sturdy neck, and strong shoulders, chest, and arms. Helen claimed her mother was a tall woman and that there were tall people in her husband's family as well. Like all of Big Momma's children, Charles was healthy, grew fast, ate all his food, and went to bed early. She said he was a good, fun-loving boy who loved to swim and ride mules.

Though only five-foot-five, Tobe Liston was a mean man who would terrorize other people's kids by unloading his shotgun in their general direction if he thought they got too close to his property. Tobe was particularly hard on his children, believing if they were big enough to go to the dinner table, they were big enough to work in the fields. In Sonny's case, that turned out to be at age eight.

"I had it tough as a kid," he said. "My father kept me busy, real busy. I didn't like it. A man's work for a youngster isn't right." All Charles had were a lot of brothers and sisters, a helpless mother, and a father who he said didn't care about any of them. "We grew up like heathens. We hardly had enough food to keep from starving and nobody to help us escape from the horrible life we lived…My father worked me hard and whipped me hard. If he missed a day, I'd feel like saying, 'How come you didn't whip me today?'"

Sonny inherited his father's mean streak. The Listons and the Holmes family lived on opposite sides of an Arkansas creek and a Holmes boy named Mitchell was trying to have sex with the Liston girls back in the early 1940s. One of those girls was Sonny's sister, Alcora. "My daddy (Mitchell) told me Sonny would be chasing him and telling him to stay away from his sister," said Alcora's oldest child, Helen. "He told me Charles was a mean sucker who wanted to fight even then."

When Sonny's mother moved to St. Louis, he said he followed her there by thrashing some pecans off his brother-in-law's tree and selling them for the price of a train ticket. Sonny always said he was 13 years old when he got there. He said he worked at a poultry house, on an ice wagon, and on a construction crew where he was treated like a man because he worked as hard as his much-older cohorts and he could hold his own in a fight. Many of those guys had been in jail or soon would be but they were the only friends Sonny had. They influenced what he did and what he thought, and for several years he didn't know there were any other kinds of people.

In the late 1940s Sonny was St. Louis' "No. 1 Negro" and he described himself as the biggest, strongest guy on the corner. In 1949 he participated in a series of muggings and robberies during which he was called the Yellow Shirt Bandit because he always wore the same yellow-and-black checkered shirt. After being caught, Liston pleaded guilty to armed robbery and was sentenced to three concurrent five-year terms at the Missouri State Penitentiary in Jefferson City. "I figure I had to pay for what I did," Sonny said later. "No use crying. I should have tried that before I did wrong."

Helen wasn't sure how this happened to her son. "I had already left St. Louis when he got into trouble. They say he confessed...I don't know. He was just a country boy. He didn't know to do nothing. I used to tell him he had to cultivate his religion. He said he would. I guess it could have been the company he kept. You know, it's sometimes the company you keep which run your luck into a bad string." As it turned out, the company Sonny Liston kept defined his adult life, framed his boxing career, and may have contributed to his early death.

Opened in 1836, Jefferson City was the oldest prison west of the Mississippi. It could house 5,200 inmates and until 1989 was the state's only maximum security prison. Anybody with a long sentence or a history of problems was sent there. Other than Sonny, its most famous inmates were Pretty Boy Floyd and James Earl Ray, who escaped from Jeff City six months before he killed Martin Luther King Jr.

During Sonny's time at Jeff City the director of Missouri's department of corrections called it one of the "roughest damned prisons in the country." *Time* later called it the bloodiest 47 acres in America. It was a bad place to be no matter how tough you were, and the guards quickly tried to break St. Louis' No. 1 Negro by tying him to bars and whipping him with ropes. Liston shared a cell with five other inmates in the all-black Housing Unit #4, which was in "a warehouse mode" back then, according to Mark Schreiber, who conducts guided tours at the now-decommissioned prison. One guy who served time with Sonny described him as a suspicious human being with an alligator voice. Liston was lucky enough to have been paroled prior to Jeff City's 1954 riot. Today his old cell is the decommissioned prison's biggest tourist attraction.

"He didn't go looking for trouble," said Edward Schlattmann, the prison chaplain and athletic director, "but he resented it when other prisoners took liberties with him and he beat them up." The prisoners at Jeff City were divided into three gangs, all of which terrorized the black inmates. For an Arkansas native like Liston, the situation was a familiar one. One day he walked across the yard and hit the leader of one gang with the back of his hand. "I'll do that every time I hear you touched a colored boy," Liston said. "If you don't like it, I'll see you down in the Hole at six." Then Liston found the other two gang leaders and did the same thing. The Hole was a storage place situated under the cell block and was the one place in the jail where inmates could usually fight undisturbed. Liking the odds, the three gang leaders accepted Liston's invitation. Less than ten minutes after the brawl began, Sonny walked up the stairs alone leaving three badly beaten men on the floor. Publicist Harold Conrad swore that the story was true.

When Father Stevens succeeded Schlattmann as athletic director, an inmate told him that Liston was the best fighter in the place. "Nobody 'round here messes with Sonny. When he walks in the yard, they part. He's something special," said the inmate. Stevens described Sonny as the most perfect specimen of manhood he'd ever seen. The Father didn't know much about Sonny's personal background when he met him. "You never do with a kid like that. Sonny was just a big, ignorant, pretty nice kid. He wasn't smart-alecky, but he got in little scrapes. Sonny was an illiterate, and these kinds (of inmates) don't know cockiness or any other emotion. They tell you nothing. It makes it hard."

At Stevens' suggestion, Sonny enrolled in the prison's school program but dropped out, according to Warden E. V. Nash. Back then, one civilian teaching instructor was assisted by several other instructors who got those jobs primarily because they were good inmates. A few years later the prison employed only civilian teachers with degrees, but by that time Sonny was long gone.

"The can was no party," said Sonny. "But after I started fighting, I had it pretty good. I could train and I had special privileges. I was like the assistant warden." Liston was assigned to the kitchen and worked on the docks unloading large crates of vegetables. He was also a runner, delivering messages or taking clothes to the dry cleaner. He said he got the second job because Father Stevens was always in his corner. "I was yard-master at the time and I remember being asked to find someone I could trust to carry the dirty clothes to the cleaning-place at the front door of the prison," said Bernard Poiry, who served 40 years at Jeff City. "Yes, I said, I know a solid, reliable bloke: Sonny."

In the years that followed Sonny always had genuine affection for Father Stevens, the man he credited with helping to turn his life around. "He was the one who got me started in fighting," Sonny told Senator Estes Kefauver in December of 1960. "They had a boxing team in there. He said, 'You like fighting so much, why don't you get into the boxing team?' I told him all right. I started fighting, and then I beat all the guys there, and he say 'I'll see what I can do for you on the outside.'"

Liston supposedly got his nickname when a small boxing instructor by the name of Joe Gonzales called him sonny boy, and the name, minus the boy part, stuck. Sam Eveland was one of Liston's prison trainers and he marveled at how quickly Sonny learned his trade. "He was the real thing right away. You'd show him a punch or a technique and by the end of the day he had it down. There's no denying it—he could hit like a mule," said Eveland. With most of the inmates watching, Liston battered the prison's heavyweight champion so badly that no one dared step into the ring with him. "They had a very hard time getting him exercise because they had to put two or three convicts in the ring to fight against him," said Monsignor Jack Maguire. "I don't think you could hurt the man," remembered Assistant Warden W. P. Steinhauser. "Whenever Liston hits you, it's just too bad."

Sonny's life changed when boxing people found out the damage he could do with his fists. After Sonny beat the eight to ten men who were brave enough to fight him (some of whom were brought in from other prisons), Stevens began to build a future for his friend. His assistant was a former St. Louis sportswriter and he called Bob Burnes, sports editor of the *Globe-Democrat*, for help.

Burnes asked Monroe Harrison, who had sparred with Joe Louis, to evaluate Sonny. Monroe had also started the career of Archie Moore, and Moore considered Harrison to be almost as great a teacher of boxing technique as he was. Harrison got Frank Mitchell, the publisher of St. Louis' Negro newspaper, *The Argus,* to drive him to the prison. He then contacted veteran trainer Tony Anderson, who brought a young pro named Thurman Wilson to spar with Liston. Shouting that Liston was going to kill him, Wilson fled the ring after two brutal rounds.

Anderson told his cohorts they were looking at a future champion. "When can he leave, Father?" gushed Harrison. "Look at that jab. Oh, you got to get him out of here." While Burnes was thinking to himself that he was looking at a man whose only chance of making anything out of his life was with his fists, Stevens turned to him and said, "What I want you to tell me is how I can get him a fight with Rocky Marciano."

Father Stevens began lobbying the parole board on Sonny's behalf and in June of 1952 the fighter was transferred to a minimum security auxiliary unit 10 miles from the prison. Less than five months later Liston was paroled into the custody of Harrison and Mitchell after serving 29 months of a five-year sentence.

His early release was due to Father Stevens, a clean prison record, and his lethal left hand. "I'm not sure we're doing the right thing," parole board member John Fels told Liston, "but I am impressed by the fact that so many people have offered to help you. Don't let them down, boy. If you do, the first minute you get into trouble, I'll see that you come back here."

Stevens personally escorted Sonny from the prison grounds to Mitchell's office and told him to always let him look at a contract before he signed it, or to have someone read it to him over the phone. Before they parted company, Sonny promised the Father he would never see him at Jefferson City again.

CHAPTER TWO

ONE BITCH OF A TOWN

On September 23, 1952, Rocky Marciano knocked out Jersey Joe Walcott to win the heavyweight title, and for the first time in 16 years the champion of the world was white. When Dwight Eisenhower welcomed Marciano to the White House, Ike expressed his surprise at how small the new champ was. At 5'10", 184 pounds, and a 67-inch reach, Marciano was such a little heavyweight that by today's standards, he wouldn't be a heavyweight at all—he'd be a cruiserweight, and a small one at that. Until 1988, boxers weighing more than 175 pounds were classified as heavyweights. As fighters got bigger, the 190-pound cruiserweight division was added to give smaller heavyweights the chance to compete for a world title. (Today, the weight limit for cruiserweights is 200 pounds.)

It was Marciano's good fortune to rise to prominence at a time when his major competitors were either old like 37-year-olds Walcott and Louis or old and natural light heavyweights like 34-year-old Ezzard Charles and the 41-year-old Moore. A new generation of formidable heavyweights was still a couple of years away; Rocky would retire undefeated without ever having to face them.

It's an open secret that Marciano's fight with Moore was fixed and that a gangster by the name of Frankie Carbo engineered it. During the 1930s and 1940s, Carbo ran boxing at the championship level. Known in the sport as Mr. Gray and The Convincer, Carbo achieved notoriety as the underworld's commissioner of boxing. He was able to control almost all of the top fighters because their managers could only secure a big bout by giving Carbo a share of their earnings. Carbo and his Philadelphia associate Blinky Palermo also insisted on acquiring part ownership of any fighter who was offered a title shot. Managers had no choice but to pay because they were afraid of the consequences if they didn't.

"Frank Carbo was the czar of boxing," said mobster Mickey Cohen. "When he came into a room, his walk, his dress, and the way he carried himself commanded the respect of everyone in that room." Carbo had been a killer for Murder, Inc. and the last of his five homicide arrests arose from a 1939 shooting for which he was indicted along with Louis "Lepke" Buchalter and Benjamin "Bugsy" Siegel, with whom he was pretty chummy. When the mob gave the order for Siegel to be killed in 1947, the FBI believed that Meyer Lansky tapped Carbo to do the job.

"The evil influence of this man for many years permeated virtually the entire professional sport of boxing," said New York's Assistant District Attorney Alfred J. Scotti. Carbo would hold court at Dempsey's Restaurant, where his guests included reporters, managers, boxing commissioners, and out-of-town associates who came to New York for the big fights at Madison Square Garden. Many state athletic commissions turned a blind eye to Carbo and some worked with or for him. An assistant Manhattan district attorney said he had evidence that most of the country's influential sportswriters were on Carbo's payroll at one time or another as well.

Novelist Budd Schulberg once described the fight game as the slum of the sports world, and for the longest time black boxers had no other place to live. The '30s, '40s and early '50s were particularly difficult times for black fighters, and they suffered disproportionately under Carbo's rule. Unless your name was Joe Louis or Sugar Ray Robinson you could only get a big fight against a white boxer if you agreed to lose. When Sonny joked that a colored guy had to knock a white guy out just to get a draw, he was referring to this earlier era. Years before Willie Reddish became Liston's trainer, he learned it too.

Ranked No. 3 by *Ring Magazine*, Willie had come close to fighting Louis for the title but as much as people loved the Brown Bomber, there would have been little promotional appeal to a title match featuring two blacks at that time. When Louis asked Willie to be his sparring partner, Reddish told him he'd fight him but he wouldn't spar with him. Instead, Reddish signed to fight "Two Ton" Tony Galento, a colorful, overweight white brawler who fought dirty and had little skill. Neither Willie's manager nor the promoter had the nerve to tell him he had to lose the fight and when they finally did, they had to cancel the bout. "When I get into the ring, I get in it to fight," Reddish told them. Other talented black fighters would agree to lose because they had to earn in order to eat.

Things like that happened all the time back then and a lot of excellent black fighters never got the money or the recognition their talent warranted. Those who did had to work for it. "I started from scratch and won the title after 16 years of being kicked around and without being given a chance to participate in real money bouts," said Archie Moore. "And yet I won the title due to perserverance and sheer ability and the affection of the sportswriters who listened to my pleas and kept my name in the papers to a sympathetic public who demanded a title fight for me." Archie was 38 when he got that fight and earned $800. Few black boxers had that kind of patience, commitment, or clout, even if they had the talent.

Jack Dempsey's former manager, "Doc" Kearns, said Carbo's group would throw guys like him a bone if and when they felt like it. According to 60-year veteran of the sport Al Certo, Carbo and Palermo often operated without written contracts. Instead, they would call a manager and ask him if his fighter wanted to fight at a specified location for a specified amount of money. "If your answer was yes, that was it," said Certo. "You knew that you would have received the $2,000, because they were men of their word."

In truth, boxing hasn't changed all that much. For the past 35 years or so, boxers couldn't get a good fight unless they did business with influential promoters like Don King or Bob Arum. So, mob or no mob, boxers and their managers have always had to negotiate with the right guys in order to get ahead.

It was Joe Louis who unwittingly gave control of the heavyweight division to organized crime. After 11 years as champ, Joe's talent began to wane and he looked for a way to relinquish his crown that would put money in his pocket. He turned to Chicago attorney Truman Gibson, who had arranged the champ's wartime exhibition bouts at army bases around the world.

Gibson worked as a special adviser on Negro Affairs for the Secretary of War and had tried to persuade the Army to utilize black troops in combat and to end segregation in the armed forces. Back in the 1940s the Army's leadership condoned segregation and didn't believe that blacks could or would function reliably in combat. Most training facilities were in the South and Gibson remembered that the Army's approach to handling black soldiers was to deputize and arm white bus drivers in military towns.

Prejudice toward blacks was so pervasive that not even the heavyweight champion of the world was immune to it. While in the military, Louis was arrested by MPs for using a "whites only" telephone and was later taken to the stockade when he refused to move to the rear of an Army bus. Keep in mind that just six years earlier, Louis did more for his country than any athlete has ever done when he knocked out the pride of Nazi Germany, Max Schmeling, in the first round.

In 1946, Gibson became the only black member of President Truman's nine-person civilian commission that studied the future of universal military training. Fourteen months later, the President adopted the commission's recommendation and issued the Executive Order that led to the desegregation of the armed forces. Gibson became the first African American to be awarded the Presidential Medal of Merit. He later lobbied Nevada Senator Paul Laxalt to get Louis buried in Arlington National Cemetery, and Laxalt got President Reagan to grant the request.

Gibson secured the exclusive services of the four leading heavyweight contenders and made it known that Louis would resign as champion after which his new company would transfer the contracts to anyone willing to pay $250,000 for the right to promote heavyweight championship fights. The eventual buyer was millionaire sportsman James Norris, a partner in a New York Stock Exchange firm who once laughingly said his family owned half the wheat this side of Quebec. When Louis learned that Norris was the promoter of famed figure skater Sonia Henie, Joe asked for a piece of Henie's contract as part of the deal. Rather than do so, Norris upped his purchase price to $300,000 in order to seal the deal.

Norris had been a boxing fan ever since his father took him to the 1919 heavyweight title fight in Toledo, Ohio, where Jack Dempsey defeated Jess Willard to become champ. After that fight, Norris dreamed of being a promoter and controlling a heavyweight champion of his own. Beginning in the 1930s, Norris, his father, and Arthur Wirtz began to acquire controlling interests in the major indoor arenas in Detroit, Chicago, and St. Louis, along with the crown jewel of venues, New York's Madison Square Garden. As a result of those acquisitions, most of the championship fights in the '30s and '40s were staged at arenas owned by Norris. Norris was a serious gambler who bet thousands of dollars each day on horseraces; there is evidence that he fixed several fights during this period.

Gay Talese called Gibson "a profound advocate of television's marriage to boxing" because Truman was the first to realize that the revenue from televised boxing matches would far exceed that which was possible from ticket sales in any arena in the country. The IBC's matches were nationally televised on Wednesday and Friday nights and reached almost a third of all households with televisions. Gibson said the IBC received $40,000 for each Pabst Blue Ribbon Wednesday night fight card on CBS, and $50,000 for each Gillette Friday night card on NBC. Boxing was television's first cash cow, and the IBC bouts were always among the top five Nielsen-rated programs. Television showcased the excellence of black fighters at a time when almost all of the professional athletes on television were white. "I'll leave it to others to assess the impact of African American excellence in the ring during the 1950s," said Gibson, "but, I think, no one should minimize it."

The IBC had the arenas and the money but realized that only Carbo and Palermo could provide the group with the four main event fighters it needed every week to fulfill its commitments to CBS and NBC. "I got the merchandise and Norris has got to buy," Palermo once said. It wouldn't be the first time Norris aligned himself with members of the underworld. He was close to crime boss Albert Anastasia and had already partnered with organized crime in horse racing and casino gambling in the Bahamas.

When Norris and Carbo joined forces, they created such a near–monopoly that from 1949 to 1953 the IBC arranged 80 percent of the championship boxing matches staged in the United States, including all 13 heavyweight title bouts; the group became known as "Octopus, Inc." Norris's ties to organized crime gave him the leverage he needed to keep would-be fight-fixers out of boxing, which was crucial since the big money in the sport now came from television contracts and ticket sales in large arenas, and a fight-fixing scandal would have torpedoed both of those.

"With all the allegations, accusations, and testimony against Carbo, no one ever successfully tagged boxing through the International Boxing Club as being crooked," wrote Gibson. "Not a single TV fight that we've put on has ever been contested as being crooked." Gibson always insisted that mob influence in boxing was relatively nothing compared to its impact in horse racing, but the cloud it cast would plague boxing and the IBC throughout the 1950s. That cloud would plague Liston more than any fighter who ever lived.

◆ ◆ ◆

"Boxing, to me, is a real good sport," said Joe Louis' wife, Martha. "It's akin to life itself. You meet life head-on, just as you meet the other boxer. There's nobody to run interference for you in either life or boxing. In almost every other sport, there's somebody you can turn to, but in boxing you can't run. You've got to face it for yourself." To put it another way, in boxing nobody has your back but everybody has a hand on your wallet.

"Most colored boys who go into boxing are poor, and boxing offers them a chance to make money, to get somewhere," Sonny once said. That was true of him, too, but he also liked boxing because it gave him something to do and that helped keep him out of trouble. He stayed at the local YMCA, worked as a furnace feeder for a steel company, and spent most of his free time listening to the radio and playing cards. Monroe Harrison talked boxing with him constantly and tried to relate to him as a father or an uncle might. "He's vicious all the way. He needs someone to help him control his emotion," said Harrison.

"He was a real bust-out kid," Barney Baker told me. "That was a bad neighborhood where he lived in St. Louis." Barney said nothing ever seemed to bother Sonny, who was so relaxed that he'd nap for an hour in his dressing room just prior to his bouts. "He was like a tiger. He could sleep on a pole. He could sleep on a picket fence." Sonny told Barney he was keeping it clean and that he was going to make it in boxing, something Baker found easy to believe because of the confidence Liston had in himself.

"The boy is crude and he's no Joe Louis yet, but he's one of the fastest big men I've ever seen," said Tony Anderson. "That's what most folks don't realize. They see how strong he is, but he's still awkward and he doesn't look fast." Anderson thought Sonny was much faster on his feet than Joe Louis was at his age, which Sonny wanted people to believe was 21. "He had a terrific jab even then," said the trainer. "He was born with it. He had a right hand, but he was afraid to use it because of the tremendous power he had."

Future welterweight champion Virgil Akins met Liston at Johnny Tocco's Gym, where most of St. Louis' best fighters trained. It seemed to Akins that Sonny was mad at the world and took it out on his fellow boxers. "He could hardly get sparring partners," said Virgil. "It wasn't no play thing. It was a war. Nobody wanted to fool with him." Wearing 20-ounce gloves, Liston broke one of his sparring partner's shoulders, and veteran promoter Don Chargin said the story quickly became legend. Within weeks, Sonny won the Ozark AAU title by default because no one would fight him.

At the National Golden Gloves Finals in Chicago, Sonny saw Rocky Marciano sitting at ringside and told himself that one day he'd be fighting for the championship of the world. Liston beat 1952 Olympic Heavyweight Gold medalist Ed Sanders before winning the title, then won the International Golden Gloves title with a one-round knockout of Europe's best amateur fighter. Sonny was being hailed as another Joe Louis and was already good enough to hold his own in workouts against the world's third-ranked heavyweight contender, Nino Valdes.

Ray Arcel never forgot the day when he first saw a huge man wrapping two of the largest hands he had ever seen. During his 50-year career, Arcel trained 22 world champions and had been head cornerman in 11 heavyweight championship fights. Even though Liston was still an amateur, he made an unforgettable impression on Arcel that day in early 1953. "It was the way he used his left hand—jabbing and hooking with it, switching a jab into a hook and back into a jab again. I was amazed!" Arcel had seen great left hands before but they were attached to world champions like Louis, Billy Conn, and Benny Leonard.

Eddie Futch was at one of Sonny's first fights and was also impressed. "He was a great prospect. I saw the potential there right away," Futch told me. Liston would need it because he wasn't afforded the protection given to most highly regarded prospects, who were able to beat up on low-quality opposition as they climbed the rankings. Future champs like Ali, Louis, Marciano, Foreman, and Tyson all feasted on a steady diet of pushovers in establishing their credentials. Following their apprentice period they would only fight big-name fighters who had long since passed their prime. In stark contrast, almost every ranked fighter Sonny would fight on his way to the title was at or near his fighting peak.

In just his sixth fight, Sonny was a big underdog against Johnny Summerlin, a highly touted Detroit heavyweight who had lost once in 21 bouts. Sonny won a unanimous decision and got the attention of boxing people all over the country. After beating Summerlin a second time, getting quality opponents to fight Liston became very difficult.

Sonny's next fight was against a tall, unorthodox boxer by the name of Marty Marshall. Frank Mitchell put Liston on the train to Detroit and told him that he and the rest of his cornermen would arrive the next day. However, when Sonny reported to the dressing room he was by himself, had to wrap his own hands, and was not happy. "A fighter's got to think about one thing before a fight—getting as evil as he can," Liston said later. "I had too many things on my mind. I was mad at my manager instead of the guy I was gonna fight. Besides, you need somebody to tell you what to do and what to look for. Monroe Harrison, my trainer, always used to yell, 'Watch out, he might be carrying a gun.' But Monroe wasn't there either."

Sonny would never forget the fourth round of that fight. "(Marshall) was hollerin' and going on and I knocked him down. He got up and I was laughing. He caught me with my mouth open and broke my jaw…least I thought it was broke. If you can't close your mouth, you know something's wrong." Liston fought the rest of the bout with his mouth open and lost a split decision. The two judges awarded Marshall the fight by scores of 78-75 and 74-73 but referee Tommy Briscoe had Sonny winning handily, 77-70.

Sonny walked the streets in pain that night and in the morning the hotel doctor gave him some pills and charged him $20. Back in St. Louis he got his mouth wired and was told he'd have to eat through a straw for five weeks and wouldn't be able to fight again for six months. When he asked his manager for the $20 he was told it came out of his end. "That's when I got mad," said Sonny. Of lasting importance was the fact that he never laughed in the ring again, and rarely ever smiled.

During Sonny's recuperation, Harrison sold his half of Sonny's contract to Mitchell for $600. Harrison said he did so because he couldn't afford the $35 a week he paid to support Liston but sportswriter Bob Burnes said Harrison told him that two guys had approached him during an earlier fight and said they were taking Sonny away from him. Organized crime attached itself to Sonny that day, and his career would forever be tainted by the men who managed it.

Mitchell had been arrested 26 times but was never convicted of anything. He was thought to be a front man for several mob-connected people, including John Vitale, a well-known labor racketeer who police considered to be the second-most important crime figure in the St. Louis area. Vitale had been jailed for forgery, carrying concealed weapons, selling narcotics, and assault and earned a reputation as a mediator in underworld disputes. He apparently was an expert in mandatory arbitration as well. In 1952, Vitale clashed with two high-ranking officials of one of the city's most powerful labor unions. Within months, both officials were shot to death. Two witnesses saw the head of one of the unions getting into Vitale's car five minutes before he was found dead in a vacant lot. Although Vitale was arrested on suspicion of murder, he was never tried for the crime.

Liston dug ditches for Vitale's cement company during the summer of 1953 and earned $65 a week. Then he worked for a year and a half in construction and as a personal chauffeur for a union president named Raymond Sarkis. "Mostly I'd drive his car," said Sonny, "a white Cadillac with air conditioning and a telephone, and the cops would see me in the summertime driving along, nice and cool with the windows all up and the cold air pouring in on me and they'd be out there sweating. I know they was jealous, and they'd even the score by pulling me in."

Of all his siblings, Sonny was closest to his sister Alcora, who had moved to St. Louis in early 1945 to find work after the birth of her first child. Born in 1927, Alcora was as tall as her brother and had the same complexion, broad shoulders, and slim hips that he did. She would give birth to 15 children but never married and always carried the Liston family name.

The eldest of Alcora's children was named after the family's matriarch and she was Grandma's pet. Helen Jean's earliest memories of her Uncle Charles were in 1954 when she was nine years old. She remembers her uncle worked on a coal truck owned by a family of Italians. The truck would drive through her neighborhood, someone would holler Sonny's name, and he'd jump on.

"He lived close so he was always around when we were kids," Helen told me. "He was driving a Cadillac when he was living here. He always liked nice cars." Alcora suggested to her brother that he give her the big, old sedan because she could fit all of her kids in it. After Liston became champ, he gave Alcora enough money to buy a big van.

"We all enjoyed Uncle Charles and his fame and fortune," said Helen's younger sister, Fannie Mae Hopkins. "He always brought us stuff, especially clothes because there were so many of us. He was a very giving person and we all loved him very much."

Alcora's three-room, second-floor St. Louis tenement had no back door and no indoor plumbing, and there were never less than 10 family members living there. "Uncle Charles was very important in my life. I looked up to him like he was my daddy," said Helen, whose real father was never around. "I could count on him. He was very dear to me." Helen believes the money Uncle Charles gave her mother was the reason they survived back then. "We were very, very poor people. He took good care of us."

Sonny would give Helen $10 or $20 and a big bag of plain M&M's every time he saw her; later on it wasn't unusual for him to give her as much as $100. Her uncle wasn't nearly as generous with her siblings, and they all complained that he never did anything for anybody but her. "I could get anything I needed from Uncle Charles. When I graduated grade school in 1959 he bought me all my graduation clothes and did the same when I graduated from high school. All I would do is tell him what I needed and he would pretty much give it to me."

Helen never heard of Sonny having bad relations with anyone in their immediate family. Though he was always happy around her, Helen knew he had a mean streak and vividly remembers the first time she saw it. Helen's stepdad fathered Alcora's last 11 children but he wasn't the kind of guy Sonny would have wanted her mom to be with. "He wasn't a go-getter, and my uncle never liked him," said Helen. "Uncle Charles didn't say anything but I could tell he didn't like him." Helen was in the room one day when Sonny was speaking to Alcora and her stepdad wanted to know what he was saying. "Sonny said, 'shut up, I ain't talking to you,' real loud, like he was gonna beat him up, and that was the end of that. My stepdad didn't say anything else. I really thought Sonny was gonna beat him up judging by the tone of his voice."

Sonny's daughter Eleanor and her mother Martha spent a lot of time at Alcora's house. "Martha would sometimes fall on hard times," remembers Helen, who always thought Martha was Filipino though her brother Henry Page insisted she was Native American. Known to the family only as Choo Choo, Eleanor was a big-bodied girl who was a few years younger than Helen. She apparently drank herself to death before the age of 50.

The police often found Sonny driving around with Barney Baker. The two met when Sonny fought on a boxing card that Baker organized as a benefit for the Teamsters. Boxing professionally as a middleweight, Baker had knocked down Max Schmeling during a sparring session and liked to tell Joe Louis that he was the one who had softened up the German for Louis' famous one-round knockout in 1938.

Baker was friends with and worked for nearly every gangster of any consequence, including Meyer Lansky and Bugsy Siegel. He was so close to Carbo that Frankie paid for his wedding reception. Barney had been jailed three times in the 1930s and used to brag that the first thing he always did upon being released from prison was to beat up the man whose testimony had put him there. He was a longshoreman and bouncer before joining the Teamsters in late 1952, where he rose to prominence as its key organizer under Dave Beck. According to Senate committees investigating racketeering in labor, Baker was one of the most dangerous men in the labor movement.

Appearing before the McClellan Senate Committee in 1958, Jimmy Hoffa said Baker worked for the Central Conference of Teamsters under his direct orders. When Baker testified, he joked his way through some intense questioning and wowed the audience by saying he once ate 38 pounds of meat at one sitting. Barney ignored the advice of his attorneys, who urged him to take the Fifth Amendment. "Little white lies don't mean nothing, not when you are not under oath," he said, explaining his approach to talking to police. In the audience, Jimmy Hoffa convulsed with laughter.

Senate Counsel Robert Kennedy savaged Baker. "Everywhere you go there has been violence. The people you associate with are the scum of the United States, and you are a part of them." Later, as U.S. Attorney General, Kennedy wrote that Hoffa employed Baker as one of his roving emissaries of violence and that his presence in a room was enough to silence anyone who might have opposed Hoffa's reign. Baker told me nobody was closer to Hoffa than he was. He believed that Kennedy and Hoffa both enjoyed their running battle and though Hoffa never said he wanted to kill Bobby, Baker told me his boss probably would have liked to kick the shit out of him.

Shortly before he died, Baker appeared before a 1978 Congressional subcommittee investigating the JFK assassination and was asked about a call he had received from Jack Ruby 15 days before Kennedy was killed. Baker testified that a mutual friend, who Ruby refused to identify, suggested Jack call him regarding trouble he was having with a union that wouldn't let him put on local talent shows at his Dallas night club. Baker told Ruby he had recently been released from federal prison and that getting involved in any labor issue could land him back in jail. Not wanting to take no for an answer, Ruby called Baker the next day and they spoke for almost 15 minutes. Two weeks later Barney was watching television with his wife when he learned that the man who shot Lee Harvey Oswald was the man who had called him for help.

Sonny's friendship with Barney colored the police department's perceptions of the fighter from the very beginning. The cops called Barney and Sonny the black and white brothers. "He stuck with me when the coppers came over to the car one time," Baker said. "We had many a barb thrown at us and Sonny once said, 'What are you gonna do, put handcuffs on us because I'm black and he's white? Ain't we supposed to talk to one another? What street am I supposed to go on?' I told Sonny not to fight cops because you don't get paid." Barney found Liston to be a highly principled man with an irresistible charm. "I liked him. He couldn't do no wrong in my eyes."

Baker said the St. Louis police department put a bulls-eye on Sonny's back and made a target out of him. The city's hoodlum squad stopped Liston almost every time they saw him, and its captain said he personally talked to him 20 times. "When I stopped him once on 10th Street, he doubled up his fists," said Detective Bob Green. "I pulled my gun and stood back. 'You better unroll those fists my man,' I told him. Why did I stop him? Just to find out where he was going." Nowadays that would be sheer harassment but in the late '50s it was standard operating procedure for a lot of police departments.

It wasn't unusual for the police to beat on Sonny. "Five coppers tried to lock Sonny," said someone who witnessed one such situation. "This ain't no bullshit story. They broke hickory nightsticks over his head. They couldn't get his hands cuffed. He was a monster." Doherty admitted to heavyweight Amos Lincoln that his cops hit Sonny with everything they had and still couldn't bring him down.

In years to come, police departments relentlessly harassed Liston in every city where he lived, and his former warden was dismayed by all of it. "There's no need to keep all the pride and manliness that was knocked out of him when he came here—knocked out of him," said Warden Nash. "Let him go and be a world champion, as long as he conducts himself properly."

Staying out of trouble was always a major challenge for Liston, no matter how hard he tried to avoid it. After winning a fight on May 5, 1956, Sonny celebrated at the house he shared with his girlfriend, Geraldine. A cab he had called was parked in an alley when a patrolman named Mello, who had been drinking, walked up and began to ticket the driver. When Sonny told Mello the cabbie was just doing his job, Geraldine said the cop called him a black-ass nigger. Mello reached for his gun and Sonny took it away from him. When Sonny released his bear hug, Mello fell and broke his leg. Liston went to Alcora's house, where he was arrested on charges of assault with intent to kill. "When the police came we had to go back into another room," said Sonny's niece Helen. "I remember my uncle cursing."

Baker termed the arrest a simple argument that the police decorated pretty good. Mitchell felt the situation could have been avoided had the officer not provoked Sonny by insulting him and Geraldine. "That would aggravate him," said Mitchell. While awaiting trial, Sonny was arrested seven more times on charges that most lawyers considered ludicrous. The St. Louis police department had declared war on Liston.

As an ex-convict, assaulting a police officer should have put Sonny away for a long time but on January 29, 1957, Liston was convicted only of the lesser charge of resisting arrest and was sentenced to nine months in the City workhouse. Truman Gibson told me that Sonny's Teamsters connections probably got him the relatively light sentence but the weakness of the state's case was also a factor. Whatever the reason, Liston's career suffered its second major interruption in three years.

In the summer of 1957, attorney Morris Shenker was contacted by a Missouri State Senator to help get Liston out of jail. Shenker's St. Louis law firm represented Frankie Carbo, Blinky Palermo, and later, Jimmy Hoffa. *Life Magazine* called Shenker *Lawyer to the Mob*. Former *St. Louis Post-Dispatch* reporter Ronald Lawrence said Shenker's financial genius rivaled that of Meyer Lansky and credited him with the idea of tapping the Teamster Pension Fund to finance much of the mob's investment in Las Vegas casinos. Shenker left St. Louis for Vegas, where he owned and ran the Dunes Hotel. When he died in 1989, the IRS said he owed the government $55 million in back taxes.

"I handled many cases for blacks in our community, so I helped him out," Shenker told me. "After he got out, he would come in to see me and I used to see him rather often. He was most appreciative toward me. You would have thought I did the world for him." The attorney remembered Sonny as being unschooled but nevertheless very nice to people.

"Sonny was just unbeatable," said Shenker. "Once he landed a punch, that was it. He realized that he had terrific strength, but if you crossed him, he wasn't able to control his temper or his emotions. That was his greatest problem. When things were right, he was extremely kind. But I knew when he would talk about other things with me, sometimes he would get all aroused to the danger point. He was real nice until something triggered him." Shenker believed the police were more afraid of Sonny than he was of them. "Physically, they couldn't stop him. They didn't want to use bullets but they didn't know how to stop him without bullets. All the police were scared of him."

"The mafia was Sonny's ticket out of poverty," said his niece Helen. "They had control over him. They got him out of prison, at least that's what I gathered from Momma." Sonny was paroled after serving seven months of his sentence and within a week was arrested twice, for disturbing the peace and for suspicion of robbery. Liston estimated he was picked up more than 50 times after his release.

"There was nothing they didn't pick me up for. If I was to go into a store and ask for a stick of gum, they'd say it was a stick-up…Them coppers just threw me in the shithouse for nothing. Just because I'm walking down the street."

Promoter Don Chargin talked to two St. Louis detectives back then and remembered that their hatred of Liston came through loud and clear. Frank Mitchell said the police told Sonny they were looking for an excuse to blow his brains out. Assistant Chief James Chapman actually put a gun to Sonny's head and told him if he stayed in St. Louis, they'd find him in an alley some night. "That's the kind of a life I had with the cops in that town," Sonny said. "They wouldn't let me live."

Liston left St. Louis for Philadelphia in the spring of 1958, having fought just once in nearly two years. When he won the title four years later, a St. Louis detective said, "He's the champion now. He should be grateful. He should be even more grateful he's alive. That was one bitch of a town then. Believe me."

The St. Louis PD's treatment of Sonny basically ended the city's viability as a boxing venue. Missouri State Athletic Commissioner Charles Pian said you couldn't get a fighter to come there knowing that the police would be watching their every move.

CHAPTER THREE

A VALUABLE PROPERTY

It's difficult to know who owned what share of Sonny's contract but it's clear he never controlled more than 50 percent of his own earnings until after the second Ali fight, when his earning potential was next to nil. "If you listen to guys talk, they'd tell you eighty-seven guys got Liston," Barney Baker told Jimmy Breslin in 1961. "They used to put my name in there, too. I'll tell you something, I wish the hell he was my fighter. You and me would be out swingin' right now."

Breslin wrote that Sonny's early boxing career was "guided by a board of directors consisting of people whose names could be found on all the better police blotters." Prior to 1958, John Vitale, Chicago and St. Louis businessman, Bernie Glickman, and a St. Louis druggist named Eddie Yawitz owned pieces of Sonny's contract. Glickman was apparently close to Chicago's mob leader, Sam Giancana, because FBI wiretaps of Giancana's office picked up Glickman complaining that he was being screwed out of his 25 percent share of Liston's contract by East Coast mobsters. According to Justice Department officials, the power struggle was ultimately settled by the underworld's 12-member "Commission" when it ruled against the claims of its Midwest members.

By March of 1958, Frankie Carbo and Blinky Palermo controlled Liston's contract, with Pep Barone being the manager of record. Barone was an associate of Palermo and served as his "detail supervisor" for several years. Sonny signed a five-year contract with Barone just hours after a fight in Chicago. It was the first time the two had met. "When I went up to fight this fight, Frank Mitchell told me it would be a man by the name of 'Pep' Barone to come up with the contract and for me to sign it and he will get me East where I can get sparring partners and more fights, a better trainer," Liston told a U.S. Senate Subcommittee in 1960. "Anyway, I wanted to leave St. Louis, so this is my chance, so I signed with him."

Sonny was moved to Philadelphia, a great fight city that has produced a disproportionate share of champion boxers and trainers. "This was home to him," said Willie Reddish Jr, whose father became Liston's trainer in late 1958. Liston hoped for a fresh start but his negative reputation followed him to the City of Brotherly Love. Local sportswriter Jack McKinney suggested that an "informal police telegraph" dedicated to Sonny operated between the St. Louis and Philadelphia police departments and he was probably right. In any case, Philly's police department hated Liston from the start.

Sonny was repeatedly stopped for speeding or told to get off the sidewalk in front of his gym. One morning he and his sparring partners did their roadwork next to a public golf course when a police car stopped him, made him assume the position, frisked him, and ticketed him for trespassing because his foot had touched the golf course grass next to the sidewalk on which he was running. Philadelphia sportswriters reported these incidents as new brushes with the law. "Oh, the police department was something back then," said Willie Reddish Jr.

Sonny made a lot of good friends in Philadelphia and he met most of them in pool halls. Pool halls were his home away from home and if he had an office, it was at a pool hall at 57th and Haverford. "Everything was about the street with him. He loved the street," his friend Tommy Manning told me. "He loved people in the street, people from the ghettos, and they looked up to him."

Manning was a 20-year-old self-professed "booster" back then and said he stole only high-end merchandise. Tommy met Sonny when he walked into a pool room at 40th and Filbert with four pairs of $150 silk pants under his arm and a 9mm pistol in his waistband. Sonny wanted the trousers and when Tommy asked for $30 a pair, Sonny said, "I ain't giving you nothin'. I'm taking 'em." Patting the handle of his revolver, Tommy said, "you can take this too." That contentious exchange began a close relationship between the two men and though Manning was always in and out of jail, every time he came out, Sonny quietly slipped some money in his pocket and never said a word.

When the Listons were out socially on Sunday evenings, Sonny would give Tommy a hundred dollar bill and ask him to escort Geraldine back home so he could continue to party. Back then, the round-trip cab ride was six to eight bucks; Sonny never once asked Tommy for the change. "Sonny had no respect for money,"

Manning told me. "He didn't care about money. I seen him lose $3,200 trying to win $75 at an Elks carnival dice game. He kept betting and losing and said to me, 'Man, you can't beat 'em.'"

Sonny would bet on almost anything. He lost his diamond ring to Geraldine when he bet her that their flight home to Denver wouldn't stop in Omaha. Gerry didn't give it a second thought but two days later they were in a jewelry store getting the ring redesigned to suit her. On his 1963 European tour, Sonny was in Belfast when a man named Patsy Quinn told him he had fathered 23 children. Liston bet the guy $500 that it wasn't true. When Sonny went to Quinn's house he was greeted by all 23 kids and he paid up "without a murmur," according to Peter Keenan Jr.

Sonny could count money but he never really understood the value of any of his interests or how to protect them. He once loaned someone $25,000 and accepted as collateral a $30,000 house that had a $24,000 mortgage. One of his managers said Liston didn't care about taxes or expenses, only the dollars he could put in his pocket and spend after a fight. However, Geraldine always made sure they banked a good portion of his purses.

The Listons lived at the Hamilton Court Hotel for almost two years and ate most of their meals across the street at the Samson, a restaurant operated by Sam Margolis and Blinky Palermo. Sonny played checkers there and shot the bull with local college students. Liston became good friends with Margolis and he respected Sam's opinions, ideas, and beliefs. Margolis had a criminal record dating back to 1937 when he pleaded guilty to operating a gambling house and was sentenced to a month in jail. In the 1940s Sam was twice arrested on gambling charges and once on charges of assault and battery but was acquitted of all three crimes. Margolis knew a lot about all aspects of professional boxing and was friends with the people who controlled it, including Carbo and Palermo.

Palermo, nicknamed The Philadelphia Sportsman, ran the city's numbers racket and also owned a Mercury dealership, where he proudly hung his state penitentiary pardon next to his dealer's license. He had been incarcerated for operating a lottery and was arrested eight more times on charges including assault and battery, operating a disorderly club, and the reckless use of firearms. In the early 1950s he had the most active stable of fighters in the country. "His friends called him "Blinky" because of his peering manner, although his rasping voice was a more striking feature of his personality," wrote Barney Nagler.

"Every time they mentioned Palermo's name in the newspapers, Liston's was put in the next sentence," wrote Jimmy Breslin. It was common knowledge to almost everyone back then that Sonny was Palermo's fighter. "Being a Philadelphian, I heard that constantly," said Liston's future business partner Bob Nilon.

Truman Gibson told me the IBC paid main-event boxers like Sonny $4,000 per fight. In states like Illinois, where boxing commissions were dedicated to the fair treatment of its fighters, Gibson would make payment directly to the boxers. In states like Pennsylvania, where commissioners were on a friendlier basis with mobsters, the IBC's payments were made directly to Palermo, who often kept more of a fighter's money than he was entitled to—including Sonny's.

Blinky relied on Liston to do him favors for which he was particularly well suited. Eddie Futch told me attempts were periodically made to get to his fighters but he learned to anticipate them, as he did when he took welterweight champion Don Jordan to St. Louis for a rematch with Virgil Akins in 1959. Futch said he always signed the register, after which he'd put his fighter in the room he had registered in and visa versa. The fighter never knew anything about it. One night, Futch got up to go the bathroom at four in the morning and heard a knock on his door. When he opened the door, a surprised Sonny Liston was standing there in his pajamas and bathrobe. "He was a quick thinker," said Futch, "and he looked past me and there were a stack of towels on the rack and Sonny said, 'Say man, they forgot to leave me a towel. I want to take a shower. How about giving me a towel?'" There was no doubt in Futch's mind that Liston had been sent to imtimidate Jordan.

During Sonny's 1956 incarceration, Jim Norris was convicted in federal court of conspiring to monopolize trade and commerce in the promotion of championship bouts. He was ordered to desist but most managers still did business with Carbo and Palermo or their fighters didn't get big fights. The most notable exception was Floyd Patterson, who won an elimination tournament to become champ after Marciano retired. Since the IBC no longer controlled the heavyweight crown, it wanted to expose Liston to a national audience as often as possible.

After four televised fights in five months, boxing fans looked forward to Sonny's ferocious, early-round knockouts. Former champs Joe Louis and Max Baer were sitting at ringside when Liston destroyed Wayne Bethea, and most of his teeth, in just over one minute. After the bout, Truman Gibson offered Patterson $250,000 to fight Liston. The offer was ignored but Sonny's performance had served notice on his fellow heavyweights that the road to the title would have to go through him. One of the first to get the message was third-ranked Willie Pastrano, who began his career as a featherweight and would later win the light heavyweight title. "I boxed heavyweight for four years till I realized Sonny Liston wasn't my cup of tea," Pastrano admitted. "When I saw him come on the scene, I said, 'I'm going back down where I belong.'"

Shortly after the Bethea fight, Liston's trainer Jimmy Wilson died, and 43-year-old Willie Reddish took over the job of refining Sonny's talent. At six feet, 182 pounds, Reddish had been a small but talented heavyweight who at the age of 23 lost an 8–round decision to Jersey Joe Walcott for a purse of $12.50. Reddish ran a successful dump truck business that could have been bigger had he been able to find employees willing to work as hard as he did. He also owned an apartment building and though he didn't need the new job, it was one he certainly wanted.

"Boxing was his life and his biggest wish all his life was to train a heavyweight," said Reddish's son. "He was thrilled when they walked Sonny into that little gym on Ridge Avenue and told my father, 'you train him now.'" Reddish got the job because of his stellar 11-year stint as a Police Athletic League trainer. "They knew my father's reputation. They picked the right guy."

The younger Reddish first met Liston in his dressing room after one of his workouts. "He was a man. He was a *man*," said Willie, who was 25 at the time, a former Army drill instructor, and a Golden Gloves light heavyweight champion. "His arms were below his knees and his hands were so big they had to get special gloves for him." Willie still remembers that his father could hardly restrain his excitement that day. "My old man says to me, 'I got him now, *I got him!*'" Back then, everyone in boxing knew how good Sonny was and how good he could become. Reddish felt like he had won the lottery.

The year Liston formally introduced himself to the heavyweight division was 1958. Archie Moore told the boxing world there was a young boy named Sonny Liston who was "blowin' like a hurricane." Former No. 1 contender Nino Valdes went to England and told that country's sporting press, "Dis Liston go bom-bom. Kiss 'em goodnight." *Sports Illustrated*'s first mention of Sonny was in its May 26, 1958 issue after he destroyed Cuba's Julio Mederos in three rounds.

Liston's rise through the heavyweight ranks was unrivaled for its swiftness and brutality. After watching Liston knock out hard-hitting, sixth-ranked Mike DeJohn in February 1959, Marciano said Sonny was ready to take on Patterson. "He can move faster than Jersey Joe (Walcott)," said Rocky, "and don't get the idea he was slow."

In April, Liston fought Cleveland "Big Cat" Williams in a battle between two of the three hardest hitters in heavyweight history (Foreman was the other). Seven years later, Williams would be knocked out in three rounds by Ali in what many people, including Muhammad, believe was Ali's best fight. In a 2006 ESPN documentary on Ali, the second round of his fight with Williams is showcased as "a signature round" in Ali's storied career. Here's why those claims are ridiculous.

The truth was that Williams was finished as a fighter and lucky to be alive when he fought Ali. A year earlier, a highway patrolman shot him in the gut with his .357 magnum when Cleve supposedly resisted arrest after being stopped for speeding. Williams died three times on the operating table, lost 70 pounds, underwent three more operations to repair kidney and colon damage, and had his right kidney removed. A bullet that broke his hip joint and paralyzed some of his hip muscles was deemed too dangerous to remove and Williams' surgeon later said it was a miracle the fighter wasn't in leg braces.

But in 1959, as promoter Don Chargin said, "Williams was an animal and the second-baddest guy around." He proved it with a vicious assault in the first round against Liston which had him giving ground and bleeding from both nostrils. "He treated me rudely," said Sonny. "If I had one weak spot anywhere in my body, my chin or my heart, it would've showed up with all the whippin' put on me in that first round. Even before I sat down, I was thinkin' to myself, 'This cat gotta put it on me like that for nine more rounds to win this fight, and I don't think he can do it.'"

Reddish told Liston he was giving Williams too much punching room, and Sonny began to score heavily with both hands when he moved a little closer to the Big Cat. The end came at 2:04 of the third round. Though Sonny maintained Williams had never hurt him, it's clear from watching the fight that Cleve gave almost as good as he got. "I knew what I was doing all the time. I knew where my corner was. That's the way I tell if I'm hurt," Sonny insisted. "After that fight, I felt I could beat anybody."

Sixth-ranked Nino Valdes was Sonny's next victim. Cuba's greatest heavyweight had ended 1953 and 1954 as *Ring Magazine*'s No. 1 contender but Marciano wouldn't fight him because Nino was just too big. Veteran sportswriter Ned Brown had been around boxers since the early 1900s and was watching the fight with Jack Demspey in the ex-champ's Manhattan restaurant. "This is the first fighter (Liston) I've seen with a left hand since they began putting these damn things on the television," Brown said. "Big guy. Looks like he's a helluva fighter, don't he?" replied Dempsey. Brown turned away from the television and said, "I don't have to see any more. I know he can fight."

After being thumbed in the first round, Sonny came out for the second round squinting and blinking rapidly. He was seeing double with the bad eye open, so he'd blink it shut. Early in the third round, Liston followed a crushing left to the jaw with a right cross that left Valdes kneeling on the canvas, propped up by the ropes. Referee Bernie Weissman had also worked Sonny's 1958 knockouts of Bethea and Mederos and came away from the Valdes fight in awe of Liston's strength. "Liston's the most powerful heavyweight I've ever seen," said Weissman. "He's a weightlifter with finesse, and you can't hurt him. When I grabbed his arm to break a clinch, it was like grabbing a beast." *Time* took note of Sonny's dominating victory with a one-column article in its next issue.

Sonny was beginning to get the respect he had always wanted. "Now, when people see me on the street, they turn around and say, 'ain't that Sonny Liston, the fighter?' I make out I didn't hear nothing but I'm smiling and happy inside. I feel important. A man ain't nothing if he don't feel important. As long as I'm fighting and making money and driving a good car and eating regular, nothing much is bothering me," he said.

Liston's occasional trips to St. Louis made him realize how much happier he was to be living in Philadelphia. Sonny was visiting his sister Alcora's family in St. Louis in 1959 when an intelligence squad picked him up for questioning. At the Senate hearings on Antitrust and Monopoly in December 1960, Everett Dirksen asked the fighter why he had been arrested.

> *Liston:* Why? That's the question I would like to know.
> *Sen. Dirksen:* That is what I would like to know also.
> *Liston:* Well, I imagine he (John Bonomi, committee investigator) got the records, why did they arrest me?
> *Chief Counsel Bonomi:* We will go into that next, Mr. Liston.
> *Liston:* Because they never told me anything. They just picked me up and put me in the can and questioned me.
> *Dirksen:* That is a form of arrest, of course.
> *Liston:* Yes. Well, the captain, Captain Doherty, told me to my face, if I wanted to stay alive for me to leave St. Louis. So he said, "If you don't, they are going to find you in the alley."

Dirksen: Why do you think he said that to you?

Liston: I don't know. Because I couldn't tell him, the questions he asked me; I couldn't tell him. I didn't know nothing about them people. [When he was picked up, Sonny had the names and phone numbers of John Vitale, Barney Baker and Blinky Palermo on him.] The only thing I tried to do is work and make an honest living. I promised Father Stevenson (sic) I would never meet him back up there. So I figured by working—I can't get no government job, so what's for me to do? Starve to death?

Dirksen: Do you think the captain took you in custody, so to speak, and put you in the can, as you say, to keep you from winding up in an alley? Was it just one of those custodial proceedings?

Liston: No. He said that his men was going to put me in the alley.

Dirksen: Oh.

Liston: And he told me one night, he said, "Lock him up, when it get dark to let him go." And so as soon as dark came they came and got me, to let me go. So I made a phone call and called Ray Sarkis to come pick me up. So he came and picked me up. He drove up in the driveway to pick me up.

Dirksen: You committed no offense, no crime?

Liston: None whatsoever.

Dirksen: That you know of. But you were picked up from time to time?

Liston: Yes.

Dirksen: Then taken down to the station?

Liston: You know they have got a few fighters on the police force and they all try to get the captain to let them take me down in the basement. So I said, "Whatever did I do that you guys would want to take me in the basement?" They say, 'You think you're tough? We'll make it tough.'"

Dirksen: Did they ever actually take you in the basement?

Liston: No. The captain, he wouldn't stand for it.

Liston no longer lived in St. Louis and wasn't under suspicion for any crime but he knew that only bad things could result from his failure to submit to questioning. He admitted making occasional social calls to John Vitale and tried to be as cooperative as possible. As far as the St. Louis police were concerned, everything led to John Vitale. Faced with going home early or spending the night in jail, Liston told them what they wanted to hear. It was important to the police department that Sonny should never forget that he wasn't welcome in their city.

◆ ◆ ◆

Liston was the world's best heavyweight but it meant nothing. Ingemar Johansson had taken Patterson's title with an unexpected third-round knockout and Ingo, as he was affectionately called, seemed far more interested in exploiting his celebrity status than in defending his title. It would be 51 weeks before Ingemar and Floyd fought again, at which time the title would change hands and trigger another automatic rematch clause. A frustrated Liston offered to fight Ingemar and Floyd in the same ring at the same time, knowing they were two of the less formidable fighters in one of the strongest heavyweight divisions in history.

No boxer *ever* dominated a division the way Sonny ruled the heavyweights in 1960. His fights were testimonials to his invincibility and his public stature increased with every win. He was being called the grim reaper of the division and was in his own words, "cleanin' out a path to the title." By the end of the year the boxing world would be in awe of him.

In February the Official World Ratings of the National Boxing Association rated Liston second, behind Johansson and Patterson. Sonny had already knocked out Cleveland Williams, Billy Hunter, and Mike DeJohn, all of whom were ranked in the top 10.

Over the next six months, Liston would knock out fifth ranked Cleveland Williams again, this time in two rounds, sixth-ranked Roy Harris in one round, second-ranked Zora Folley in three rounds, and beat newly second-ranked Eddie Machen by decision, clubbing all but the unwilling Machen into submission. Folley, Machen, and Williams were dangerous fighters who Patterson refused to fight, and while Floyd took 12 rounds to subdue Harris, Liston needed only one.

"No one wanted to fight Folley, Machen, and Williams," Ernie Terrell told me. "Folley and Machen were top-shelf fighters. Only old Archie Moore knew more boxing moves than they did." Williams and Folley are best known for their nationally televised title fights against Ali in 1966 and 1967. They were both near the end of their careers and their fights with Ali thankfully provided them with the only good payday they ever had. However, Zora was almost 36 and the Big Cat's body was much older than his 33 years when they fought Ali. Nevertheless, many consider those fights to be Muhammad's finest performances, and Angelo Dundee said Ali never looked better than he did against Folley. When Liston fought Zora and Cleve, they were both dangerous opponents. By the time they fought Ali, all they had left were their reputations.

"I never fought anyone as stout as him," said Folley after being stopped by Liston. "I figured I'd make him miss, but he didn't miss enough. I knew I could outbox him. I didn't plan on opening up until the seventh or eighth round. But something happened. We didn't do it. He's too big, too strong, to let him crowd. I made my biggest mistake getting up against the ropes. I should have stayed out and boxed. He's too strong."

Seven weeks later, Liston fought Eddie Machen in a fight he optimistically called his "last elimination." At his best, Machen would have given Joe Louis all he could handle. Eddie was such a talented boxer that Liston's people made sure the fight contract included a provision for a rematch in the event that Machen won. Unfortunately, Eddie hurt his upper right arm six days before the fight and because the injury never improved, Machen knew he had no chance of beating Liston with only one arm. He fought anyway, but if the injury had been to his left arm he would have pulled out of the fight.

Such is the importance of having a healthy left hand in boxing. Had Eddie been at full strength, this could have been a memorable fight for all the right reasons. As it turned out, it was memorable only because of the way Sonny responded to Machen's tactics.

The best Eddie could hope to do was survive and the best way to do that was to make sure Sonny didn't fight his fight. To that end, Machen taunted and angered Liston throughout the fight by cursing him, calling him names, bull rushing and tackling him but he truly infuriated him by kissing him on the neck. "He was so mad at the way the fight was goin', and the fact that the referee was interfering with him, he just got plum thick and thought of nothing but knocking him out," said Willie Reddish. By the end of the fight, the pro-Machen crowd was rooting for Liston, who won a unanimous decision, losing only the two rounds that were taken from him because of one-point deductions for low blows.

Sonny was pissed because he equated Machen's tactics with cowardice. He didn't like having to endure question after question about his inability to knock Machen out. "You want me to get in there and fight by myself?" said Sonny. "When the other man keeps runnin' and won't fight, how you gonna make a fight? I'd felt better if I'd lose, if it's a good fight…Guess he was tryin' to make me angry. Never paid no attention." Nobody who saw the fight believed that last sentence.

Machen had shown that getting Sonny to fight angry was a smart move because it exposed the only significant weakness in his armor. Angry boxers tend to fight more like amateurs than professionals, and Sonny was no exception. If Liston fought *his* fight he couldn't be beaten, but if he lost his composure a master boxer like Machen could turn it to his advantage. Though Reddish told reporters his fighter would never again lose his cool, Sonny would do it again three-and-a-half years later—and it would cost him his title.

By the end of 1960, support for Liston's right to fight for the heavyweight title had peaked. *Ring Magazine*'s Nat Fleischer said no heavyweight had ever done more to earn a title shot than Sonny. As a matter of fact, no one has ever come close. *Sports Illustrated* editorialized that as long as the law had nothing to charge Liston with, he was entitled to a shot at the title. "Sonny Liston is the number one contender for the heavyweight boxing championshp," echoed *Boxing Illustrated*. "He is also an ex-convict. We don't think the one has anything to do with the other, and we hope that the only record of Liston's considered in connection with his claim to a title shot is his ring record."

Remarkably, *Ring Magazine* and the New York Boxing Writers' Association unanimously named Patterson their Boxer of the Year by virtue of his knockout of Johansson in Floyd's only fight of the year. It was now clear to Sonny that his toughest battle would take place outside of the ring, though it's doubtful he knew just how difficult it would be. In spite of being the undisputed No. 1 contender, Sonny would have to wait another 22 months before Patterson agreed to fight him. Not since Jack Johnson chased Tommy Burns halfway around the planet in 1907 and 1908 had the world's best heavyweight waited so long for his shot at the title.

In the meantime, Liston would have to defend himself in front of the U.S. Senate when a Subcommittee on Antitrust and Monopoly convened to determine how much influence organized crime had on boxing. Former Vice Presidential candidate Estes Kefauver of Kentucky chaired the hearings. He had twice chaired the Senate's hearings on organized crime during the 1950s and was also a very dedicated boxing fan. It would soon become clear that Liston's rise to prominence had precipitated the hearings.

Former IBC president Truman Gibson was the first to testify. He was grilled about his associations with Carbo and admitted that the IBC decided to live with him to guarantee the availability of quality fighters it needed for its twice-weekly television shows. He acknowledged that the mob could cause the IBC trouble by having a fighter fake an illness or by having workers generate a strike at one of Jim Norris's arenas. However, he repeatedly said that neither Carbo nor anyone else had been allowed to influence him or the decisions he made.

Norris testified behind closed doors after three doctors claimed a public hearing could endanger his already-poor health. Norris had survived two heart attacks and suffered from coronary artery disease and hypertension. He said he reluctantly developed a relationship with Carbo to fulfill his television contracts and claimed he had angered Carbo in 1952 when he offered J. Edgar Hoover $100,000 a year for ten years to run the IBC, crack down on hoodlums, and clean up boxing. Norris denied having any ownership of Liston's contract and said he'd never even met him.

When Pep Barone was subpoenaed to appear before Congress, his doctor sent the committee a letter that said that two psychiatrists had concluded he was suffering from depression, was incapable of testifying, and would need several weeks of continued hospitalization. Frank Mitchell and John Vitale pleaded the Fifth Amendment to all 61 questions asked of them. Blinky Palermo also invoked the Fifth Amendment on boxing questions and his associations with other people in the sport. Gibson had already testified that his contact for Liston's fights was always with Palermo and that Blinky told him he had a piece of the fighter. The five-foot tall Palermo would only say that he was 55, the father of five, and a resident of Philadelphia. His attorney was Morton Witkin, who would become Sonny's lawyer a year later.

Frankie Carbo was brought from Rikers Island, where he was serving a two-year term for arranging matches and managing without a license. Carbo congratulated Kefauver on his recent re-election but refused to answer questions about his boxing associations or activities. When subcommittee investigator John Bonomi declared that almost every leading manager or promoter in the United States was either closely associated with or controlled by Carbo, Frankie smiled.

The stream of uncooperative witnesses prompted Kefauver to subpoena Sonny to testify. Introducing himself as Charles Liston, the fighter was polite and respectful and the composure he exhibited impressed and surprised everyone. Within three minutes, the Senator was complimenting Liston for being cooperative, forthright, frank, and open.

Sonny was represented by Philadelphia attorney Jacob Kossman, who had also represented Blinky Palermo, but not at these hearings. "Mr. Liston wants to answer any question that the chair will ask. He told me that," said Kossman. "We appreciate it," said Kefauver. "He is recognized as a very fine boxer; the uncrowned heavyweight champion, he has been called." Kefauver told Liston he had information that indicated that Palermo, Vitale, and Carbo shared in his earnings. "I only know what I got on paper," replied Sonny, who insisted he was simply trying to work and make an honest living. Asked if he thought people like Carbo, Palermo, and Vitale should be connected with his management, Sonny said, "How could they all? Gee whiz, there wouldn't be nothing left for me. What's the use of me fighting?" When Kefauver asked him if he thought hoodlums should be banned from boxing, Sonny said, "I cannot pass judgment. I ain't been perfect myself."

Asked what he felt could be done to improve his sport, Liston said he'd feel obligated to the public to fight the No. 1 contender when he became champ. "Boxing is in a bad way. Only thing to bring it back is to get a champion like Joe Louis. He would fight anybody and everybody and just fight. I mean, not play around and pick his opponents." Sonny supported the idea of a national boxing commissioner to regulate the sport as long as it was someone with a boxing background, rather than a politician. Without a boxing background, Liston said it would be like letting a truck driver pilot a jet. Asked what he wanted most at this time, Sonny said, "the title." Senator Everett Dirksen described Sonny as short on words but long on clout.

Senator Kefauver took the unusual step of speaking to Liston from his heart.

> You had a hard beginning, you have had a hard time, you have made many mistakes, which you readily admit. You had a rough economic situation. You have undoubtedly been taken in by many improper people who made connections with you whether you knew it or not.

Apparently, the St. Louis police, or some of them, think that you may be beyond redemption, but I think that you have got a lot of good in you.

I'd like to see you have whatever chance you are entitled to, the championship or any other way. I don't usually moralize with witnesses or try to give them advice, but I think that your lawyer might go along with the suggestions that I might make.

I think it would be an awfully good thing for you to get back in touch with Father Stevens or some good man of the clergy who might be recommended in Philadelphia. Tell him that you want to get a manager who is absolutely clean, no record, fully licensed; someone that you can trust without any question, who will advise you correctly.

You say you have counsel about your investments, but I would be certain that you don't meet the plight that Ike Williams did, making an awful lot of money and losing it and winding up in later years with nothing.

Maybe there will be some good office of the law who you could consult with once in a while as to who your associations are, whether they are people that you ought to be associated with.

I hope that you will do these things because if you don't do them, you might wind up not being eligible to fight anywhere.

I think if you follow that kind of advice, boxing commissions will take that into consideration and overlook some of the past mistakes you have made, if there is a real effort to follow the counsel and advice of these good people with whom you might be associated.

I know that you appreciate the fact that there are many young people interested in boxing, who look up to the champion or to the contender for the championship, the heavyweight, so that you have a real responsibility and a real opportunity. But you are going to have to shake off the Palermos, the Vitales, and some of these people who have leeched themselves on to you. They have taken advantage of you and that has to stop, if you are going to get a chance. I don't mean to be lecturing you, but I hope it might be of some benefit to you."

In closing the hearings, Kefauver said Carbo's influence with promoters, managers, and matchmakers continued in spite of his imprisonment. He called Carbo, Palermo, and Vitale as vicious a group of racketeers as had ever appeared on the boxing scene. Fearful of their power if Liston became champ, Kefauver proposed creating a federal boxing commission to eliminate monopolistic influences from the sport.

After the hearings, the National Boxing Association's members voted unanimously in favor of Sonny receiving a title shot. However, the issues raised by the Kefauver hearings provided Patterson with an excuse to avoid fighting Liston. The people behind Liston controlled many other big-name fighters and there probably wasn't a major boxer in the previous 25 years who didn't have at least one underworld figure involved in his management. But Sonny was the only one who anyone sought to punish without any evidence of personal wrongdoing. The fact that Sonny had twice served prison time caused many of his critics to think he was unfit to challenge for, much less hold the heavyweight title.

Floyd arrogantly signed to fight Johansson for a third time. "If that Cus had his way, I couldn't even buy a ticket to watch Patsy fight," said Sonny. It may have occurred to Liston that Cus was a monopolistic influence on boxing all by himself. He froze out all the great black fighters, and the press never took him or his fighter to task for it. The way I see it, D'Amato was a little dictator and Patterson was a little coward.

Promoter Chris Dundee said the 1960 Olympic light-heavyweight champ Cassius Marcellus Clay appeared to be a lot more interested in getting in the ring with Sonny than Patterson was. "Clay wants to spar with Liston," said Dundee. "He says he wants to try him on for size." Clay had already talked his way into a sparring session with Johansson during which he made the Swedish fighter look more like an inexperienced pro than a former champ. "By the end of the first round I had him pinned against the ropes, all shook up and very mad," said Clay. "And he hadn't put a glove on me at the end of the second round."

Most of the boxing establishment dismissed the sparring session as a bad day for Ingemar, rather than the emergence of a highly talented young heavyweight. In truth, Johansson was slow, easy to hurt and, apart from a good right hand, lacked any real talent. Patterson couldn't demonstrate that in three fights with Ingo; Clay had been a professional for six months and he proved it in less than six minutes.

After Floyd stopped Ingemar in the sixth round, he was asked about defending his title against Liston and responded by saying he didn't want to get bumped off. "I'm the only mob he's worried about," replied Sonny. "As far as I'm concerned, Patterson is just afraid to fight me. That's all, and that's his way of avoiding me." A lot of other people felt the same.

Dewey Fragetta was a New York matchmaker who booked fighters all over the world. He had promoted a show in St. Louis in 1955 that had Liston on the undercard. "I took one look at him and I came back here the next day and had lunch at Dempsey's and I told everybody I had just seen a guy who would kill Patterson," said Fragetta. "It's the same thing now. Liston will ruin him. So it's only logical they're going to have all sorts of reasons why they can't let him fight for the title. But the main one is they don't want to get beat." Nevertheless, Liston's managerial history was Patterson's trump card, and Floyd wasn't the only one who played it.

World Boxing Association President Charles Larson promised to do whatever he could to prevent Liston from getting a title shot. He called Patterson a fine representative of his race and said the heavyweight champion of the world should be the kind of man America's children could look up to. Larson's thinly veiled bigotry reflected the sentiments of a large segment of white America, who would rather have their children look up to a paper champ than to a truly great athlete who happened to scare the crap out of their parents. But Sonny believed that public opinion would force Patterson to fight him—and he was right.

People were disenchanted with Patterson, whose manager had avoided every major contender, all of whom were black. D'Amato always made sure to match Patterson with fighters he was sure to beat while formidable, proven contenders like Folley, Machen, Williams, and Liston were passed over. Two years earlier when top-ranked Machen and second-ranked Folley fought to a draw, D'Amato arrogantly and self-servingly declared: "This eliminates both!" Folley's manager, Al Fenn, was so frustrated that he asked Congressman Stuart Udall to see if he could somehow prevent Patterson from ducking his fighter.

For two years D'Amato used the rematch clauses with Johansson to protect Floyd. Now Cus feigned righteous indignation that a man with Sonny's background could ever be considered for a shot at the title. The guy deserved to be slapped. Everyone in boxing knew that Cus acted the way he did because Patterson was not a formidable heavyweight. His championship credentials were suspect for three major reasons: his relatively small size, the quality of his opposition, and his weak chin. Floyd won a gold medal in the 1952 Olympics as a middleweight and for most of his early title defenses, was within seven or eight pounds of the light heavyweight limit of 175. Floyd could have been one of the greatest light heavyweights of all time but D'Amato knew that the money and power in boxing resided with the heavyweight champion and those who controlled him.

Like Marciano, Floyd became champ mainly because there were no good big men around at the time. He won the title Rocky vacated by beating 42-year-old Archie Moore. His first defense was a tenth-round TKO of Tommy "Hurricane" Jackson, a 185-pound journeyman with little skill. His second defense was a sixth-round knockout of Olympic heavyweight champion Pete Rademacher, in Rademacher's *first* professional fight. Patterson's only 1958 fight was a 12th-round TKO of Roy Harris. The champion's 1959 campaign began with an 11th-round KO of 8th-ranked Brian London, followed by his unexpected loss to Johansson in June. His only 1960 fight was a knockout of Johansson to regain the title. All of Patterson's title opponents were second-tier heavyweights and all of them knocked him down. Not coincidentally, except for Jackson, all of them were also white.

"I have a little dislike for Patterson, but it's not because he wouldn't agree to fight me for so long but because he hasn't fought any colored boys since becoming champion," said Sonny. "Patterson draws the color line against his own race. We have a hard enough time as it is in this white man's world."

Liston had run out of rated contenders who were willing to fight him. All that remained of the division he destroyed were a sorry collection of white pushovers who decided it would be healthier and far more lucrative to wait and hope that D'Amato would select them as fodder for Patterson. Sonny found himself in a Catch-22 predicament: by firmly establishing himself as the world's best heavyweight, he had convinced D'Amato that he was a fighter to be avoided at all costs. Sonny's no-win situation was clearly illustrated by the comments of Dan Kilroy, chairman of the California State Athletic Commission. Kilroy said that Liston could fight in his state only if he proved he had rid himself of his underworld ties, something good old Dan didn't think Liston could do "without a machine gun."

Skinny Davidson, who trained light heavyweight champ, Harold Johnson, summed up Sonny's situation. "Look, there's a lotta talk about Sonny's hooked up with the mob—even the Mafia. If he is, there's nothing he can do about it. That's boxing. He's trying to live around it, but people don't seem to want to let him."

CHAPTER FOUR

GUILT BY ASSOCIATION

In his 1963 Liston biography, *The Champ Nobody Wanted*, Doc Young observed that those who made a defense for Liston comprised one of the country's smallest minorities. In truth, Liston's toughest fights were always outside of the ring and in the court of public opinion. Before he won the title and after he lost it, Sonny's press coverage was probably worse than O.J. Simpson's was during his murder trial (the difference being that Sonny didn't deserve the treatment).

"To most white reporters, a Negro athlete is a clown. A Negro athlete is not worth taking seriously," *SI*'s Jack Olsen once told Liston. Reporters may have thought Sonny was a clown but he was a Negro they always took very, very seriously. No athlete was ever vilified more viciously and unfairly by the press than Liston. Among other things, Sonny was called an inferior Negro, less than human, slow-thinking, a primitive in a primitive profession, a latter-day caveman, a savage, glaring-eyed gorilla, a rogue elephant, a congenital thug, a cop hater and stronger than a yoke of oxen and just as dumb. Unfortunately, I could go on. Most of Liston's press coverage was devoid of fairness and accuracy. And it bothered the hell out of him.

Early in his career Liston grew so tired of responding to writers' questions that he'd sometimes shut his eyes, lean back against a wall, and fall asleep. He once said a newspaper man would look up at the sun and ask him if the sun was shining. It wasn't long before scribes began venting their displeasure by focusing on Liston's criminal record. "They constantly ex-convict these fellows," said Liston's former warden, E.V. Nash. "Why not recognize the fact that he's served his time?"

But sportswriters were also scared of Liston, so much so that some of them soiled themselves in his presence. Making reporters feel uncomfortable and scaring them with his glare was Sonny's way of paying them back for creating such an unfavorable public impression of him. His age and his mob associations were responsible for most of the bad press but what all black fighters faced was articulated by Liston to British sportwriter, Reg Gutteridge, in 1963, when he said, "You're just like all the other white guys, you think us blacks are just big hairy apes." Sonny, of course, was King Kong and if a writer didn't call him that, chances are he was thinking it.

Budd Schulberg could have been speaking for most of this country's press when he called Liston the meanest and most hated man to hold the heavyweight title since Jack Johnson. "Those were the days when he was regarded as the personification of evil," wrote Jack Olsen, "and the journalists, including me, crept about him and were hesitant to ask incisive questions." Olsen was one of a handful of white writers who treated Sonny with respect. As far as most sportswriters were concerned, Liston was simply too big, too black, and too damn good.

Jack Saunders was the secretary of the Pennsylvania State Athletic Commission and was impressed by the way Sonny parried inappropriate or hostile questions at press conferences. He found Sonny to be a quiet, sensible guy with wit and humor, rather than the hardened criminal that the media portrayed. "Don't think that Liston is an irresponsible dummy who doesn't know what he is doing," echoed *Ring Magazine*'s Dan Daniel. "He is sharp, he is alert, and he appreciates what he is saying and what somebody may be trying to make him say." For the most part, though, Sonny received respect and fair treatment only from black and female journalists.

Most boxers like to talk about their sport with people who know something about it, whether they're reporters or simply fans. But talking about their personal lives is and has always been something quite different. "There used to be a direct path to fighters and they would talk a lot and freely with reporters about boxing," Mark Kram wrote in *Ghosts of Manila*. "Not so with how they were formed or grew up; they became reticent or they didn't know how to answer, perhaps because to some of them their origins were so hideous that they looked upon it as another lifetime." More so than athletes in other sports, many fighters have spent much of their lives trying to overcome their pasts. People can't change their histories but there's nothing that says they can't rise above them. Sonny was never given that opportunity.

"If you're going to understand the kind of man I am, you got to get one thing straight," Liston told reporters. "I say what I mean because I don't know no other way. If I got something to say I don't pussyfoot around. I say it. That's it." That attitude didn't sit well with sportswriters, many of whom sought to inflict as much damage on Sonny's reputation and character as they possibly could. "The public instinctively dislikes Liston and that's grossly unfair," wrote Arthur Daley in the *New York Times*. "The average fan doesn't even know the man. One really has to know Liston to dislike him with the proper intensity." The truth of the matter was that Daley and other schmucks like him had no idea what kind of man Sonny Liston was.

Liston rarely revealed anything about himself in public, but all of his friends described him as a very good man. Willie Reddish said any man who cared for his wife and mother like he did, had his heart in the right place. "The guy's really got a big heart," said veteran trainer Skinny Davidson, "but if they keep on talking about him and writing about him like they do in the hometown papers, then he's got to get a complex of some kind and that's what happened." Novelist James Baldwin considered Sonny to be a very complicated, very dedicated, and very spiritual person and liked him a lot. "Say the guy had a good heart, that he's comical and you won't be wrong a little bit," said Liston's attorney Mort Witkin.

"Sonny was all right!" Willie Reddish Jr. told me. "You couldn't have met a nicer guy. I can't speak anything bad about Sonny Liston. I was around him a lot and I never heard him speak a bad word about anyone." Angelo Dundee said beneath Liston's tough exterior was a sensitive, caring man. "Despite what everyone said, Sonny Liston was the nicest guy in the world," said Irish Bobby Cassidy. "I think everyone was fooled by his glare. He was just a nice guy, one of the nicest boxers I ever met."

Former heavyweight champ Ernie Terrell insisted Sonny was nothing like his fighter's persona. "He was relaxed, but if he didn't know you, he'd put on a face." Ernie remembers walking down the street with Sonny and some other fighters, talking freely and being totally at ease. When Liston saw a group of guys coming toward them, his attitude would do a 180. "He'd put on a 'What these guys want?' face,'" said Ernie. "After the group passed he'd come back and it was like he was putting air back in a tire, as far as his demeanor was concerned. He was not that guy walking down the street. He was all right!"

Father Edward Murphy of Denver said reporters were lazy and would rather bring up the bad things in Liston's past than to give him credit for changing his life and achieving his goals. Sonny told friends he was hurt by the newspaper articles that dwelled on his criminal past. "The newspapers always put me down as a bad guy," he said. "You can't live it down." He believed he had already paid a heavy price for those wrongs and felt like he was being crucified.

Geraldine said her husband used to talk to sportswriters until they started making stuff up. "You gonna say what you gonna say anyway, so you say it," she remembers Sonny telling them. Geraldine said that sportswriters' lives probably wouldn't look very clean under the same kind of bright spotlight that was shined on her husband. She probably felt greater resentment toward the press than her husband did, feelings that she harbored until her death in 2005.

Sonny Liston was a man who simply did not like to talk. "He was a reserved sort of fellow," said Jefferson City's assistant warden, W.P. Steinhauser. "He was the sort of fellow you almost had to draw a conversation out of." Wary of people he didn't know, Sonny spoke only when spoken to and only after a pause that most people found unnerving. "Actually, we have never talked to Liston," said World Boxing Association president Ed Lassman. "You can't talk to him. He doesn't answer you. He just lifts his head up and stares at you."

Attorney Mort Witkin remembered the time Sonny came to his office and sat for 43 minutes without saying a word. Witkin was watching the clock; those were billable minutes. A Seattle sportscaster once spent three hours with Sonny in order to produce a six-minute television feature. When Liston addressed the student body of an Iowa high school, he spoke for 30 seconds. "I keep my speeches like my fights—short," he told the students.

"I don't talk to my wife. Why should I talk to a man?" Sonny once said, a sentiment confirmed by Geraldine who said she'd ask her husband a question, he'd give her an answer and that was it. "He never talked much as a kid and he still don't," said his mother. When he first started training with the ex-champ in 1968, George Foreman said Sonny gave him three sentences worth of advice and didn't say another word to him for three months. "Sonny Liston was Sonny Liston," said George. "He didn't say nothin'."

Contrary to public opinion, Sonny wasn't stupid, and there was nothing slow about his mind. "He's not dumb by any means. He's pretty shrewd," said Father Stevens, who described Sonny as nobody's fool. Father Murphy found Sonny to be a bright man with great native intelligence that couldn't be accurately measured because of his lack of education. Sportswriter Jack McKinney said Sonny was "a deeply sensitive guy, with an I.Q. (had there been a way of measuring it) that was probably higher than that of any boxer I've ever known, before or since."

Former light heavyweight champion Jose Torres said he never met a baseball, basketball, or football player who was more intelligent than Sonny. "He was so smart, it wasn't even funny," said Torres, who claimed sportswriters either couldn't or wouldn't understand that Liston had difficulty articulating his ideas because his vocabulary was somewhat limited. Sonny mispronounced a lot of words and he was very self-conscious about it. Instead of corporation, he'd say cooperation; he'd call Roquefort dressing, rockfort dressing; he referred to plastic surgery as plaster surgery. Nevertheless, when he'd hear a word he didn't understand he'd ask someone for its meaning and use it properly when the opportunity arose.

Tommy Manning believes Sonny had a photographic memory and his friends would marvel at the way he could repeat the routines of black comedians down to the last detail with perfect inflection. Publicist Ben Bentley said Liston could tell you the names of almost all of the sportswriters sitting in the first three rows of ringside. "He fools you," said Willie Reddish. "He's so aware of what's going on. He sees things before other people can see them, or remembers things other people forget."

"He was always comfortable," said Henry Winston, who was close to Sonny in the late 1960s. "Here was a man who was psychologically strong, mentally never wrong. He would act like a man with wisdom and common sense. There weren't any big words, just down-to-earth conversation." Winston told me he never met anybody who was more honest with himself than Liston was. "You come with the BS and he was gonna straighten you out," said Tommy Manning.

Constantly portrayed as mean and even barbaric, Sonny was compassionate, polite, and exceedingly friendly—unless he drank too much. "I know he ought to be above reproach," said Geraldine. "I know he ought to be better than other people, but sometimes he do get into things." In truth, Liston was a principled man, a friend of the underdog, and anxious to prove to people that he was deserving of their respect.

Sonny always said meeting his wife was the best thing that ever happened to him. "She was there when the going was rough," he said. "When I was in jail she came every visiting day, never missed." His niece Helen believes they met at a grocery store where Geraldine worked as a cashier but Geraldine told *Esquire's*

Bruce Jay Friedman that she met Charles when he was a munitions worker and she worked for S&W Foods. Geraldine was born in 1925 though she always claimed she was born seven or eight years later.

All of Sonny's friends were fond of Geraldine. "She was a very nice lady and she loved her Charles as far as I could tell," said Willie Reddish Jr. Tommy Manning said Geraldine treated him like the mother he never had. Ernie Terrell went out of his way to meet her, a move that ingratiated him with Sonny. "When you do that, you're pretty much all right with the family," said Ernie. "He had a good wife. She knew how to handle him." Liston's friends said Geraldine was always a very positive influence on him and if she didn't like you, he wouldn't like you either. "When he was nothing, she never complained and was always loyal and devoted to him," said Liston's publicist, Ben Bentley. "No wonder Sonny is crazy about his wife."

Geraldine always called her husband Charles. She said her husband loved to tease her when they were first married. "He'd come into the house without me knowin' and I'd be hummin' and singin' and all at once he'd tiptoe up behind me and scare me to death. His mother said he used to keep her jumpin' all the time. I hear a noise now and I say, 'All right, Charles, come out.'" Gerry remembered how excited she was when his name was flashed on the television screen in advance of one of his early bouts but she rarely watched him train and never attended or listened to his fights. Instead, she'd distract herself by reading, cooking, or cleaning while waiting for his call. She said Charles was an easy man to live with but she'd get mad at him if he was late for dinner. "We get along good," said Sonny.

"He was the most feared man, but Geraldine was his boss," said Lem Banker. Liston's first manager, Frank Mitchell, referred to Gerry as Sonny's right arm and she'd read his mail and write his letters. "I think Sonny is living down his past and his wife is a fine influence on him," said attorney Mort Witkin. "She's tried in many ways to help him and it shows. Sonny appreciates it and talks about it."

In 1961, the Listons bought their first home for $15,000 in an integrated, middle-class neighborhood in West Philadelphia. Their car was a nondescript Ford sedan. Willie Reddish Jr. visited the Liston's home on many occasions and said Geraldine had decorated it beautifully though Sonny personally chose the busts of Aphrodite and Buddha that adorned their living room.

As a neighbor, Sonny was so quiet and inconspicuous that many people wondered if he ever talked at all. "Few of us got to know him personally," said

Georgianna Myer, "but we all got used to seeing him come up and wave a cheery hello to us. The smile always followed and we'd smile and wave back. It's a pleasure to have a neighbor like that." Gloria Wilkins lived two doors down from the Listons and said Sonny was always friendly and always smiling. "We never had a minute's trouble with him in any way."

Liston's close friend, Mrs. Martha Malone (Joe) Louis said Sonny was considerate and affectionate to his wife. He did most of his wife's shopping and while she'd buy one dress at a time, he'd always come home with three or four. Geraldine said her husband had great taste. When times were good, Sonny repainted Geraldine's Cadillac convertible shocking pink to match the color of her favorite sweater. "Charles is awfully generous," she said. "Never once has he told me what I should or shouldn't spend, never once." She said Sonny added a diamond to her wedding band every year and remodeled her engagement ring several times.

Nevertheless, Geraldine had to accept her husband's serial infidelity. "As long as he's married when he comes home. Ain't no man married when he's away from home," Geraldine once said. "He acts like he loves me, whether he does or not, and he takes care of home and that's all you can ask of a man." A lot of men and women would take exception to the first part of that statement but Geraldine had to believe it in order to keep her marriage together. When Jack Olsen asked Sonny if he engaged in any other sports, he said "broad jumping—jumping from one broad to another." Gerry was in the room when Sonny said that.

Liston's sexual appetite may have been as prodigious as his talent and anybody who saw him in the shower would tell you he had the biggest penis they'd ever seen. He was one of the great playboys of the 20th century and if he didn't sleep with as many women as Wilt Chamberlain did, it wasn't for a lack of effort. When a woman would complain that he came and she didn't, he'd tell her champs come first.

"He had a tremendous magnetism that was quite astonishing," said British promoter Mickey Duff. Fellow promoter Mel Greb said "the smell of white pussy was like chloroform to him." Liston boxed to make a living but he lived for sex. When asked in 1968 what he would do if he were as rich as Bobby Kennedy, Sonny smiled broadly and said, "I'd buy me the finest pussy in the United States of America."

Geraldine and Charles had no kids of their own but he fathered several children out of wedlock. Sonny's youngest daughter, Choo Choo, lived with his sister Alcora for several years and a son named Bobby lived with the couple in 1960 and was claimed as a dependent on the Listons' 1960 tax return. A man named Charles Liston lives in Chicago and his striking resemblance to his father lends credence to his claim that Sonny was his father. There is also a man in Gary, Indiana who Sonny's niece Helen saw as a small boy and immediately knew he was fathered by her Uncle Charles. The boy's mother was married at the time and denied it. A son named Sonny Liston Jr. died in Oklahoma City in 2008 at the age of 58.

Five days before Sonny won the heavyweight title, his son William Wingate was born. William was only eight when Sonny died and his earliest recollections of his father were when he was five or six years old. "Based on what my mother told me, I know for a fact that we didn't want for nothing. I can't tell you what it's like to grow up hungry. We were well, well taken care of. I had the best clothes, I had the best toys."

William is his father's son in more ways than one. Until recently his 6'1" body resembled that of his father's. William's ring size is 13 and though his hands are not quite as big as his dad's, his forearms could pass for biceps. Not too many years ago William hit former heavyweight contender Bert Cooper's chin so hard that the EMTs broke two ammonia capsules under his nose and still couldn't revive him.

When William saw an ESPN special on Sonny several years ago, it was the first time he really felt like his son. "I looked him in the eye and it was like I was looking in the mirror," he told me. William is a warm, sweet man who knows so many people that he says he can pretty much go from Philadelphia to New York shaking hands. Apart from his closest friends, almost nobody knows that Sonny Liston is his father. When he was growing up, he didn't either because the name of his birth father was a family secret. "I really thought he was just a friend of the family," William told me. "All I knew was I liked him and he liked me. We just clicked from the beginning." Sonny's black Cadillac convertible with red leather interior reminded William of the Batmobile.

Sonny may have loved kids more than any athlete ever did, and the feelings were always mutual. "You should have seen him with the kids. Boy, did he love 'em," said Joey Curtis, president of the American Veteran Boxers' Association. Children never saw the menacing look that other people did and if there's such a thing as an automatic uncle, Charles Liston was that man. "Funny thing," Sonny once said, "adults think I look mean. How come I don't scare the kids? Maybe they got more courage." He liked that kids had their own way of thinking and that they weren't jealous people. He willingly signed autographs for his younger friends because they had "a future" and he wanted every kid's childhood to be the opposite of his. "You think you've got it bad," he said after visiting a hospital for crippled children. "You go there and you know you've never had a dark day."

A little red-haired kid became good friends with Sonny while he was training for the Patterson fight. "He's nice," said the kid. "We talk a lot. No, never about boxing. Mostly just about things. You know, like he was a friend of mine." Over the years Sonny had high-profile friendships with several white children and ironically, this was the one area of his life that wasn't criticized. People either didn't know what to make of these relationships or realized that since the kids adored Sonny as much as he adored them, it would have been foolish to make an issue out of it.

Liston met 11-year-old Mike Zwerner in Miami Beach while training for the Patterson rematch. The Associated Press called the boy Sonny's mascot. Jack Zwerner was a successful businessman and felt the friendship his son had with Sonny could only be good for him. "You can ask why doesn't he take a colored kid around with him?" said Mr. Zwerner. "This is to show that he is impartial. He knows that some colored people resent it. Sonny has nothing to gain." When Mike's summer vacation began, Sonny insisted that he fly to Denver to stay with him and Geraldine. Liston bought Mike a motor scooter and they rode around the neighborhood together with Sonny seated behind his young friend, using his feet as brakes.

Peter Keenan was also eleven when Sonny went to Glasgow, Scotland to spar on one of his father's programs. "He arrived at my dad's home in Kelvinside. He called me 'Petesie' and insisted that everywhere he went on the tour, I should accompany him." Sonny flew Petesie to his Denver home for Christmas that year, where he was greeted with a big, well-lit 'Happy Xmas Petesie' sign on Liston's roof. He had been in Denver for three weeks when the elder Keenan received the Listons' request to legally adopt his son. Within 48 hours Petesie's dad arrived to take him back to Glasgow.

◇ ◇ ◇

Sonny earned $39,000 in 1960. It was the most he had ever earned but Gerry said she'd choose poverty over prizefighting. "I'd much rather live simply without this anxiety and torment," she said. Sonny, however, was prepared to do whatever was necessary to get a title shot, and that meant getting rid of Pep Barone. "The way it is now, Patterson won't fight me because of the men he says are behind Pep," he said.

The men behind Pep—Carbo and Palermo—were on the verge of being convicted of extortion in trying to become part owners of welterweight champion Don Jordan. They would receive sentences of 25 and 15 years, respectively, and their personal relationship at that time was strained, to say the least. Carbo had managed to avoid New York's ten-count indictment for almost a year by hiding out in an associate's New Jersey home and was taken into custody only after Palermo gave the FBI the address.

In April, Liston asked Barone to sell him his contract and threatened to quit boxing if Pep sold the contract to someone else. "Sonny wants to be free," said Barone. "He says he won't let me sell him to anybody else—like a slave. If he means what he says about quitting, there'd be nothing in it for either of us." Liston agreed to pay Barone $75,000 with $18,000 up front and the rest to be paid over the next two years.

Now Sonny felt he'd done everything that had been asked of him, but D'Amato threatened to sue anyone who tried to "impose" Liston on his fighter. Nevertheless, Patterson had painted himself into a corner from which there was really no escape. If Liston's next manager had no baggage and Floyd still refused to fight him, it would show that Sonny's managerial connections were only an excuse to hide Patterson's fear of getting in the ring with him.

When people learned Sonny was looking for a new manager they literally beat a path to his door. He received managerial offers from Marciano, Louis, and Sugar Ray Robinson among others. Many who crowded into Liston's relatively small home over a three-day period weren't even involved in boxing but everyone was interested in negotiating some kind of an agreement with him, including would-be promoter Robert Nilon. Nilon and his brothers Jim and Jack ran a lucrative catering business. They had operated the concessions at the Army-Navy football game, Ringling Bros. circuses, and Billy Graham rallies, and once handled the feeding of employees during the construction of the hydrogen bomb plant in Augusta, Georgia.

The Nilons wanted to branch into championship boxing events and had unsuccessfully attempted to bring the second Patterson-Johansson fight to

Philadelphia the previous year. To curry favor with Liston, Nilon would get him tickets to different sporting events but the fighter always turned them down. Nilon said Sonny wasn't interested in football, baseball, or any sport other than boxing. "Sonny wanted to fight—period!" said Bob.

Sonny surprised the boxing world when he signed a 30-month contract with 50-year-old George Katz, giving his new manager 10 percent of his purses. Katz was a diminutive, pompous picture framer who told the press he hoped the high-profile nature of his new job would help him meet women. Katz's claim to boxing fame was getting Gil Turner a welterweight title fight, and his reputation for screaming loud and long on behalf of his fighters appealed to Liston. What Sonny wanted and needed from a manager was very basic, never disrespect him, always have his back, make sure he fought on a regular basis, get him good money, and get him the Patterson fight as soon as possible.

Liston and Katz testified under oath that neither had a silent partner, and the Pennsylvania State Athletic Commission approved their contract and issued Sonny a license for the first time. Patterson sent his congratulations to Liston and announced he would ask Kefauver's Senate Committee if it approved of Sonny's choice. When Kefauver heard that, he wrote Floyd saying it would be unconscionable to deny Liston a title shot and that he should fight him immediately. "Is my house clean enough now for him to give me a fight or was he only looking for an excuse to duck me?" said Sonny. "I don't see how Patterson will be able to walk down the street now, unless he gives me a fight." Or unless Sonny provided Floyd with an excuse not to fight him, which is exactly what happened.

In the first of two questionable arrests, Liston was standing in front of a drug store signing autographs and answering questions about the possibility of getting a fight with Patterson when a black police officer told both he and the fan to move along. Cracking down on loitering was a priority for the Philadelphia police department at the time. "What is this, Russia or something, you can't stand on a street corner?" asked Liston. "If I'm not allowed to stand on the street corner and talk to people, then I might as well be in Alabama." The cop told Sonny to move on or get locked up and arrested him when he told the officer he must be kidding.

The desk sergeant heard Liston's story and dismissed the incident as a misunderstanding. However, when Sonny insisted on a lift back, the police charged him with "corner lounging" and locked him up. Four hours after the arrest, a magistrate came to the police station to hear Liston's side of the story. Sonny said people who paid taxes had a right to stand any place they wanted and that the cop should have asked him and the fan what they were doing before he got tough. He received a brief lecture and was released. Two days later, Athletic Commission chair Alfred Klein wrote Liston a letter warning him to stay out of trouble. The World Boxing Association considered corner lounging to be such a serious crime that they immediately dropped Sonny from their ratings. I couldn't make this stuff up if I tried.

Sonny's friends were amused by the second incident, which they still call "the lark in the park." In the early-morning hours of June 12, Delores Ellis was driving home through Fairmount Park when Sonny flashed his car's spotlight on her Cadillac, and his passenger, Isaac Cooper, ordered her to pull over. Sonny would later say Cooper had told him he thought the woman was a prostitute. When a park guard drove up, Sonny and Isaac were arrested and charged with impersonating an officer, resisting arrest, conspiracy, and operating a motor vehicle without lights. The headline of Dan Parker's column in the *New York Mirror* the next day read, "Liston Proves Himself Unworthy of Title Shot."

After a two-week continuance, the judge ruled that Liston and Cooper had been guilty only of errors of judgment and dismissed the charges. However, the matter was far from over. When the State Athletic Commission ordered Liston to explain the arrests under oath, Sonny apologized for his behavior, waived his right to a hearing, and threw himself on the mercy of the commission. He got none and was suspended, a ruling that was effective in all 50 states. A lot of people knew those arrests should never have been made—and they wouldn't have been if the police weren't out to get Liston.

Philadelphia was home to the world's best heavyweight but it's clear the city didn't want him any more than St. Louis had. Local trainer Skinny Davidson was embarrassed by the way his city treated Liston. He knew that Sonny was trying to carve out a better place for himself, but he also knew that a lot of people didn't want him to succeed. "You want my personal opinion?" he asked a reporter. "The law has made Liston what he is by harassing him. And that's that."

Sonny said the publicity hadn't done him any good and insisted the situations weren't as bad as the newspapers said they were. "People are easily led against you and it's harder to get them to go along with you," he said. Knowing he needed damage control, Sonny flew to Denver in search of guidance and rehabilitation from Father Murphy, who he had met while training for the Folley fight. Murphy preferred the word reorientation to rehabilitation because the latter meant changing a man's character, which he said Liston didn't need to do. For three hours every afternoon, another priest taught Sonny to read using the flash card system; Murphy said he learned quickly. He characterized Liston as a "big, soft boy who has been kicked around since he was born. If only they would give him a chance."

The Listons lived in a house next to the rectory of St. Ignatius of Loyola Catholic Church along with four priests and the family of the church's caretaker. Sonny helped out by cutting the lawn of the church's school grounds, taking out the rectory garbage, and waxing the floors. Sonny would take a heavy, old-fashioned school desk in each hand and carry them out two at a time until he had cleared the floor.

After his morning roadwork and breakfast, Sonny would converse with visitors or talk with Murphy. In the afternoon he'd work out for two hours at nearby Lowry Air Force Base and on weekends he'd visit the church's mountain retreat. He quickly earned the respect of everyone including a lot of police officers.

Murphy received criticism from several friends for helping Sonny but the priest spent enough time talking to him to realize that the fighter had a strong desire to do good things. "He wants to be liked and he wants to do something for his people so they will be proud of him," said Murphy, who was impressed by the way Sonny spoke with the boys at his church complex and urged him to join the fight against juvenile delinquency. "He told them they can't make it if they don't behave themselves. They listened to him."

Sonny's relationship with Father Murphy was such a positive experience that he announced he would enter the priesthood when he retired from boxing. Told that his being married to Geraldine prevented that, he joked, "I guess I have to get rid of her now." According to his friend and sparring partner Foneda Cox, Liston thought the world of Father Murphy and when Sonny thought highly of someone, he valued that person's advice. "I feel I have found a true friend for the first time," Liston said of Murphy. "I feel like a new person."

New person or not, Liston couldn't stop drinking. Tommy Manning said Sonny would drink hard liquor and a lot of it, "but he'd walk out just as straight as I was and I didn't drink back then." Henry Page saw his Uncle Charles get drunk on more than one occasion when he visited the champ in Denver in 1963. Sonny had switched from Canadian Club to vodka by that time. "He'd drive his Fleetwood and I'd be riding with him and he'd put the bottle down when he passed a car so no one would see him," said Page.

Tommy and Henry never saw Sonny's dark side but other people who knew Liston would tell you that he was a heck of a nice guy unless he drank too much. IBC President Truman Gibson described Liston as an unbridled drinker. "If he had a drink it would mean the whole bottle," Gibson told me. "When he was bad he was really, really bad." Alcohol tends to bring out the worst in people, and Sonny was no exception.

While training for a fight, though, Sonny was able to stop drinking as if turning off a faucet. He'd never allow people whose approval and acceptance was important to him see him drink. "We used to go away for weekends in Los Angeles and Houston, and he never took a drink in front of me," said Liston's good friend Lem Banker. "And we used to go out a lot." Close friends Davey Pearl and Ash Resnick told me the same thing.

When the District Attorney in Philadelphia discovered that the initial hearing was held 30 minutes ahead of schedule and that no Assistant DA had been present, he decided to reopen a closed case and re-arrest Liston on charges of resisting arrest and turning off car lights to avoid identification. Both charges were misdemeanors, punishable by as much as three years in jail and a $500 fine.

At a juryless trial on September 27, Sonny was represented by the son of a Philadelphia Congressman, and Father Murphy was one of several character witnesses who testified on the fighter's behalf. Sonny took the stand and said his companion believed he knew Mrs. Ellis and that was why he stopped his car near hers. He insisted he never attempted to avoid identification and claimed the headlights got turned off by accident. "A jury would certainly render a verdict of not guilty and that's what the verdict is," said Judge Joseph E. Gold. He also noted that if Sonny hadn't been involved, the whole case would have been disposed of in a magistrate's court which, of course, it already had been two months earlier.

Before the day was over, Delores Ellis filed suit against Liston in Common Pleas Court seeking more than $5,000 in punitive and compensatory damages. Ellis claimed invasion of privacy, mental anguish, severe shock to her nervous system, loss of work, humiliation, and mental suffering. By the sound of it, had Sonny actually gotten out of his car, Ms. Ellis might have dropped dead on the spot. "Man, am I glad the woman back there wasn't white," Sonny said later, "because they sure would have hung me and called me another Jack Johnson."

Three weeks later, the Athletic Commission voted to reinstate Liston when it learned of a proposed closed-circuit doubleheader involving him and Patterson at separate locations. Sonny's $75,000 payday would be the largest of his career by far and he also got Patterson's promoter to promise him that he would get Floyd to finally give him the title shot he deserved.

Liston's opponent was German heavyweight champion Albert Westphal, who looked like a shorter version of wrestler Gorgeous George. Sonny called him Quickfall. At the weigh-in, Westphal asked Sonny why he looked so angry. "You'll find out tonight," was the response. Then Liston went home and hosted a party where he selected the music while everyone else celebrated in advance by drinking champagne. Sonny ate his usual steak dinner and took a nap.

That night, Liston landed a paralyzing right hand to the German's left cheek, a punch that Willie Reddish said was the hardest Sonny ever landed. Westphal went down hard on his face in the center of the ring with blood oozing from his left ear and was counted out at 1:58 of the first round. Reddish prayed silently for the German's survival. When Westphal finally regained consciousness, it was several minutes before he was able to leave the ring under his own power. "My body feels good," said Westphal, "but my soul not so." Joe Louis laughed when he heard the way Westphal responded to the thought of a rematch. Joe said it was the first time he ever heard a fighter say, "No, I don't want no more."

Liston and his handlers went to the press room to watch Patterson defend his title against Tom McNeeley, a white, unranked former Michigan State football player and 10-1 underdog. It was as though Patterson and D'Amato were thumbing their noses at every black contender. Like his son Peter who fought Mike Tyson a generation later, McNeeley couldn't fight a lick. What's more, the fight had been moved from Boston to Toronto after Massachusetts boxing officials refused to allow D'Amato to use his own referee for the fight.

The bout was a major embarrassment to the sport of boxing. McNeeley made faces and threatening gestures at Patterson but it was all downhill for him after the bell rang. Sonny was amused that Patterson tried to help his opponent up after three of his nine knockdowns, as if he had nothing to do with putting him on the canvas. Asked what he thought of Floyd's performance, Sonny simply said, "Tell you what I think? You want me to blow my chance of getting a fight with this guy?"

Sonny had visited D'Amato in New York and the report of this meeting was intentionally distorted either by a writer or by Cus. Whoever the guilty party was, the description of the meeting is highly unflattering to Sonny, yet is repeated to this day. As the made-up story goes, Liston appeared unannounced in D'Amato's apartment causing little old Cus to clutch at his heart in distress. "Is you is or is you ain't gonna give me a shot at the title?" the fighter supposedly asked.

Fight historian Jimmy Jacobs lived with D'Amato and was present the day Sonny visited. He told me the scene that I described to him never took place. "Liston wanted to fight for the heavyweight championship of the world and he asked why he couldn't," said Jacobs. "Sonny was extremely polite. His demeanor was, in my opinion, impeccable."

Cus told Sonny to get himself a new manager who wasn't controlled by hoodlums and suggested that Liston send him a list of managers' names for inspection and that he would put a circle around one of them. "Ain't that nice," said Sonny. "What you mean is that you want to control me." The two shook hands and Sonny left the apartment convinced that Cus was nuts, as did a lot of boxing people who referred to D'Amato as the "crazy man." After the meeting D'Amato told the press that the fight could be signed as soon as Liston did what Cus told him he must do.

"D'Amato has never told me anything," said Sonny. "All he keeps saying is Liston knows. I *don't* know. Cus says when I do whatever *it* is I can sign for the title fight tomorrow. But when tomorrow comes, *it* is always tomorrow." When he returned to Denver, Sonny began dreaming about fighting Patterson but always woke up just before the contracts were signed.

Katz's pompous personality grated on Liston and the two never got along. Sonny also found it unacceptable that Georgie never called him while he was in Denver. Most important, Liston felt Katz had done nothing to get him closer to the Patterson fight. "I have to wait between fights," Sonny said. "They don't come often. That's how I got into trouble the last time, too much loafing around. All I want to do is fight in the ring. I want to fight Patterson. Then there is no trouble, just fights."

Sonny began to rely on Bob Nilon's 40-year-old brother Jack on managerial matters. The Nilons met Father Murphy at the U.S. Open in Denver, and the priest recommended Jack to Sonny even though he had no experience in the fight game.

Married and the father of six, Jack was the son of an Irish-born blacksmith and had his share of fist fights growing up. Always on the lookout for a way to make money, he began selling newspapers at the age of 11 and claimed to have supported himself ever since. After the war, Jack and his brother Jimmy used their $45 bankroll to set up a shack next to the shipyard selling sandwiches and coffee. In a few years they had built a very successful business.

Sonny liked Nilon and called him his investment adviser. The fighter delegated to Nilon all the things for which he had no aptitude and told him to do whatever he thought was right. Nilon always felt Liston needed a business manager more than he did a fight manager and while that may have been true, the future would clearly show that it would have been in Sonny's best interests to keep the two functions separate. In the final analysis, Nilon thought of Liston as a way for he and his brothers to control the promotion of heavyweight championship bouts.

Just ten months after signing with Katz, Sonny agreed to a five-year contract with Nilon, making him his sole and exclusive manager. Katz told the Boxing Commission that Liston was free to negotiate future contracts without him. In return, Sonny agreed to fulfill the terms of Katz's contract by paying him 10 percent of his purses until their contract expired on October 23, 1963. Newspaper reports had Nilon paying Liston $125,000 or $150,000 for his contract.

Sonny was beginning to see the light at the end of the tunnel when Nat Fleischer threw the editorial weight of *Ring Magazine* behind him. Ring had received hundreds of letters, most of which said Liston had earned the right to fight Patterson. It was getting a lot harder for D'Amato and Patterson to hide behind Sonny's mob connections. Blinky Palermo was appealing his conviction and that legal fight consumed most of his resources. "All he can see is those 15 years in the can," said a fight manager who knew him. "Blink has mortgaged his house. The poor slob is broke—he's in tap city. He couldn't care whether Liston lives or dies." Palermo's financial situation was so dire that he asked Jack Nilon to try and get him a job. "He said he would do anything," Nilon later told a Senate committee. "He said he would dig a ditch. I distinctly remember."

For the first five years of Patterson's championship tenure, D'Amato shrewdly refused to let his fighter defend the title against any contender aligned with the IBC. By doing so he was able to justify ducking the fighters who could beat Patterson since all of the major contenders had managers who were controlled by Carbo and Palermo. After ruling the roost with a natural light-heavyweight and making both of them a fortune, D'Amato acted like the heavyweight title was his own personal possession. But the world would soon learn that D'Amato's business methods were no different than those of the people he criticized.

In 1958, Bill Rosensohn tried to get D'Amato to defend Patterson's title against Johansson. He got nowhere until he met a mobster and friend of D'Amato who told him that he and another mobster could get him the bout if Rosensohn gave each of them a piece of his company. Rosensohn got the bout but had to give up a majority ownership of his company in the process. Having lost control of his own firm, Rosensohn told his story to the New York Attorney General's office.

After the fight, an investigation by New York's District Attorney determined that the main decision-maker in Rosensohn Enterprises was actually D'Amato, a violation of the law that prohibited managers from having anything to do with the promotion of his fighter's bouts. The little dictator's hypocrisy had been exposed and D'Amato's managerial license was revoked for acts detrimental to boxing. But it was far from an isolated incident on Cus' resume and at least three of Floyd's opponents admitted to being victimized by D'Amato.

First, Johansson said he only got his title by agreeing to have two of Cus's friends serve as his manager and cornerman. Second, when Patterson fought British heavyweight Brian London the challenger was forced to be trained by another one of D'Amato's associates. After the fight, London claimed that he was promised a rematch with Patterson if he let D'Amato take care of his management. Third, Roy Harris had received similar treatment when D'Amato forced him to accept Charlie Black as his manager as insurance against a possible upset. Had the mandatory rematch taken place, Black would have received 10 percent of Harris's purse.

People now knew that Cus had been eager to break up the IBC's monopoly so he could set up his own. *Ring Magazine* called it one of the biggest hoaxes in boxing history. Even after he fell from Floyd's good graces, Cus did everything he could to prevent Patterson from fighting the man who had done more to earn a title show than any fighter in history. Cus had a lot of influence among the country's sportswriters and boxing commissioners, many of whom were only too glad to bad-mouth Sonny at his request. By now, however, a lot of people believed that if Patterson continued to duck Liston, it could only be because he was afraid to fight him. "Not even the bitterest of Liston's enemies will deny the legitimacy of his claim to a championship fight, so long as we allow boxing at all," wrote *Look's* senior editor Sam Castan.

Sports Illustrated called the debate over Liston's right to fight for the title "sport's livliest moral controversy" and sought the opinions of prominent people in and out of the sport. Comedian Dick Gregory and Harlem Congressman Adam Clayton Powell said Liston should have an opportunity to prove himself regardless of his past. "Whether he wins or loses, he will have a new future," said Powell. "If he doesn't have that chance, you will be sending him back to where he came from." Powell and Gregory were both black; the opinions of most of the whites *SI* surveyed were far different.

International Olympic Committee president Avery Brundage, a Nazi sympathizer, said it would be a mistake to permit a man "with a record of this kind" to fight for the heavyweight championship. California State Athletic Commissioner Harry Falk suggested his state might license Liston in a year or so if he got a job and behaved in an exemplary manner. In Falk's view, "someone with a record of that nature will be hard to rehabilitate or reform." Branch Rickey, the man who made Jackie Robinson the first black major league baseball player, referred to Liston as "a character of that type" and chided Patterson for stooping "to that level." Robinson was also troubled by Sonny's record but took solace in his belief that Patterson would demolish him.

"A fighter with Sonny's ungovernable temper and gutter-type sportsmanship would be a dangerous man in the wrong sense of the word on the heavyweight champion's throne," wrote Dan Parker. "I wish with all my heart that Patterson would win," echoed former champ Johansson. "Boxing is not a sport for ladies, but you have to keep a standard and it would hurt boxing if Liston is champion." Those were interesting words coming from a man who was disqualified from the 1952 Olympic Games for cowardice.

When Jack Dempsey went on record against him getting a title shot, Sonny returned fire. "Dempsey was a draft dodger in the First World War, or so they said. What right has he got to squawk about me getting a chance at the title?" An incensed Dempsey responded by calling Liston "a big, stupid guy." In contrast, Rocky Marciano was careful not to say anything inappropriate about Sonny. "I wouldn't want Liston to carry scars because I said something unfair and perhaps helped to deny him a chance at fighting for the heavyweight title," said Rocky. "Who knows how Sonny thinks, how he would think if he became champ? I leave that to fortunetellers."

The Pennsylvania Athletic Commission took so much heat for reinstating

Sonny that its chairman felt the need to speak to the country's sports community in a letter to *Sports Illustrated* in early March. "I would like to set the record straight on what motivated myself and my colleagues to reinstate Liston," wrote Alfred Klein. "After mature consideration and a very thorough investigation we concluded that in the ring he could make something of himself, whereas, if he were to be denied an opportunity to make a living in the field in which he was obviously best qualifed, the frustration, disappointment and disillusionment that would follow would smash his morale and might possibly cause him to regress."

Nevertheless, Liston wondered what he had to do to get a title fight. "Put on a straightjacket, somebody say. Tie my right hand behind my back, somebody else say. They're joking, when all I want is to fight." The National Boxing Association (NBA) threatened to strip Patterson of his title if he didn't sign to fight a credible opponent by March 13, 1962, but that meant nothing to Sonny. "I wouldn't have the title like that," he said. "I would want to hold my head up as a champ."

Nat Fleischer wrote that any commission sanctioning another fiasco like the McNeeley match should be dissolved for the good of its own state and for boxing. The truth was that Patterson had disrespected the title by thinking he could do with it as he damn well pleased. But it was now clear that the public wouldn't pay to see any more title defenses against unworthy opponents. The truth was that D'Amato knew his fighter couldn't beat Liston—and Patterson knew it as well.

Watching the December closed-circuit fights at the White House, President Kennedy pointed out the obvious, saying it would have been a better show if Liston had fought Patterson and McNeeley had fought Westphal. Patterson heard about Kennedy's remark and during a visit to the White House quietly told the President that he had decided to fight Liston. JFK reportedly told Patterson he needed to beat Sonny for the good of the country and of boxing.

Geraldine was at home listening to the radio when she heard that Patterson had agreed to fight her husband. Sonny was on a plane at the time and received a message to call his wife when he landed. "He thought I was kidding him," remembered Gerry. "It was big news for us."

After they signed the contracts, Liston followed Patterson to the door, put his arm around him and with what Floyd described as a sort of gleaming smile in his eyes, thanked him for giving him the chance. Sonny believed the real obstacle to the fight had been D'Amato but judging from the contract negotiations, Sonny greatly underestimated Floyd's reluctance to fight him. Patterson abused his championship position more than any fighter ever had. While demanding he get 45 percent of the live gate and 55 percent of the ancillaries (non-live gate revenues), Patterson punished Liston by insisting he get only 10 percent of both, even though all of Patterson's previous challengers had received 20 percent. "He said he'd fight me for nothing," said Floyd. "Now he can put up or shut up."

Sonny settled for 12.5 percent, which he considered to be "crumbs," and his unhappiness with the terms of the contract bothered him throughout training. "I only want to be comfortable for the rest of my life and provide for my family," said Sonny. "I don't hate Floyd but I certainly do not like him. I believe he could have given me a fairer percentage of the gate." Liston had earned less than $200,000 in fighting all of the serious contenders that Patterson had ducked while himself amassing career earnings of over $4 million. Floyd later had the gall to say that he gave Sonny a title shot because he felt sorry for him.

The promoters wanted to stage the bout in New York City, so Sonny applied for a license there. Publicist Harold Conrad had been hired to "paint the prison stripes off Liston," and the promoters were so confident he had succeeded that they placed a deposit to reserve Yankee Stadium for a September fight. However, the powers that be had decided long before that Sonny Liston would never fight in the state of New York. It was public knowledge that Commissioner Farley was opposed to licensing Sonny, and that Commission chairman Kruelwitch had called him coarse, brutal, ignorant, and friendless.

Following public testimony, the three-man Commission sat around and talked for two hours to convey the impression that they had seriously and fairly deliberated the question at hand. Then they distributed copies of their decision and left the building. "We dissected his vitals and laid them out for all to see," a mean-spirited Krulewitch would later remark. The Commission wrote that Liston's history of past associations provided a "pattern of suspicion" and they couldn't ignore the possibility that Liston was controlled by organized crime. Nat Fleischer said the press was entitled to know whether the Commission possessed such proof, but none was offered.

Sonny's attorney termed the action unfair, unjust, and un-American. To this day, he remains the only heavyweight champion never to be licensed in New York. Krulewitch wouldn't even allow Liston to be introduced before a main event when he attended fights at Madison Square Garden! "I don't think I should hold it against the people there," said Sonny. "When I walk to my seat people stand up and clap and say encouragements to me. One night it took me 20 minutes to get outta the lobby in the Garden because there was so many people wantin' to shake my hand and give me encouragements."

That diplomatic response notwithstanding, Sonny was upset at the decision. "To me, boxing was a sport, like baseball," he said. "When a man steps up to the plate, he either hits that ball or he don't. That's what he's judged on, not who he is or where he came from. It seems like there's more politics than sport in boxing now." Asked about New York's denial after he won the title, Liston said, "it was kind of sad that they did it."

Gerry was furious and like her husband, she too could cut to the heart of the matter in a few words. "Do they think Charles is so bad he can come in for just one night and turn the whole town rotten?" she asked. Apparently Governor Nelson Rockefeller did, since it was widely believed that he had dictated the Commission's decision. Gerry insisted Sonny's past would be forgotten if sportswriters weren't always bringing it up. "It's like they don't ever want him to be good," she said. "Many nights we talk it over. Sonny knows himself, and he knows if he becomes champ he only wants to live to make everybody realize he's a better person. He just doesn't like to talk much. If he wins, we'll feel its God's will. If he loses, we'll feel its God's will. I'm praying he'll win. Mostly, I'm just glad all this tension will be over."

That same day, the *Washington Post* reported that two of the three District of Columbia Boxing Commissioners were in favor of licensing Liston. Sonny had written Patterson and the D.C. commissioners to assure them they wouldn't have to worry about criminal elements if the bout were held there because it was home to the FBI. J. Edgar Hoover was livid when he saw the article. "Just how blind can those 3 mice—the Boxing Commissioners be!" Hoover wrote at the bottom of the page. "Let me have summary of Liston and his managers." The result was a three-page, single-spaced memo detailing Sonny's criminal background, his underworld management, and his chances of securing a title fight with Patterson. According to the memo, the FBI's criminal intelligence surveillances had picked up considerable information regarding the activities of Liston and the people around him after he turned pro in 1953.

On May 2, the *New York Times* editorialized in favor of the Commission's decision. The thought of Sonny Liston becoming champ bothered the *Times* so much that they called for the abolition of professional boxing. In California, State Athletic Commissioner Douglas Hayden said his state's thinking on licensing

Liston was the same as New York's. However, the athletic commissions of eight other states, including Pennsylvania and Illinois, expressed their interest in hosting the bout.

With that assurance, Harold Conrad went to see Chicago Mayor Richard J. Daley. Daley had already given the promoters his unofficial approval to bring the fight to Chicago and when Conrad started to sell Daley on the benefits to his city, the mayor cut him off. "Never mind all that," he said. "I just want to know one thing. Is this going to be a good fight? I don't want this town's image loused up." Conrad told Da Mayor it was going to be one of the greatest fights of all time.

CHAPTER FIVE

THE CHAMP NOBODY WANTED

During his career Liston engaged the services of so many lawyers that one of his managers claimed he had attorneys on attorneys. Almost all of those relationships ended badly but Sal Avena was an exception. Liston and Avena had developed a strong rapport after being introduced by Sam Margolis and in early May, Sonny asked Sal to drive him to his training camp in Fallsburg, New York.

Willie Reddish Jr. helped his dad set up the camp and remembers that everyone was confident that Sonny would win the title. The fact that Liston's living quarters were decorated with pink petunia wallpaper didn't bother him at all. The Pines general manager was pleasantly surprised when he found out Sonny was "a great guy, friendly and obliging as you please." The Bear was relaxed and approachable, and townspeople were happy to have him around.

Sonny's breakfast consisted of five strips of bacon, three soft-boiled eggs, two glasses of fruit juice, and two cups of tea. He juiced his own carrots and thought coffee was bad for the nerves. Sonny brought 50 or 60 of the finest steaks to training camp packed in dry ice. His dinner consisted of salad with olive oil, lots of green vegetables, and two pounds of steak cooked close to rare. "That's why they have training camps," said Sonny. "They take away women and feed you raw meat, and this puts you in a fighting mood. It makes you angry and brings up the evil inside you, so that when the man in your corner say, 'Go in and kill 'em', you do."

Geraldine insisted she was a bigger eater than her husband was. His weight never topped 235 pounds and he perspired so heavily that he lost weight faster than his handlers would have liked. Before fights, Gerry would stop making the pies, cakes, and cobblers that her husband loved so much (and he'd also lay off of the occasional quart of ice cream). Sonny said he didn't get hungry because he kept thinking about the fight.

The promoters wanted Liston to set up his Chicago-area camp next to Joliet State Prison, thinking it would be the perfect backdrop for a man with his history. That didn't sit well with Sonny, who chose to train at the defunct Aurora Downs racetrack, 45 miles west of Chicago. Liston began his day at 5:30 in the morning by running 5 miles on the track bed of an abandoned railroad. His gym workouts started promptly at 2:30 p.m., when he'd walk over to the phonograph and play either *Night Train* or *It Ain't Necessarily So*. People could watch him train for 99 cents, a real bargain since anyone who witnessed one of Sonny's workouts would never forget it.

Each day Reddish hurled a 16-pound medicine ball at Liston's midsection 25 times from a distance of 2 feet. Willie would wind up as though he were a baseball pitcher and Sonny liked to joke that the only reason he did the medicine ball exercise was because his trainer was having trouble sticking to his diet. A stint on the speed bag was followed by several minutes of shadow boxing in the ring, which he'd enter by scissor-kicking himself over the four-foot ropes without using his hands. A few rounds of sparring were followed by several minutes on the heavy punching bag. Then Sonny would jump rope for as long as 22 minutes without stopping, his face always expressionless. He ended his workouts with a neck-flexing headstand on a rubdown table.

"Sonny has made himself what he is today by training as hard as any man I ever saw," said Reddish, who had seen all of the great fighters train. Liston always kept his body at or near peak condition. Over one 12-fight period his weight was never less than 209 and never more than 212. He usually trained so hard that Willie had to order him out of gym. Sonny's idea of being self-indulgent was taking a few days off between hard fights. "Some fighters have to be driven, but he's not one of them," said Willie. "He's got a remarkable sense of self-discipline and, like he says, he knows his own body better than anyone."

Joe Louis said Sonny was the hardest trainer he'd ever seen. When it came to punching the heavy bag and shadow boxing, Liston did three or four rounds to every one Louis did. "When I was training, I'd rather box ten rounds than go 15 minutes with the rope, and he doesn't even breathe," marveled Louis. *Sports Illustrated* referred to Sonny's rope skipping as "menace personified," and Marshall Smith described him as being as nimble as Nijinsky in an exercise usually practiced by little girls.

Sonny always compared fighting to going to war and his ring strategy was a simple one. "I don't believe in waiting until I get into trouble," said Liston. "I fight to keep out of trouble and I fight to get out of trouble. I fight my own fight. I always fight my own fight. Never mind what style he has. It doesn't matter what the crowd is like, whether they're for me or not for me. I just go in and fight my fight." And that is the crux of the matter. If Liston fought his fight, no one could beat him, especially over the eternity that is euphemistically known as a 15-round fight.

Sonny called his group of handlers Bums Incorporated and for the most part Sonny used the word bum with genuine affection. In addition to Reddish, Liston's training team included Joe Polino, the camp manager who also functioned as cut man and straight man for Sonny's skits. Sonny's camp secretary was Archie Pirolli, who Reddish called "pencil man" because he'd stay up late signing Liston's autograph. Everybody counted on Archie to take care of all the little details. Ex-fighter Teddy King served as equipment manager and official photographer and meticulously timed every portion of Sonny's workouts. Bill Morefield was camp cook while Raymond (Muncie) Munson, who managed the pool hall where Sonny had his "office," served as Liston's personal assistant. Also in camp were two big Chicago policemen who had been assigned to Liston by the Illinois Attorney General at Sonny's request. Both men carried guns and were under orders to stay with Sonny from morning until night, every day until the fight.

John "Moose" Grayson was one of Liston's bodyguards and the two became good friends. That would change when Liston sexually assaulted Grayson's wife, Pearl, on March 29, 1963. The assault came to light six months later when Mrs. Grayson sued the new champ for $100,000. She claimed she was a passenger in Liston's car when the fighter "willfully and maliciously assaulted and beat and inflicted bruises upon her body and caused her personal injuries." No complaint was filed with the police at the time of the assault; Mrs. Grayson's attorney said he agreed to delay filing the lawsuit after conferring with Sonny's manager, Jack Nilon. A cash settlement would be reached with the Graysons. Surprisingly, the story got very little attention and most of it was in black publications.

Geraldine was in training camp because her husband wanted her there. "I want her with me all the time," he told reporters. "I want you to know about my wife because she is important to me." Gerry said Charles seemed happier when she was with him than when she wasn't. The Listons stayed in separate quarters but spent most of the day together. She also cooked all of his meals. Nobody around could recall a training camp in which a fighter's wife had been present all the time.

To relax, Sonny watched television, listened to music, lagged coins, or rode a bicycle. He enjoyed swimming and dancing and said Ray Charles was his favorite singer. Bad weather, cigar smoke, and reporters would put Liston in a foul mood but his handlers knew he'd cool off fast. The occasional blow-up was quickly followed by an apology, usually with money attached to it. Sometimes Sonny would talk for an hour with the policeman at the front gate because he figured the man was bored. He gave $10 to a sparring partner he'd beaten at cards because the guy helped him pass the time. When a young fighter came to camp and couldn't hold his own with other sparring partners, Sonny hired him as assistant to the camp cook rather than send him away with a handout. All of his handlers insisted he was a regular guy.

Liston's relationship with the press had always been an adversarial one but now he had the upper hand and he laid down three basic rules. First, he would no longer answer questions about his past. At The Pines he talked about his prison time by saying he ran with a bunch of bad, stupid kids and was thankful that he got another chance. At Aurora Downs those questions were no longer tolerated. "There's no use to keep reminding him that he's an ex-convict," said E. V. Nash, Sonny's warden at Jefferson City. "Nobody knows it better than he does."

Second, Sonny would not permit anyone to touch him, even in jest, and anyone who tried got a very rude awakening. There would be no tapping him on the shoulder and no slapping him on the back. Only his friends could do those things and apart from Philadelphia writer Jack McKinney, Sonny had no friends in the press.

Finally, the press could only interview him immediately after his daily workouts. Sonny generally would not talk to white reporters one-on-one, which led to his being known as Malcolm X at press headquarters. "He reminded me of some fierce African tribal chief," said publicist Harold Conrad. "And those sportswriters gave him plenty of respect in his presence."

Even so, reporters belabored the obvious, asking Liston questions he had long since tired of answering. "When I nod and grunt, it's my way of saying I don't want anything to do with you," Sonny would say. "That's as diplomatic as I can be." At times he would chastise the press for inventing stories about him, a journalistic sin that many reporters evidently felt was their prerogative when it came to Sonny Liston.

The constant negative reporting had an effect on how blacks looked at Liston. Fifty years earlier, Jack Johnson was passionately hated by whites but enjoyed the love and support of the vast majority of his race. Antipathy of Liston, however, transcended racial lines. "If Liston had a saga, the average Negro wanted none of it," wrote Norman Mailer. He said just about every black person he talked to in Chicago was rooting against Sonny. "It was not only the grey-haired Negroes with the silver-rimmed glasses and the dignity of the grave, the teachers, the deacons, the welfare workers, the camp directors, the church organists who were for Patterson, but indeed just about every Negro one talked to in Chicago."

Floyd admitted Sonny was a fighter without a flaw but his attempts to sound confident were absolutely ludicrous, even delusional. "I not only believe I can take Liston's punch, if he lands it, but I think I can hit harder than he can," said Floyd. "The only thing that will bother me is if he fights as good as he says he will. If that happens, nobody's going to beat him—even with a slingshot." The thought that Goliath would prevail bothered a lot more people than just Patterson. Floyd said so many people wanted him to beat Liston that the bout seemed more a matter of state importance than a fight.

"It has been predicted that if Liston became champion it would be a greater blow to boxing than the death of Benny (Kid) Paret," wrote McKinney. Nobel Peace Prize winner Dr. Ralph Bunche and NAACP President Percy Sutton were among the black leaders who felt Liston would hurt their quest for equality. "Hell, let's stop kidding. I'm for Patterson because he represents us better than Liston ever could or would," said Sutton. Thirty years later Sutton helped organize a parade to honor Mike Tyson upon his release from prison after serving three years on a rape conviction.

"The NAACP didn't want Patterson to fight me for the title," said Sonny. Worse yet, the group had lobbied against Liston getting his title shot. "They wanted to make this a political business. They wanted to take the sport out of it. When Joe Louis was fighting, they didn't ask a man's past." After he won the title, the NAACP asked Sonny for a $500 donation, which they might have gotten had they asked him directly instead of his attorney.

The reaction Liston got from blacks hurt him deeply. "Colored people say they don't want their children to look up to me," Sonny told James Baldwin. "Well, they ain't teaching their children to look up to Martin Luther King, either…I wouldn't be no bad example if I was up there. I could tell a lot of those children what they need to know because I passed that way. I could make them listen." One day at his training camp he spoke to 38 kids from a boy's reformatory and told them winning the title meant more to him than what Martin Luther King was fighting for. "This fight's going to be for my whole life," said Sonny.

Prior to each workout Reddish would ask, "Who's got The Bear today?" and one fighter would wince more than the others. Liston's sparring partners called him T.C. which was short for Top Cat. It's the most impressive nickname a fighter can have, and Sonny was the only one who ever earned the right to be called it. He was particularly hard on his sparmates while training for Patterson and they fled his camp on a regular basis. "Those boys don't like to work with me," Liston would often say.

Promoter Don Chargin told me it was well known in boxing circles that Sonny had to pay sparring partners much more than other contenders did. He battered them so badly that some of them actually hid from him. "You can't get sparring partners for him," said assistant trainer Archie Pirolli. "These fellows get $50 to $60 a round, they have no expenses, and they get the best of food but when I call them they say 'Archie, how would you like to just drop dead?'" With the heavyweight title being so close that Liston could taste it, there would be no letup on these guys whatsoever. "I feel it comin' on," Sonny told reporters as fight day neared. "I'll get to feelin' pretty evil the last few days or so before the fight. I'll pull inside myself to build up a good hate and I'll be pretty hard to live with."

Floyd knew he was doomed. Six days before the fight one of the promoters asked Conrad to get him a makeup man for Patterson. Conrad connected him to a friend at a local TV station who called Conrad the next day to let him know Patterson had asked to be fitted with a phony beard. Conrad swore his friend to secrecy, afraid of the negative effect on the gate if the story got out.

Sonny wore gloves that were custom-made an inch wider than normal to accommodate his huge fists. The gloves made by Everlast were too small for Liston, who preferred ones made by Frager. Everlast padded their gloves with curled horsehair while Frager used foam rubber padding. D'Amato argued that Liston's knuckles would be closer to the surface of the gloves made with foam rubber than they would be in the ones with horsehair and insisted that Everlast make new ones for the challenger. Eventually, the Illinois commission ruled that each fighter could choose his own gloves, and Sonny used the situation to pull one of his best practical jokes.

When the gloves were delivered for inspection, Nilon complained that they were a quarter ounce too heavy, and Joe Polino shouted that Liston wasn't going into the ring with gloves over the regular weight. "What's the difference for a quarter of an ounce?" asked the commission's chief inspector. "You ain't weighing diamonds." The ensuing screaming match lasted a couple of minutes before Liston walked in and asked what the hell was going on. Sonny put on one of the gloves, said it still didn't fit, and looked around the now-quiet room.

Geraldine was amused because no matter how many jokes Liston pulled on sportswriters, no one ever seemed to see them coming. "You felt you were looking at a creation," wrote Mailer. "And this creation looked like it was building into a temper which would tear up the clubhouse at Aurura Downs. One knew he was acting, and yet everyone in the room was afraid of Liston."

Suddenly, Sonny calmed down and agreed to use the gloves. But, as the officials prepared to leave, Liston said he'd changed his mind and intended to use a pair of specially made gloves. The officials froze until two of Sonny's assistants walked in carrying a white, five-foot boxing glove while Liston and his handlers laughed heartily. "Very unusual fellow," said D'Amato. "He's more intelligent than I thought. Good sense of humor."

Nothing entertained Sonny more than his own jokes and he loved to play tricks on people. Sonny once got arrested when he shook hands with a policeman with a buzzer in his hands, a prank that cost him a few hundred dollars in fines and legal fees. He carried a two-headed quarter, owned a trick pen that splashed disappearing ink, and loved a phony camera that squirted water on the person he pretended to be photographing. One of Sonny's handlers said giving fighters toys was a good way to keep their minds off the fight, and it seemed to work for the Bear.

Most people would have been surprised to learn that Liston's sense of humor was an integral part of his personality. "If he was sitting here he'd be telling some kind of joke. He was a guy that liked to have fun," his friend Tommy Manning told me. British promoter Mickey Duff said Liston was the funniest guy he ever hung around with. Legendary Las Vegas casino executive Ash Resnick said when Sonny was with people he liked, he was the funniest guy he knew.

Sonny loved to intimidate people but his good friend Henry Winston said it was all a big bluff. "You'd think he was very serious when he stared you down, but he was really just having fun," said Winston. "He carried a pistol all the time but it was a blank, not a real one. I'll never forget one day a guy was screaming at a lady on a sidewalk and Sonny jumped out of the car and cursed the guy and told him to leave her alone. He pulled his gun, fired it twice, and said 'get out of here' and the guy took off." Liston sometimes drove his car onto the curb just to scare someone. "He was having fun but he'd make you run," said Winston. "He really got a kick out of those kinds of things."

Sonny loved his training camp skits, which always rattled sportswriters, almost all of whom feared him. In one skit, Liston would feign rage over a supposed screw-up by Joe Polino and climax a heated exchange by hitting him. Polino would catch the blow with his palm alongside his face, spit out several white beans, stagger back, pick up a conveniently placed golf club or baseball bat and advance toward Liston, whereupon Sonny would pull out his blank-filled pistol and shoot Polino down in his tracks.

Earlier in training camp, A.J. Liebling asked Harold Conrad to introduce him to Liston. As they sat down for a cup of tea, Sonny started yelling at Polino. "I ain't gonna give you the five bucks, you cheap muzzler! Not if you live to be a hundred." Polino slapped Liston across the shoulder, causing Sonny to take the same, small blank-filled revolver out of his robe as Polino ran over to Liebling and kneeled behind him. When Liston aimed and fired, the frightened writer fell backwards, drenching himself in tea and leaving Sonny stomping his foot and laughing hysterically. "You come see us again," said the fighter. "You come back."

On the drive back to Chicago, Liebling told Conrad that because of Liston's prison record, he had believed the act was real and was praying that Sonny had good aim. Liebling took it a lot better than most sportswriters, who really disliked being fooled by a man who they considered to be devoid of intellect and humor.

◇ ◇ ◇

A heavyweight title fight used to be the world's most highly anticipated sporting event. It produced an excitement that was so palpable it bordered on dread and there was nothing that came close to equalling its importance with the average sports fan.

Heavyweight title fights may not be that way now but every fan from the eras of John L. Sullivan to Mike Tyson experienced that feeling. The first Patterson-Liston fight was certainly no exception. Indeed, it was the most symbolic boxing match since Joe Louis defended his title against Germany's Max Schmeling 25 years earlier.

Shortly before the fight Sonny felt everyone was against him. He admitted he had little regard for other people's feelings and wanted to get even with somebody, anybody, for the life he had lived. "You become resentful when you have nothing to look forward to," he said. "You find yourself actually hating people who are making progress and have security. I was like that and so were all my friends. I realize now that a man can't be successful or happy with that attitude. Whatever happens, win or lose, I am positive that Sonny Liston is going to be a better man."

What Sonny wanted most was to make a place for himself in society and live a reasonably normal life. America had treated him as a second-class citizen at best. At worst, he was thought to be a stain on the fabric of American life. He hoped he could get a fresh start and a chance to change the public's perception of him if he won the title. He knew that most people thought there was nothing good about him. "All them things people they say and they write, they all be gone when I'm the champ," he said. "I'll show people what kind of a fella I am. Be a champ, act like a champ."

Such honesty had no effect on the press, who continued to hammer away at the negative themes they had cultivated. Red Smith told his readers that Patterson was a thoroughly decent human being and that Liston was a jailbird. That was relatively mild compared to the words of a national news magazine. "The image of Floyd Patterson, heavyweight champion, is one of gentleness and everything that is good," wrote *Newsweek* in the lead of its lengthy pre-fight story. "The image of Sonny Liston, heavyweight challenger, is one of viciousness and everything that is evil."

Viciousness in a professional prizefighter is, of course, a far more valuable commodity than gentleness, and Liston probably had more of it than any fighter who ever lived. But *Newsweek's* characterization of him as evil typified the unfair press coverage Sonny received throughout his career. Only an animal could be this tough, they seemed to imply, and a vicious animal like Liston was apparently as bad as it could get for white America in the late '50s and early '60s.

"The white public saw him as evil, a naked example of unconsolable black hostility," wrote Mark Kram. Leroi Jones compared Sonny to "the big black Negro in every white man's hallway, waiting to do him in, deal him under, for all the hurts white men have been able to inflict on his world." That's how Liston was always viewed and it helps explain why few people today know anything good about the man.

Chicago's Comiskey Park was unseasonably cold on the night of the fight.

There was a doctor for each corner, a neurosurgeon at ringside, and the Illinois Boxing Commission had two ambulances standing by to take injured fighters to a local hospital. Earlier in the day, people learned that heavyweight Alejandro Lavorante was near death from injuries he had suffered in a bout four days prior. After the fight, Patterson's mother admitted that she had worried about her son fighting Liston after learning of Lavorante's situation. "Everybody was so concerned," said Mrs. Annabelle Patterson. "He's so big-g-g." Still, most of the boxing world thought enough of Patterson's abilities that the pallor of death was not hanging over this fight.

Frank Sinatra had closed-circuit TV piped into his Los Angeles home, charged 100 friends $50 each to watch the fight, and donated the money to charity. Barney Baker told me that Sinatra thought the world of Sonny. The White House had been wired for the telecast, as was Patterson's home in New York. More than 600 writers attended the fight, the largest press assemblage in boxing history. Many of them were serious writers like Norman Mailer, Truman Capote, James Baldwin, and William F. Buckley. Cassius Clay and Angelo Dundee were also in the audience.

Because of the weather and very little local press coverage, fewer than 19,000 people paid between $10 and $100 to see good try to conquer evil. The final odds made Liston a 7 1/2 to 5 favorite, only the third time in history that a challenger was favored to win the heavyweight title. There was little betting action as people apparently were afraid to risk their money on Floyd and unwilling to profit off of Sonny. In truth, the odds should have been 50-1 because Liston simply could not lose this fight!

Sportswriters have a rich history of consistently picking the loser in championship boxing matches and, lo and behold, 51 of the 83 polled picked Patterson to win. It was wishful thinking, of course, and boxers knew better. "Somebody's going to be humiliated so bad the public won't stand for another fight," Archie Moore said with certainty. "Sonny figures to win easily," said former featherweight champ Willie Pep.

In his hotel room, Sonny listened to some blues as he lay on a 7-by-7 foot bed that had been built in 1929 for an imperial potentate of the International Shriners. He became angry thinking about the weigh-in when he and his handlers had made their way down a flight of stairs to a mob scene in his dressing room. "Too many people around," growled Sonny. "I could have got stuck by somebody up there." He told his handlers to make sure that nobody got near him on his way to the ring.

The mood in Liston's dressing room was almost festive with "Night Train" blasting from the record player. Ringside physician Dr. Nicholas Casciato took Sonny's blood pressure and asked him how he felt about the fight. "Doc, no 185-pound motherfucker can beat me," replied Liston. Truer words have never been spoken; Sonny could just as well have been referring to Dempsey and Marciano, neither of whom were anywhere near as talented as Patterson.

Seated on the rubbing table Liston bowed his head and asked Father Murphy to give him a blessing. On the way to the ring Sonny told Nilon if he didn't knock Patterson out in the first round he'd lie down in the ring in disgrace. According to playwright August Wilson, Attorney General Bobby Kennedy stopped by Patterson's dressing room prior to the fight and told Floyd to keep the title in the country. Patterson was so gripped by fear in his dressing room that Dr. Casciato had to enlist D'Amato's help to take the champ's blood pressure.

Life Magazine had gotten permission to attach microphones to the ring posts and planned to record the conversations of each fighter's corner between rounds. Liston arrived first in the larger-than-normal 22-foot ring that D'Amato had demanded and was met by far more boos than cheers. One minute later, Patterson was greeted by a roaring ovation. As usual, Floyd never made eye contact with his opponent but those at ringside who saw his eyes got a glimpse of a terrified man.

As the fighters waited for the opening bell, Patterson danced around in his corner while Sonny stared at him. Liston always said this fight would be a short one and he was about to make the prediction come true. "My plan is to go right out at the opening bell and get what's coming to me and give Patterson what's coming to him," Sonny had said. He knew he was already heavyweight champion of the world. The next couple of minutes were necessary merely to authenticate the transaction.

When the bell sounded, Patterson charged from his corner and missed with his signature leaping left hook to Liston's head. When Sonny landed his first jab, he knew Floyd would be easy to hit and he wasn't the least bit worried about Patterson's punches.

"Soon after I connected with that first left jab, I threw a left
hook that landed on the side of his face and he clinched. The referee

said break, and Floyd stepped back quickly. Then we squared off again, and I threw a short right uppercut. It was a good punch, very good, but he took it well. I followed it up with another left hook that landed high on the head, around the temple, and he clinched again as he fell in toward me. This time, when the ref yelled break, Patterson didn't want to. I had to punch him off. He fell against the ropes and it was then that I realized he was hurt. He was stunned and his legs sagged. I hit him with the third left hook and he went down. The way he fell, I knew he wouldn't get up."

Patterson hit the canvas directly in front of his wife and mother, who were seated at ringside. In Los Angeles, Frank Sinatra sprang to his feet and pumped his fist in joy. When Floyd got to one knee, Sonny thought he looked like a man reaching for the alarm clock while he was still asleep. Patterson was counted out for the first time in his career and the ex-champ's personal physician said he was glad Floyd didn't beat the count because he could have been badly hurt. The referee bluntly said Patterson would have been murdered if had gotten up. "I saw his eyes and he wasn't in any condition to continue," said Floyd's mother.

Sonny reacted with a show of joy not seen since he won the National Golden Gloves title in 1953. He walked across the ring and sincerely thanked Patterson for giving him a shot at the title. Patterson had avoided this day for almost three years but Sonny would never have more respect for Floyd than he did at that moment because he came to fight. "There's a difference between having fear in you and being a coward," Sonny said. "I can have fear in me, too, and that kind of fear is good. Then I'd go into the ring and because I had this fear I'd try to take the other guy out as quick as I could. Patterson had fear in him but he wasn't no coward."

Listening to their radios, the inmates at Jefferson City cheered wildly for their former brother. "I can bring 200 men into this office and they'll all tell you they were Sonny Liston's cellmates," Liston's former warden said. The inmates, though, were pretty much alone in their enthusiasm. The announcement that Sonny Liston was the new heavyweight champion of the world was greeted by near silence in the cavernous Comiskey Park, where Joe Louis had knocked out Jimmy Braddock to win the title 25 years earlier. Soon, waves of angry boos filled the night air. At one closed-circuit outlet in Harlem, the 3,000 blacks who paid $6.75 to watch the fight sat in stunned silence for several seconds before venting their displeasure. "The forces of evil had triumphed," *Sports Illustrated's* Robert Boyle said later.

Joe Louis had predicted the fight's outcome and was amused by the public's reaction. "It's funny," he said, "but when I knocked out Schmeling in one round, everybody thought it was a great fight and they were tickled to death."

The fight's gross revenue of $4.8 million was the most in boxing history. A total of $665,000 came from the live gate, the rest from 260 theaters that carried the fight on closed-circuit theater TV for nearly 600,000 paying fans. Patterson's earnings were estimated to be a record $1.2 million; Sonny was expected to earn $282,000.

As soon as the fight ended Treasury agents seized the promoter's half of the proceeds in 217 cities in 48 states, the largest such action in the history of the IRS. A provision of the tax law known as "jeopardy assessment" allowed the IRS to demand immediate payment of any taxes due on income if it believed that collecting the tax might be jeopardized by waiting for the taxpayer to file a return. After his third bout with Patterson, Johansson fled the country owing $600,000 in taxes. An IRS spokesman said that the fight's promoter and closed-circuit firm had also failed to file income tax returns the previous year.

When Patterson finally unlocked his dressing room door, he told reporters that Liston could be a good man if given the chance to show it. He had told Sonny the same thing in the ring following the fight. "I think it will surprise a lot of people, if only they'd believe Liston was any kind of a human being," said Floyd. "I really was surprised that he stood up for me like he did," Sonny said later.

The ex-champ had made no plans for a victory party but had parked two cars near a side entrance prior to the fight. One of the cars would have taken him back to his hotel if he had won. The other car, his Lincoln Continental, had a packed suitcase in the trunk and a full tank of gas to begin the trip home to New York. Patterson got in the Lincoln, put on the beard and mustache he had stashed there, and began driving home. The world learned of his disguised escape the following day, only because an Indiana state trooper pulled him over for speeding.

Sonny answered questions politely and with humor and said he believed his faith in God had something to do with his victory. "The public owns the title and I brought it back to the public. The title is for all the people. I won't make a challenger wait as Patterson made me wait." Liston said he would fight the contenders "as they list them in the book," starting with the No. 1 contender. That said a lot about the kind of man Charles Liston was. Whether it was due to his two-and-a-half year wait as the No. 1 contender or simply a reflection of his own sense of fairness, Sonny held firm to this conviction. He did so shortly before the first Ali fight, when Eddie Machen came to one of Sonny's training sessions and tried to goad him into a title shot. "When you get to be No. 1, I'll fight you," Sonny told Machen. "Clay is No. 1 now, ain't he? Then work your way up to No. 1 and you'll get your chance. I can only fight one man at a time and he has to be No. 1!" No other heavyweight champion ever came close to showing such respect to his fellow competitors.

The new champ called his mother and said he was a little tired but felt fine. She told him to be a good boy and to use his earnings to buy a house. "He asked how I was doing," said Helen Liston. "I told him. Then, he said, 'Well, I'll be seeing you,' and that was all."

Winning the title was sweeter than Liston ever thought it would be. Throngs of people at his victory party asked for handshakes and autographs, and Sonny denied no one. Sonny kept signing, smiling and chatting, basking in the respect he had sought for so long. "I only got one man to thank for what's happened to me— me," he would later say, and that's what made this all the sweeter.

The following morning in his hotel lobby, the well-dressed, new champ shook hands with A. J. Liebling as if the two had been old friends. Liebling said Sonny patted a child on the head and broke into a run to give money to a panhandler before hotel security could throw the guy out. In the hotel's coffee shop he passed out ballpoint pens bearing his name but when a woman offered to pay his check, the new champ politely refused by saying it might cause tax problems with Uncle Sam. "Boxing buffs searched today for the scowling, growling fist fighter they had known Sonny Liston to be," wrote Robert Teague of the *New York Times*. "Instead they found a jovial, dignified talkative chap who might seem out of place in the ring."

Sonny made his way to the press conference, surrounded by a group of serious-looking Chicago cops. As they approached the ballroom, Harold Conrad saw that Norman Mailer was sitting in Liston's seat, drunk as a skunk. The novelist hadn't slept since prior to his celebrated debate with William Buckley two days earlier and seemed oblivious to the insults of some of the 300 reporters in the room. Norman didn't respect boxing writers as journalists and said the geezers among them looked like old cigar butts. He cared not a whit about their opinion of him, but he had also apparently entered the Twilight Zone. Mailer had picked Patterson to win by a six-round knockout and was insisting that the Mafia had surrounded the ring and cast an evil eye on Floyd. Since Patterson had distanced himself from D'Amato, he could not be helped by the man who Mailer said knew more about warding off the evil eye than anyone alive. He later admitted that his rantings were demented.

Conrad managed to convince the angry police contingent to let him handle matters his own way. He told Mailer he was screwing up his press conference and implored him to leave Liston's stage. "Fuck him," said Mailer. "I ain't moving." When Conrad said the cops were ready to work him over, Mailer told him to fuck the cops. Then Conrad remembered seeing a picture of a man who was carried out of a Montgomery Ward stockholder's meeting in his chair after refusing to leave. He instructed the police to do the same, which they did, amid wild cheers from the press corps. From that day on, Sonny always thought of Norman as the son-of-a-bitch who tried to ruin his press conference.

Sporting his huge smile, Sonny took the high road and praised Patterson as a good fighter and a gallant man. He said the shortness of the fight belied how much time and aggravation he had gone through just to get into that ring. He also thanked the people who stuck with him through the years and said he was glad to have proved them right.

"I have reached my goal as heavyweight champion," he said proudly. "When you reach your goal, you represent something and you have a responsibility to live up to it. As champion, I can do something good for somebody else. Right now I'm in the good light, but there are people who don't want me to be there. Regardless of them, I intend to stay there and I promise everyone that I will be a decent, respectable champion. If the public allows me the chance to let bygones be bygones, I'll be a worthy champ. If they'll accept me, I'll prove it to them."

Most of all, Sonny wanted to let black Americans know they needn't worry about him interfering with their progress. "I want to go to colored churches and colored neighborhood groups," said Liston. "I want them to see me and hear what I have to say, what I have to promise." He had been hurt by stories in black newspapers that said "the better class of colored people" were hoping and praying he would lose.

"I remember one thing so clear about listening to Joe Louis fight on the radio," he told Jack McKinney. "I can't remember a fight that the announcer didn't say about Louis, 'A great fighter and a credit to his race.' Remember? That used to make me feel proud inside. Of course, I don't mean to be sayin' I'm just gonna be the champion to my own people. It says now I'm the world's champion and that's just the way it's going to be."

Joe Louis said something that was ignored by every reporter except *Jet*'s Bobbie Barbee. "Sonny could do more for boxing than any champion in the history of the fight game," said the former champ. "He can set an example to kids everywhere that anyone can pull up and make something of themselves." Joe realized that Liston could become an even more transforming figure as champ than he was and believed that Sonny was capable of becoming someone who everyone could have admired and looked up to, and not just for his ability to fight. "Liston has a chance to exemplify what boxing can do for the tough kid who starts out the wrong way," echoed Jimmy Breslin.

Most of Sonny's adult life had been a quest for respectability, recognition, and the opportunity to share in the American dream. Like all of us, he was his own best advocate and his own worst enemy. His was a sport whose history was replete with second chances for men born on the bad side, and most of the greatest fighters of all time were afforded at least one. Liston had every reason to expect that he'd be given a second chance but the new beginning would not be forthcoming from either the police or the press.

Newsweek's terse two-sentence review of the fight referred to the new champ as a "hulking ex-convict." His victory actually heightened the animosity of the best-known national sportswriters. "If Floyd Patterson were a cop, Sonny Liston would be in the cooler again," wrote Red Smith. Murray Kempton said the world now had a heavyweight champion on the moral level of the men who owned him. "So it is true," wrote Philadelphia sportswriter Larry Merchant, "in a fair fight between good and evil, evil must win." For a celebratory parade to honor the new champ, Merchant suggested they use shredded warrants of arrest for confetti. If any of those writers were half as good at their craft as Sonny was at his, they'd need a storage unit just to hold their Pulitzer Prizes.

On the day Sonny was to fly home to Philadelphia, newspapers all over the country reported that Attorney General Robert F. Kennedy had canceled plans to attempt to get James Meredith admitted to the University of Mississippi, saying this particular attempt was called off because of the possibility of major violence and bloodshed for the citizens of Mississippi. Kennedy said he was sending several hundred more federal marshals to Memphis, Tennessee, for possible use in enforcing the federal order in the Meredith integration case. The powers that be in Philadelphia were about to show a similar lack of enthusiasm toward Liston's return, but without the violence.

Sonny had heard that the city would celebrate his return with a parade and he believed it. It was a reasonable assumption since Mayor James Tate had congratulated Sonny with a telegram that said his feat demonstrated that a man's past didn't have to dictate his future. On the flight home, Liston gave a lot of thought to the speech he would give and rehearsed it in front of Jack McKinney. "My heart ached for him," said McKinney, "because I already knew the mayor's office had nixed the idea of a reception and none of the local media would cover his arrival."

Upon landing, the champ saw that only about 50 people had turned out. "There's nobody here," Sonny said to his wife. McKinney saw the hurt look in his friend's eyes. "He was extremely intelligent, and he understood immediately what it meant. He was still the bad guy. He was the personification of evil. And that's the way it was going to remain. He was devastated." Jack Newfield said it showed Sonny that he would never be able to overcome "the outlaw image of negativity."

Athletic Commissioner Alfred Klein praised Sonny as a great champion and predicted he would make everyone, including his detractors, proud of him. When Jack Nilon insisted he say a few words, Liston smiled, hugged his wife and thanked everyone for coming out. Then he walked to a reception room where he spoke with reporters for 10 minutes. "Being the heavyweight champion hasn't changed me," he said. "I'm just Sonny. I'm going to be the same."

As he left the airport, Liston told McKinney that he'd continue to do the same things he had always done, like stopping in the drugstore, talking to neighbors, and buying the newspapers. "Then I'll see how the real people feel," he said. "Maybe then I'll start to feelin' like a champion. You know, it's really a lot like an election, only in reverse. Here I'm already in office, but now I have to go out and start campaignin.'" It was a campaign he couldn't win as evidenced by an editorial in one of the local newspapers. "Many persons will find precious little to cheer about in having an unsavory character like this occupying the lofty position of world's heavyweight champion," stated the *Philadelphia Inquirer.*

Sonny was so disappointed by the non-reception that he couldn't sleep that night. "He called me about one or two in the morning and asked me to come on over," said his good friend Willie Reddish Jr. "We just sat there and talked all night. He talked about how disappointed he was by the turnout but we mostly talked about nothing, just talked." They talked until the sun came up and Willie had to go to work.

CHAPTER SIX

CHAMPION FOR LIFE

A hugely unpopular black ex-convict with organized crime associations not of his making had an unbreakable grip on the most prestigious individual title in sports. Calls for the abolition of boxing were heard in all parts of the country, and Sonny thought he knew why: "Because they know that no white man is going to be heavyweight champion for a long time to come. And they don't go for that."

Oddsmakers made Liston a 7-to-1 favorite for a rematch that most people considered pointless. The new champ said they could put the fight in a phone booth and it wouldn't sell out. However, Patterson and D'Amato had worded the fight's contract so that it would have cost Liston $1 million to get out of the return bout. Madison Square Garden's matchmaker Harry Markson was convinced that Patterson wanted a second fight simply to prove that he wasn't afraid of Sonny. He offered Patterson a $150,000 guarantee against 32.5 percent of the gross to fight Cassius Clay but withdrew the offer when Floyd tried to dictate Clay's percentage, just as he had done to Liston.

The truth was that Patterson always had far more power outside of the ring than in it and he knew his ironclad rematch contract guaranteed him another big payday. Contenders like Machen, Folley, Williams, and Clay could have beaten him, so if he were going to lose his next fight Floyd figured he might as well get paid as much as possible. And that meant a rematch.

Former heavyweight champs had mixed feelings about the new champ. Jack Dempsey said he picked Liston to win but hoped he was wrong. "I think he'll develop into a fighting champion, but then he may set us all back 50 years in the boxing game," said Jersey Joe Walcott. "A fighter's a fighter. He'll be good.

People will come to see him fight," countered Jimmy Braddock. "All right, it would be better if Liston were not world champion," said Max Schmeling, "but there he simply is. He should be left in peace."

"Being black in this country is hell," Sonny told Carlos E. Russell of the *Liberator*. "And it makes no difference if it is in the North or the South." Liston preferred the South because at least there he knew where he stood. "Our people has got to stop being like crabs in a bucket. The more one tries to get out, the more the others pull him back in." Former heavyweight champ Jack Johnson was severely criticized for preferring the company of white women but Liston admired him for it. "He didn't take nothin' from nobody," said Sonny. "I like Johnson for the way he was, you know, a proud man. He was proud and anything he wanted, he went after, no matter what. More Negroes should be like him, instead of being like crabs in a bucket."

Given the way Sonny talked about changing, and changing people's attitude toward him, I believe he sincerely wanted to do both. Was he capable of changing that much? I think so. Were people willing to change their attitudes toward him? Not enough so that he'd notice. For the most part, winning the most coveted title in sports did nothing to alter people's opinion of Liston. "In this world, if you're colored, anything you do has to be twice as good as the white man," said Sonny, who might have succeeded if he only needed to be twice as good.

Jet Magazine wrote that a Mexican promoter wanted Sonny to appear in exhibition matches but that Mexico had refused the request because it thought Sonny would set a bad example for its youth. Jack Urch of the California State Athletic Commission asked an assistant U.S. attorney general for help in initiating a major new investigation of Liston. Urch wanted some unspecified information he believed to be in the possession of Attorney General Robert Kennedy. "A proper investigation of Sonny Liston at this time is a tremendous investigative challenge to any single state agency," wrote Urch, "but perhaps through the Bureau of Criminal Identification and Investigation, or perhaps through an association of State Attorney Generals, or through the cooperation of the Federal Government, some assistance can be given." Apparently, some people in high places thought Sonny had committed a crime by winning the world heavyweight boxing title without official permission and sought to punish him for it.

The police were not about to change their opinion of Liston either. All of Philadelphia's patrol cars carried a picture of Sonny in their visors, lest some of the department's rookies be unable to identify the world's most famous black athlete. Within two weeks of winning the title, Sonny was arrested again by the Fairmount Park police, who said he was driving at a suspiciously slow speed. "I'm not anti-cop, but some police take themselves too seriously," the champ told *Sports Illustrated*. "If we didn't have cops the world would be in a terrible fix... Everyone would have to go around wearing a gun. Most cops is good guys, but some of those people think them badges makes them big shots."

Philadelphia was Sonny's first real home but he couldn't live there anymore. "I didn't have to leave," he told the *Liberator*. "I left because I wanted to. They kept investigating and I got tired of that." The Listons moved to Chicago, a city that Sonny said had always been good to him. They rented a 21-room mansion that was previously occupied by musician Ahmad Jamal. Located at 4900 S. Greenwood in Chicago's Kenwood neighborhood, the house is less than two blocks from President Obama's home.

Joining the Listons were Geraldine's mother, a niece, and two members of his inner circle, Teddy King and Foneda Cox. While the champ signed autographs and posed for pictures with kids, four squad cars pulled up and parked for several minutes before moving on. Sonny had yet to spend a night in his new city but he could sense that life in Chicago wasn't going to be much different than it was in Philadelphia. Less than six months later he would relocate his family to Denver.

Sonny decided to buy himself a new Cadillac every year and he apparently never used the same color combination twice. He considered his car to be his office and he preferred that people call him there rather than at home. His car phone number was listed but his home number wasn't. His new black Fleetwood had a white leather top and was equipped with a television set and telephones in the front and back seats. He added his personal touch by placing a crucifix on the dashboard, little boxing gloves on the rearview mirror and a small metal plate on the driver's side inscribed, *This car was specially made for Sonny Liston*. He made sure it was always washed with a special soap, and pity the person who washed it with anything else.

Sonny's previous car was a dark blue Cadillac Coupe de Ville, which he bought on Christmas Eve of 1961. While preparing for the Patterson fight, he told his trainer he'd give him the blue Caddy when he won the title. Sonny handed his trainer the keys to the Caddy at a dinner that Reddish's ex-wife gave for the new champ. Willie Jr. remembers his dad proudly bragging that in order to defeat

Sonny, someone would have to go into the deepest jungle, find a gorilla, and shave the hair off of him. Willie Reddish was black and this was just one of those powerful compliments paid to Sonny by members of his profession.

Winning the title made Sonny more willing to talk about himself than he ever had been. "I have accepted without whimpering all the punishment dealt to me for the mistakes I made voluntarily when I was growing up," he told Wendell Smith. "The others, which were the result of bad advice from insincere associates, disturb me greatly because now I find it hard to believe that I was such an easy sucker for their schemes. When I hear people say this is a hard, cruel world, I know exactly what they mean."

When *Ring Magazine* interviewed the new champ for a story entitled "The Look of Meanness," Sonny told Nat Fleischer that he hoped people would look up to him like they'd looked up to the great champions of the past. He pulled an article from his pocket, the writer of which described Sonny as polite, human, and a quick thinker who used good logic and was often witty. Liston said those kind words meant the world to him. "I am uneducated," he admitted, "but I'm not a mean man unless I'm molested."

Sonny used his intimidating look to convey the message to sportswriters and others that they "must not take liberties" with him by prying into his personal life or constantly bringing up his past. Liston offered to make a deal with the press. If he did something bad, he wanted them to tell the world about it, but if he did something good he wanted them to tell the world about that, too. He was offering his huge right hand in friendship to anyone who would accept it.

Columnist Drew Pearson was president of the District of Columbia chapter of Big Brothers and believed Liston deserved a second chance and said so publicly. Soon after he spoke with Liston, Pearson proposed that the Patterson rematch be staged in D.C.'s new National Stadium, with part of the proceeds going to keeping boys out of trouble. In a telegram to Pearson, Sonny said nothing could make him happier than to accept his offer though Floyd had the right to select the date and location.

Fighting in the nation's capitol could have been a game-changing event for Liston. He would have delivered a unique State of the Sport message in less than three minutes without uttering a word. He would have shaken the hands of President Kennedy and Sen. Kefauver and the photo of him standing in front of the Lincoln Memorial would have given us an enduring image of two American giants 100 years after the signing of the Emancipation Proclamation. The world's most important athlete would have been seen as a man of substance and goodwill and he would have been honored to lead the fight against juvenile delinquency as a member of Big Brothers' national board of directors. A lot of wonderful opportunities might have opened up for the former Black Public Enemy No. 1, if only Sonny and Floyd had fought the rematch in Washington DC.

Sonny wanted to defend his title three times a year. He talked about fighting Johansson or light heavyweight champion Harold Johnson but said his first choice would be Clay. "He's young and if I wait too long, age may catch up to me like it did Archie Moore," Sonny said referring to Clay's recent fourth-round stoppage of the 48-year-old Mongoose. After the fight, Clay bragged he was ready to fight Liston but privately he said, "Are you crazy? I can wait."

Liston's second title defense would be promoted by his own company, Inter-Continental Promotions (ICP). ICP was incorporated in July of 1962 by Jack Nilon's brothers, Bob and James, and held the exclusive rights to promote Liston's title fights for the next seven years. The company was predicated upon Sonny winning the title and would become active when he beat Patterson again. Liston's involvement in the company was motivated by one basic thought. "I'm going to promote my own fights so I don't have to wait for my money," he said.

The Patterson fight had been a very bad financial experience for Sonny. He had to wait more than three months before the government released most of the money they had seized and, even then, Patterson's contract required that most of Sonny's purse went into escrow to guarantee the rematch. "I'm kind of mad because this guy (Patterson) wanted the same promoters even after they were the cause of our money being held up by the government," said Liston. "They had no right holding my money."

Despite winning the most prestigious individual title in sports, Sonny's gross income on his 1962 tax return was $44,000 and his purse was less than one-fourth of Patterson's record $1.15 million. The Nilons used the bad experience of the first fight to convince Liston that the only way to guarantee timely payment of his money would be to have his own promotional company. They conveniently ignored the fact that being champion would prevent what Patterson had done to Liston from happening to him again and Sonny bought it hook, line, and sinker.

Bob Nilon initially wanted 52.5 percent of the stock for setting up and running the corporation, but Sonny found it unfair that he was to get less than half of the corporation's stock when he was doing all of the fighting. Eventually, he was given 50 percent of the stock and the title of President but his position had no real power. Nilon had the bylaws drafted so that the authority of the corporation rested with him by virtue of his controlling three of the five directors: himself, his brother Jim, and ICP's secretary and attorney Garland Cherry.

"No one can ever point to Sonny as another sorry example of a boxer who earned a fortune and wound up broke," Cherry would later say. If anyone ever wondered why Liston hated attorneys, this quote of Cherry's would be an excellent place to start doing the research. Having an interest in his own promotional company seemed to be a good thing in a sport where athletes were constantly being screwed. Unfortunately, Inter-Continental would prove to be one of Sonny's greatest disappointments. He had been led to believe that the corporation would give him control of his future fights and greatly enhance his earning potential. If the Nilons were anywhere near as good at promoting as Sonny was at boxing, it may have turned out that way, but they weren't and it didn't. Inter-Continental would end up costing Liston hundreds of thousands of dollars, perhaps even millions, thus accomplishing the opposite of what he thought it would do.

Boxing suffered another serious blow in March when Davey Moore died from the head injuries he suffered in losing his featherweight title to Sugar Ramos. Less than an hour after the fight, Moore lapsed into a coma from which he never emerged. Four professional boxers retired from the ring upon hearing of Moore's death, and state representatives in Ohio, New Jersey, Maryland, and California introduced bills to outlaw boxing. The sport was reeling and some boxing people feared that Patterson could be the next ring fatality at the April 4 rematch with Liston in Miami.

In February and March, Liston and Clay were training at Miami's Fifth Street Gym at separate times. As he often did, Clay would watch Sonny train and try to irritate him. "You ain't so hot," said Cassius on one such occasion. "Yeah?" responded Liston. "I could leave both legs at home and beat you." Saying he could beat the champ, Clay began to climb through the ropes, at which point Liston pivoted and charged toward Cassius, causing the kid to tumble back through the ropes and out of the gym.

Sonny attended the closed-circuit telecast of Clay's fight against Doug Jones. Before the bout, Cassius shook hands with people on street corners, did as many interviews as he could, and even entertained a group of beatniks by reading poetry about himself at The Bitter End in Greenwich Village. Because of Clay's non-stop efforts at building the gate, Madison Square Garden sold out for the first time in six years, in spite of a newspaper strike. "I only wish that Cassius Clay were quadruplets," said a California matchmaker. "It was like the old days," said Jack Dempsey after the fight. "I haven't seen so many regulars at a fight show there in years. That kid's good for the sport. He's something, isn't he?"

Doug Jones had recently lost a decisive 15-round decision to light heavyweight champion Harold Johnson and had never weighed more than 185 pounds for any fight. Not even Jones considered himself a threat to take Liston's title but he was good enough that Liston's manager tried to discourage Clay's syndicate from making the match, knowing that a loss could torpedo a possible fight with Sonny. As it turned out, Jones came close to altering the course of boxing history when he landed a hard right to Clay's head in the first round that hurt Cassius and wobbled his legs. "I knew I had been hit," Cassius said after the fight, "and I also knew one more like that and I'd be on my way to Louisville." Clay won the next two rounds but couldn't deliver on his pre-fight prediction of a fourth-round knockout. Rounds five through seven were not good for the young fighter and the crowd abandoned Cassius and began cheering for Jones. "I knew he was making me look bad," Clay admitted.

Prior to the eighth round Angelo Dundee told his fighter he could kiss Tomato Red goodbye. Tomato Red was an $8,000 Cadillac convertible that Clay's sponsoring group had promised to buy him after he won the fight. "Dundee shook me up," said Cassius. "I came out in the eighth saying, 'So long, Dougie—hello, Tomato Red.'" As he waited for the official decision, Cassius circled the ring with an uncharacteristic scowl on his face. Even though the referee scored the fight 8-1-1 for Clay, had he not won the final two rounds on the scorecards of the two ringside judges who scored the bout 5-4-1 in his favor, Cassius would have lost the fight. *Sports Illustrated*'s Huston Horn described the reaction of the Garden crowd as unbridled outrage as people screamed, "Fix!" while littering the ring with whiskey bottles, lots of trash, and even a switchblade knife. Dundee told his fighter that he looked like an amateur.

"Clay never hurt me at all," Jones said after the fight. "He was barely hanging on at the end. Clay has no chance at all to go 15." Jones looked forward to a rematch (which he'd never get) and said he'd work on hitting Clay when he pulled back, which the young fighter did often. "He's far from the best boxer I ever fought,"

Jones added. "He's really not much."

Veteran referee, Ruby Goldstein, considered Clay to be a combination of a young Ray Robinson and Floyd Patterson. "He's kind of a picture fighter," said Goldstein. "He's the kind you got to say to yourself, he can't miss. But with these picture fighters, how can you tell? One minute they're everything. The next minute they're nothing." Asked how good Clay might become, Dempsey said, "Who knows. But it would be ridiculous for him to get in there with Liston now."

Cassius was uncharacteristically humble at his press conference. "Tell them I did my best," he said. "And tell them I ain't Superman. If they think I can do everything I say I can do, then they're crazier than I am." For the first time in his professional career, Clay's confidence had been shaken and his resolve was being tested. He was in need of a pep talk and he gave himself one on the drive back to Louisville.

Sonny thought Clay had won the fight but he wasn't impressed. "He can't punch. He don't know how to duck. He don't even know how to run. He don't know much about doing anything. He showed me one thing though. I'm liable to get locked up for murder if I fight him." Calling Clay's performance awful, SI's Robert H. Boyle and Mort Sharnik said it proved that the top-rated contender to Liston's crown was made of papier-mache. According to Huston Horn, "it was a sorry showing for the man who thinks he is ready for Sonny Liston...The idea that Clay will meet Liston by fall, gives one the shivers."

Sonny's demeanor had improved so dramatically that people could scarcely believe their eyes. He joked with customers in stores and posed for photographs, telling people he'd like to fight Patterson and Clay at the same time. After Clay's poor performance against Jones, Sonny believed there were no serious challengers in sight and he basically stopped training. In six weeks he was in the gym only five days, and his penchant for Miami's nightlife was no secret.

Sonny's reluctance to train was due in part to a knee injury he suffered by swinging a golf club while holding his 11-year-old friend Mike Zwerner. An X-ray revealed a slightly torn ligament in his left knee, and Sonny was forced to stop training for 17 days. His personal physicians thought cortisone treatments would heal the injury but two Miami Beach Boxing Commission orthopedic surgeons found unmistakable evidence of cartilage damage. "It is our opinion that this knee should have the benefit of surgical procedure and that if such is done, a period of at least six months should elapse before he might be in shape to indulge in any scheduled boxing match," said the Commission's report. Jack Nilon said the surgery would probably take place in Chicago within a week.

According to Angelo Dundee, a knee operation could have ended Liston's career. "Few fighters have been able to keep fighting after having knee trouble," said the trainer. Sonny flew home to Chicago convinced he could avoid surgery if he rested his knee, and he was right. Because Miami Beach lost most of its seasonal residents after Passover, the postponement meant the fight had to be moved. Even though the Miami boxing commission knew Liston's injury was legitimate, they would never forgive him for costing Miami the rematch and would punish him for it when the opportunity presented itself less than a year later.

During Sonny's convalescence, the Listons bought a $28,000 home in Denver on the street where Sonny's good friends Joe and Martha Louis lived. The house had a second living room and full kitchen in the basement so his daughter Choo Choo and Geraldine's niece Connie had a place to entertain their friends. There were color televisions in every room except the kitchen.

Sports Illustrated's Barbara La Fontaine was given a tour of the house and thought Sonny seemed most proud of a hand-carved jewelry box made by an inmate of a Colorado prison. She described their den as a long, large room whose walls were adorned with pictures and paintings of Sonny as champion and a statue of President Kennedy. The living room had a leopard skin rug on which Sonny would stretch out to watch television, and he watched the films of the two Patterson fights all the time. Sonny cut the grass and rode his bicycle around the block but generally had little contact with any of his new neighbors. The Listons had a German shepherd they loved but gave him to a friend when the dog kept chewing up their redwood fence.

Las Vegas was chosen as the new site for a July 22 fight and was the first time that the city would host a heavyweight championship fight. Sonny met Irving "Ash" Resnick there, a former Original Celtics basketball star, who ran the Thunderbird Hotel. Ash came to Las Vegas in the 1940s and was an important figure at seven major casinos, most prominently at Caesars Palace, where he served as assistant to the President and in charge of all casino operations. Ash organized the first high-stakes trips for gamblers, for which he coined the term junkets, and initiated the city's first baccarat game at the Dunes.

Beginning in the early 1960s Ash promoted 19 world championship fights and more than anyone else helped establish Las Vegas as the fight capitol of the world. "All the athletes used to visit Ash and congregate with him," Ash's widow Marilyn told me. "He always had mostly athletes around him." Teams and individual athletes would stay at Resnick's hotels, and if you saw Ash in a restaurant, there was a good chance a star athlete would be at his table.

Ash was dear friends with a lot of world champs including Louis, Liston, Marciano, Sugar Ray Robinson, and Ali. Marilyn said the young Ali fell in love with Ash when he came to train in Las Vegas after winning his gold medal at the Rome Olympics. "I used to cook for Cassius back then in our first house. His sponsoring group would bring him over and he'd watch me make the salad. Ash would bring the steaks home and I'd cook his steak, which he liked done medium. We had just bought a German shepherd and Cassius was always petting on that dog." Ali was so close to Ash that he invited the Resnicks to come with him on his first honeymoon.

By any standard, though, Resnick was closest to Louis. The two met in 1942 while waiting in line for their Army physicals where they discovered they knew a lot of the same people. Ash was the best friend Louis ever had and as bad as Joe's last years were, his life would have been an unmitigated train wreck without him. "Joe had Ash. He always had Ash," said Marilyn.

Louis would travel with the Resnicks and they would share a large, two-bedroom suite at the finest hotels. Joe was a big tipper but it was always with Ash's money. "That's not enough of a tip," Louis would say while taking another $20 out of Ash's hand to give to the doorman. "Joe never had any money," said Marilyn. "All he ever needed was a golf cap, a pair of slacks, a shirt, and a set of clubs. That's how he lived."

Caesars Palace rented a home for Joe and hired his wife Martha to do some of the hotel's legal business. Joe used the reported $50,000 salary that Caesars paid him as a greeter to buy drugs. Ash hated drugs and Joe knew it was the only thing his friend wouldn't buy for him. A lot of drug dealers from the West Side would come over to sell Joe drugs; Marilyn remembered a time when Joe and the dealers were walking a few steps behind her and her husband. "When Ash saw a guy try to slip something to Joe, Ash grabbed him and threw him down the steps," she said. "The dope did Joe in."

Ash threw Joe a 65th birthday party two years before Louis died. *Jet Magazine* did an article on that party and the main photo is one of a weak-looking Louis lying in bed, being visited by Frank and Barbara Sinatra. Lounging on the left side of Joe's bed is his dear friend Ash, who is smiling broadly. Their friendship is one of the great untold stories in sports.

It's safe to say that no child was ever closer to more great fighters than Ash's oldest daughter Dana was. For starters, Rocky Marciano was her godfather. She also has wonderful memories of the practical jokes that Joe Louis played on her, often in cahoots with her father. There were many times when the three of them would be walking hand-in-hand down a street and Joe and Ash would lift Dana up, put her in a trash basket, and keep right on walking for a few steps. "That was their favorite thing, and I fell for it every time," said Dana.

Dana would accompany her dad on "collection trips" where he'd play golf with people who owed the casino money. The collections could amount to between $500,000 and $1 million, and Ash would put the cash in Dana's Barbie case and have her carry it on the plane. "They didn't go through your luggage back then," she told me. Dana was not yet four when Sonny came to Vegas and the two quickly became friends.

Sonny and Ash grew close at the same time that Liston's relationship with Jack Nilon went south. To a man like Sonny, Ash's close friendship with Joe was the best possible reference a man could have. The Dunes wanted Sonny to train at their hotel, and Nilon promised to make it happen. Knowing that the publicity would be tremendous for the hotel where Liston trained, Resnick got Sonny to agree to stay at the Thunderbird. Resnick told me he went out to the airport by himself to pick up Sonny and found a big contingent from the Dunes waiting to take the champ to their hotel. When Nilon and Liston deplaned, Sonny asked him where they were going and was told the Dunes. "I only go with Ash," said Sonny, who walked past the Dunes' people and got into Ash's T-Bird. Nilon was furious but he was powerless to do anything about it.

The Thunderbird put Sonny in the cottage Bobby Kennedy stayed in, and casino executive Vince Anselmo equipped it with a slot machine in which the jackpot symbol was three pictures of Clay. Anselmo said Sonny hit the jackpot twice and played the machine like an old lady in tennis shoes. The champ told his people to get him a fight with Johansson or Clay as a birthday present. "The only thing I'd have to do with Clay is a lot of roadwork, because he's gonna run like a thief," said Liston.

Archie Moore wasn't so sure about that. Though he had been embarrassed by Clay eight months earlier in what Liston said looked like a grandfather fighting a grandson, Moore knew as much about the fine points of boxing as anybody who ever fought. "Sonny would be difficult for him and I would hesitate to say he could beat the champ," said Archie, "but I'll guarantee you he would furnish him with an exceedingly interesting evening." Very few people gave any credence to Moore's analysis, and none of them were in Liston's camp.

Clay had asked his Louisville sponsors to fly him to Las Vegas so he could watch the champ train, harass him, and let the world know the real fight was yet to come. He attended many of Liston's workouts, often standing within inches of the ring ropes. His heckling of the champ was generally relentless but everyone in Sonny's camp considered Clay to be more of an annoyance than a serious contender. "The women will ruin him long before he gets up there," said Reddish. "Ugly fighters are the best." Nevertheless, the sporting press paid more attention to Clay than they did Patterson because as Ali said later, people can't stand a blowhard but they'll always listen to him.

In a fairly well-known incident, Liston walked up behind Clay in the Thunderbird Casino and tapped him on the shoulder. When Clay turned around, Liston slapped him with the back of his hand. Sonny told a visibly shaken Cassius he did it because he was "too fucking fresh." As he left the casino, Liston said, "I got the punk's heart now." The next day, in broad daylight, Liston urinated on a copy of *Time* that had Clay's picture on the cover.

Not long after the casino incident, Willie Reddish devised a practical joke for Sonny to play on Clay. Willie told Cassius that Liston was gambling at the Thunderbird and suggested he do the same. Figuring Clay would go, Reddish gave Sonny a blank-filled pistol that he had secured for the occasion. Liston was shooting craps when Clay arrived and immediately began taunting the champ. Most people stopped gambling to see what was happening but Sonny remained cool. "I want you out of town by sunup tomorrow," Clay said. "Las Vegas ain't big enough for both of us." Suddenly, Liston pulled the pistol out of his pocket, pointed it at Clay's head, and pulled the trigger. Two loud BANGS rang out. Clay ducked and a chill ran down his spine. Two more loud BANGS had Clay leaping over tables and scattering chips and cards all over the floor. Clay was ducking and dodging all the way out to the street as Liston fired two more shots.

Clay's heart was racing and his hands were shaking when he got back to his hotel room. "I was thinking maybe I should leave Liston alone. I knew I was only acting crazy, but he might be crazy for real." He was still shook up an hour later when a reporter told him the gun contained blanks and it was all a practical joke.

Newsweek finally gave Sonny some credit in its pre-fight story. "Liston came to the crown wearing horns. He is no longer the object of such fierce contempt. Nor is he the object of fierce admiration. He is, if anything, an object of curiosity. And the curiosity focuses, first, upon his talent. Sonny Liston could be the most talented heavyweight fighter who ever lived." Joe Louis predicted that Sonny would take out Patterson the first time he hit him.

On the day of the fight, black leaders decided to call off a demonstration that would have focused attention on the lack of job opportunities for blacks in the Las Vegas gambling industry. That morning Sonny played with young children at the hotel pool and said his mental state was much better than it was for the first fight. A few hours before the fight, the Listons dined in the Thunderbird's restaurant and could have passed for tourists.

By fight time, the odds were 5-1 and most of the writers polled by UPI picked Sonny to win by an early knockout. A sold-out crowd packed the Las Vegas Convention Center where the seats were priced from $20 to $100. After comedian Shecky Greene finished the first of his two shows at the Riviera Hotel he took a cab to the fight. "Keep the motor running," Shecky told the taxi driver. "I'll be right out." Sure enough, Shecky was back at the Riviera in plenty of time for his second show.

Liston's close friend Father Murphy stood quietly in the back of the arena. He had decided not to use the ringside ticket that Sonny had given him. "By the time everyone gets seated, the fight will be over," predicted Murphy. "I wouldn't want to get crushed when they start climbing into the ring." Murphy's instincts were telling him to bet the collection plate on this fight.

Sonny calmly clipped his fingernails in his dressing room. As far as this fight was concerned, it was just something he had to do and he was glad the wait was over. "Well, let's go down and cross the railroad tracks and stop in at the pay station," said the champ as he began to make his way to the ring.

The booing of Liston when he entered the ring was so intense that A.J. Leibling thought the crowd resented Sonny's competence. Sonny even got a rude reception in his new town of Denver, where capacity crowds booed him at the city's two closed-circuit outlets. The Convention Center crowd booed again when Liston was introduced and their reaction only strengthened his resolve. If the public wasn't with him now, he thought to himself, they'd just have to swing along till somebody else came along to beat him.

After being introduced, Clay had a short conversation with Patterson during which Floyd pointed his right hand toward Sonny. Clay nodded, took two steps toward Liston's corner, comically threw up his hands in horror, and leaped over the ring ropes as though he were terrified. He knew that the police had orders to keep him away from Sonny and he'd already decided that the time to make a scene would be after the fight rather than before it.

Much to the crowd's chagrin, it quickly became clear that Patterson had no chance of winning the fight. Sonny had a huge smile on his face when Floyd was counted out at 2:10 of the first round after being knocked down three times. As he had in Chicago, Floyd got up one second too late to beat the count. Several years later he would claim that he finished all of his fights on his feet.

Even before the official announcement, Clay jumped in the ring, grabbed a microphone, and called the fight a disgrace. His rantings were so loud that Howard Cosell had to finish his interview with Sonny in the champ's dressing room. When Liston's cornermen held up an oversized newspaper headline that read *Clay has a big lip that Sonny will zip*. Cassius grabbed the paper and ripped it to shreds. "Can you believe this guy?" Sonny said to Reddish. Angelo Dundee remembers Sonny walking over to Cassius and calmly saying, "Don't get hurt now, little boy. We're gonna make a lot of money." Clay continued to scream insults in the general direction of Liston after the champ left the ring. "Liston scares me sometimes," he admitted, "but I'll just laugh at him."

Sonny had become the first heavyweight champion to stop a challenger in the first round of his first title defense. That meant little to the crowd, which booed intensely as Sonny left the ring, though a group of policemen tried to shake his hand as he made his way back to his dressing room. Given their reaction, it seemed that Las Vegas was the perfect place for Sonny to call home.

The first thing Sonny said at his post-fight press conference was that he was anxious to get home to his lovely wife. The champ wore slacks, a blue denim shirt, and a straw hat with a feather in it and looked like he'd spent a casual evening with friends. He expressed disappointment that he wasn't able to hit Patterson with what he considered a really good punch and said he could have beaten him with one hand. Sonny also revealed he had injured his left elbow in training and had flown in his personal doctor from Detroit to treat the problem. "I'm telling this for the first time," he said. "There was a chance the fight might be called off. We kept it a secret."

A reporter asked the champ if Patterson had fought better this time. "Didn't you see the fight?" Sonny shot back. When asked if Patterson should retire, Liston diplomatically offered, "Who am I to tell a bird he can't fly?" Asked how long he planned on holding the title, Sonny said, "That's like asking God how long you want to live—as long as I can." This was Sonny Liston—direct, diplomatic, philosophical, and honest. More than anything else, though, it showed how important being champion was to him.

Then someone asked Liston if he thought there was any significance to the pointing gesture Patterson made towards him while talking to Clay. "It's like this," Sonny said. "You see, once there was these guys and every night they used to steal some ham from the butcher's freezer. Well, the butcher caught wise, see. And one night he was waiting in the freezer when the two guys showed up. Anyway, the first guy sneaks up to the freezer and puts his hand in to get some ham. Wham! The butcher swings his cleaver and chops off the guy's hand. Well that guy he pulls his arm out real fast and he says to the other guy, 'I got mine, Buddy, you get yours.'" Liston roared, as did his listeners. Several seconds later, many of those who had laughed grew uneasy as the meaning of Sonny's parable began to sink in.

Reached in Newcastle, Arkansas, Helen Liston said she was proud of her son, but not his vocation. She hadn't seen or listened to either Patterson bout and had learned of the outcomes from neighborhood friends. "I don't like fighting," she said, "but I can't tell my boy how to live his life."

After the fight, Patterson lived alone in a two-room apartment at the rear of his house. He told Gay Talese he would give anything just to be able to spar with Liston where nobody would see them. "All I want is to prove to myself that I could get past the first round," said Floyd, revealing a humiliation that would haunt him for the rest of his life.

Clay went to Sonny's victory party, hoping to make the champ mad. "Come on over and sit on my knee and finish your orange juice," said Liston. After receiving the title belt from Nat Fleischer, Sonny waved it over his head and told Cassius it was something he'd never get. "Listen, kid. You'd better fight my trainer instead of me. You'd still lose, but at least you won't get killed."

The reviews of the fight underscored Liston's dominance. "It must now be admitted that he is a superb fighter," wrote *SI*'s Robert Boyle. "He is huge yet lithe, a rare blending of strength, balance, and reflexes." *Time* compared Liston's performance to a man killing a rabbit with a stick. Marciano said Sonny was so big and strong, it was almost like he was walking through his opponent. *Ring Magazine*'s

Nat Fleischer called Liston one of the greatest power punchers in history and speculated that Patterson wouldn't survive the first round if they fought another six times. Sportswriter Jerry Izenberg believed Sonny would be heavyweight champ for life.

"Patterson didn't have a chance against him and neither would I. It would be suicide to enter the same ring," admitted Johansson, who said Jack Nilon had offered him a million dollars to fight Liston. "I like money, but not that much. I don't want anything to do with him." Heavyweight champs do not say things like this. Years later, a boxer who fought on one of Johansson's cards in Sweden said Ingemar talked about Sonny like he was a god. Even Cus D'Amato acknowledged Liston's talent, saying he compared favorably with any heavyweight champ, including Louis.

Liston's camp was worried that Denver would ignore his return home. When Mayor Tom Currigan learned of this, he had his aides call his supporters to urge them to greet the returning champ. "Gee whiz, Geraldine, look at all the people! Here they come," a gleeful Liston said as the plane taxied to the gate. More than 1,500 people greeted the champ; the mayor said all of Denver was proud of him. The reception was in stark contrast to the cold shoulder Philadelphia gave Sonny after he won the title. "I was thrilled," said the champ. "It's one of the nicest things that ever happened to me."

Sonny thanked the crowd for the welcome, then cut a huge chocolate cake decorated with boxing gloves and inscribed, *Welcome Home Sonny*. "I'll cut Clay in half like this cake," Liston joked, brimming with happiness and confidence. The Listons talked about the reception late into the night and Gerry said they were both thrilled beyond words. Sonny told her he could live in Denver for the rest of his life and that he wanted to build a $150,000 home there raised high so he could see the mountains. He was counting on the Clay fight to help him pay for it. "Clay's the nicest thing to come along since Christmas," said Sonny. "I would say Clay has a lot to learn. I hope nobody teaches him before I get to him."

You may remember that someone almost did. Cassius was in London for his June 18 fight against British heavyweight champion Henry Cooper where he infuriated the fight crowd by entering the ring wearing a crown. Making as many enemies as possible would mean that the next time he fought in England, more people would come to see him get beat. And the tickets would cost a lot more.

At 185 pounds, the mediocre Cooper was small, easy to hit, and bled more than any other fighter. Clay boasted that the Englishman would fall in five but by attempting to carry Cooper to the predicted round, he almost lost the fight. Near the end of the fourth round, a badly bleeding Cooper landed a left hook to Clay's jaw that sent him to the canvas. The Louisville Lip was extremely lucky for two reasons. Had the ropes not broken his fall, his head might have hit the canvas very hard. Second, the knockdown occurred just before the round ended, denying Cooper the opportunity to press his advantage. "Thank God for the ropes. Thank God the bell rang," Angelo Dundee said after the fight. According to Dundee, his fighter slumped on his stool like a sack of potatoes as fellow cornerman Chickie Ferrara worked feverishly to revive his fighter by dropping ice cubes down his trunks, breaking smelling salts under his nose, and massaging his shaky legs.

Midway through the fifth round, a cut over Cooper's right eye was bleeding so badly that many in the pro-Cooper crowd of 55,000 people were imploring the referee to stop the fight. Cassius said he could actually hear Cooper bleeding. Clay's fifth-round TKO did nothing to convince anyone he belonged in the same ring with Liston and it actually further damaged his already-tarnished reputation. A majority of boxing people believed Clay's rise to prominence had been due more to his style in and out of the ring than his boxing skill, and the Jones and Cooper fights confirmed the notion. "I don't think he ever crept into the national consciousness as anything but a burlesque act, comic relief, a hype job, till he fought Sonny Liston," wrote *L.A. Times* sportswriter Jim Murray.

The truth was that Cassius Clay had everybody right where he wanted them.

The Nilons were looking to hold the fight on September 30 in Philadelphia's Municipal Stadium. They had selfish reasons for wanting to do this: their catering company handled the stadium's parking and all of the concessions. However, scheduling the fight before Sonny's 30-month managerial contract with George Katz ended in late October would have required Liston to pay his former manager 10 percent of what figured to be a huge payday. Managers are paid to look out for their fighters and it was Jack Nilon's responsibility to point out to Liston what he stood to lose under the proposed timetable. But blood is thicker than water and Jack chose his brothers' interests over Sonny's.

After Clay's bout against Jones, Bob Nilon had phoned William Faversham and was told that the entire Louisville Sponsoring Group, including Angelo Dundee, was opposed to Cassius fighting Liston. Nilon told Faversham their fighter was a bubble that was about to burst and that he could approach his fighter's future in two ways. If Clay didn't fight Liston, he would have to fight some of the other contenders, like Cleveland Williams, Zora Folley, or Ernie Terrell. Nilon offered the opinion that Clay would probably lose to the first good heavyweight he fought.

Second, if Clay actually was a good fighter and could make a credible showing by going seven or eight rounds with Liston, he wouldn't lose any prestige as a fighter and would guarantee himself a lucrative, if not spectacular career. ICP offered Clay 22.5 percent of the gate and in mid-July, Gordon Davidson told Nilon his group was inclined to accept those terms and sign for the fight.

Clay's backers were some of Louisville's most distinguished and successful citizens. Faversham had boxed at Harvard but that represented the sum of the group's experience in the sport. Though short on boxing knowledge the group understood money. Ten of their 11 members were millionaires and they were looking to maximize Clay's purses, as well as their 50 percent share of his ring earnings. They each invested $28,000 to finance Clay's boxing career and protected their investment by taking out a $300,000 insurance policy on their fighter's life. Since Cassius had already been ticketed twice for speeding and liked to shadow box an imaginary Liston while he was driving, they also took out a $300,000 accident policy.

Apart from wanting to make money, the group said they wanted to prevent Clay from falling victim to the "jaws of the hoodlum jackals" that had glommed on to Liston. "The Kefauver hearings were still fresh in everyone's mind," said LSG attorney Gordon Davidson. "The disadvantages of boxing and the effects on fighters were still fresh to the general public and it was thought that this group, composed of corporate executives and men of substantial means, who had no great profit motive, should form a group and sponsor Clay." They seemed to have done right by their fighter.

Marciano had spent a week in Louisville and heard only good things about Cassius. "There's no drinking, girls, late hour shows," said Rocky. "He's being taken care of just right by his management. He doesn't have to worry about his family or about walking-around money. He's a contended fighter who really wants to become champ." Cassius lived such a chaste existence that Angelo Dundee said a lot of people thought his fighter was gay.

Around this time, Clay's backers received word that Congress would pass a bill in 1964 permitting the averaging of income over several years and they decided it was in their fighter's best financial interests to wait for a 1964 fight date. The personal income tax rate was oppressively high back then. When negotiations resumed in September, Davidson told Garland Cherry that his group was no longer interested in fighting for the 22.5 percent they had agreed on and felt that their fighter was worth 25 percent or even 30 percent. "The Nilons explained to me they were having a problem with Liston going above 22.5 percent," said Davidson. Inter-Continental told him that Clay wasn't about to get any more money and wished him and his fighter well.

Davidson was merely expressing the wishes of his group's fighter. "I have talked too much and worked too hard to take a low cut," Cassius was quoted as saying. "I built this fight up and I will tear it down. Let me lay it on the line. Liston either meets my price or he can dance elsewhere for peanuts." The 22.5 percent that Clay thought was peanuts was actually the highest percentage any challenger had ever been guaranteed. Since Cassius had yet to fight a major heavyweight contender and had almost lost to a couple of also-rans, Liston and the promoters were justified for holding their financial ground.

Sonny could have defended his title against somebody else on home TV but opted for a September exhibition tour of Norway, Sweden, Denmark, Finland, and Great Britain. When the trip became public knowledge an agent in the FBI's London office alerted J. Edgar Hoover saying that a higher-up in England had read that Liston had a criminal record and requested that a copy of Sonny's fingerprint record immediately be furnished to the London office. Why the British government felt threatened by Sonny's visit is unclear but the declassified portions of Liston's extensive FBI file clearly indicate that they were.

The tour was reminiscent of one in 1911 when people cheered as heavyweight champion Jack Johnson smiled his way through the streets of London. A similar excitement was generated by Sonny's visit and to his great surprise no one in England asked him about his past. Working out in front of 11,000 people at London's Wembley Pool, Liston bowed to all four corners of the audience and took several curtain calls. "I appreciate you coming here tonight," Sonny told the crowd. "You people shows up better here than they do back home. That's the truth, and the truth don't hurt no one."

In Glasgow, Sonny rode down the town's main street on a white horse in full Highland dress with a flask of alcohol under his kilts. Thousand of cheering people lined the streets to cheer him. In Belfast, Sonny caused something of a scandal when he kissed a white model from a local clothes shop, and the model was promptly fired by her employer. According to the tour's organizer, Peter Keenan, Sonny was disturbed by and couldn't understand the bigotry he saw in Belfast. "He thought only blacks were treated badly," said Keenan. "He kept talking about the march Martin Luther King was organizing and how he really wanted to be back home for it."

However, Sonny knew he couldn't go on that or any other Southern march. "They don't fight fair," he said of the police there. "They don't fight my kind of fight. I ain't got a dog-proof butt. Some cop puts a hose on me, and I'll forget where I am." Liston believed in the concept of an eye for an eye. If someone burned his house, he'd burn theirs. If they tried to beat him, he'd beat them.

Sonny met privately with Johansson in Stockholm, after which Ingemar said it was possible that he would come out of retirement. When Jack Nilon said Liston would defend his title in Britain against Brian London if the terms were right, Sonny said he'd gladly fight London and Cooper in the same ring at the same time. Sonny's string of one-round knockouts could have gone on for quite a while against the likes of Johansson, London, and Cooper and there were a lot of such fighters around. "We had nobody anywhere good enough to fight him," admitted British boxing promoter Mickey Duff.

Every notable heavyweight champion in history fought much less than the best available challenger in his first title defense, and nobody ever complained about it. It was the accepted prerogative of any new titleholder to take what amounted to a victory lap with an easy fight—and they all exercised it. Jack Johnson fought Victor McLaglen, Jack Dempsey fought Billy Miske, Joe Louis fought Tommy Farr, Floyd Patterson fought Tommy Jackson, Joe Frazier fought Terry Daniels, George Foreman fought Jose Roman, and Larry Holmes fought Alfredo Evangelista. After return bouts with the previous titleholders Gene Tunney fought Tom Heeney, Rocky Marciano fought Roland LaStarza, and Muhammad Ali fought George Chuvalo. Sonny would have been well within his rights to follow the same course as his predecessors; this would have provided him with some very easy money. Fighting Johansson in Sweden would have been Liston's best possible payday given Ingo's popularity there.

The tour was cut short when Sonny unexpectedly flew home to Denver. A British boxing writer claimed that Liston had quarreled with Jack Nilon, and Liston's publicist, Ben Bentley, said he had never seen Sonny in such an angry mood. Sonny said he was leaving because of the illness of his daughter, Eleanor.

Until then, few knew that Liston was a father. Bentley, Nilon, and Sonny's sparring partner Foneda Cox said they knew Sonny had two daughters, the oldest being a 19-year-old who, according to an article in an Hawaiian newspaper, was the product of an earlier marriage. It was reported that she was going to a business college, taking pre-law classes, and had applied for a job with the FBI.

Sonny jogged down the passenger ramp into Denver's terminal. As the press ran after him, Sonny stopped and told reporters he was ashamed to be in America. When asked why, he said, "You ought to be able to figure that out. You should see the way they (the British press) treated me. It made me ashamed to be from America." A fellow passenger told UPI that a young girl on the plane had asked Liston for an autograph. When he declined, the girl asked where he had been and Sonny replied: "In Alabama."

Sonny was distraught over the bombing of a Birmingham church that had killed four young black girls. This affected Sonny more profoundly than anything ever had. He would have much rather killed the murderers than to have to speak on behalf of the country that had long tolerated and fueled the depth of racial hatred needed to commit these crimes. The following day Geraldine told the Associated Press that Sonny had been deeply disturbed by the Birmingham bombing. "You should hear the things they ask you there, about the race problem," she said. "They kept bugging him, and he finally said, 'I can't take this anymore.'"

Sonny remained in seclusion for two weeks before speaking at a press conference organized by a local boxing promoter. "People asked a lot of questions about the race problems over here," said Sonny. "The questioning was real bad after the bombings. Everywhere I went, they would ask me over and over, 'What about the Alabama bombing? What do you think of it, Sonny?' I've never been afraid in the ring, but I used to get real nervous when they'd start asking me about the race problem because I just didn't know how to answer them."

Liston said he couldn't sleep, had terrible headaches, and decided he needed to come home. He didn't expect to be greeted at the airport and didn't feel like talking to anyone about the Alabama bombing. "If I hurt anybody's feelings, I'm sorry," said Sonny. He called the people of Denver wonderful and said his family wanted to stay there permanently. He also said the reception he got after the second Patterson fight made him happier than winning the title in the first place.

Sonny's sensitivity to America's racial problems actually heightened his unpopularity. In a column titled "Sonny Needs To Grow Up," the *Denver Post*'s Jim

Graham wrote, "If his temper trantrum of last Wednesday is any indication of the 'new' Liston, then the sports world ought to pack it in as far as calling him by the name of 'champion.'" Graham went on to say, "Since when does a two-time loser take it upon himself to judge the whole of American society? There are an awful lot of Americans who are ashamed of Sonny Liston. He hasn't exactly made his supporters or the people of the United States proud of him."

What exactly had Sonny done wrong? What offense had he just committed? What part of Liston's reaction to the Birmingham bombing was not admirable and laudable? What part of his words and sentiments was not an honest expression of the way every Black American felt? I sometimes wish I could have been at a subsequent press conference as Sonny's rep, and ridiculed the hell of that little impotent butterball Graham, and a hundred others just like him.

It had been a year since Liston won the heavyweight title but the second chance he longed for was not happening. He felt the fans treated him like dirt and he was still bitter five years later when he told sparring partner Ray Schoeninger that everyone acted like he had stolen the title. "I didn't expect the president to invite me into the White House and let me sit next to Jackie and wrestle with those nice Kennedy kids, but I sure didn't expect to be treated like no sewer rat." He knew he was nobody's good guy.

In Sonny's case, being the most feared man on the planet made him a highly unmarketable figure. Ed Sullivan invited the Bear on his show to jump rope for a couple of minutes but that was the extent of his television exposure. Rocky Marciano once said that while popularity would never give you ability, ability would put the crowd in your corner almost all of the time. But the public never embraced or even warmed to Liston, a fact that *Esquire* learned the hard way at a time when the magazine's circulation was at an all-time high.

"In 1963, *Esquire* editor Harold Hayes decided to rethink the covers of the magazine and George Lois devised a Christmas cover that was outrageous," photographer Carl Fischer wrote in his description of the event. "The unthinkable conceit was to show an unlikeable, intimidating black man as Santa Claus." Liston was the perfect choice for that cover but he wouldn't travel to New York for the shoot so Fischer set up an impromptu studio in Las Vegas at the Thunderbird Hotel.

"Liston had not been told that he would be wearing a Santa Claus hat, of course. That was the usual subterfuge of Harold Hayes, who feared that famous subjects would discuss the picture with agents or friends and would refuse the egregious situations which *Esquire* wanted to see on its covers...*Esquire* had the foresight to hire the respected ex-heavyweight champion Joe Louis, who was admired by Liston, and who worked in Las Vegas, to attend the shooting and to use his persuasive powers, if required. They were required." Even so, if not for Ash Resnick's three-and-a-half-year-old daughter, Dana, the shoot may have never taken place.

"Liston was angry and dismissive when the idea of wearing a Santa Claus hat was brought up. I quickly offered to do the cover without the hat (a delaying tactic to keep him from abruptly leaving) and started taking pictures. Liston had brought a friend's child with him and I suggested taking souvenir snapshots of them together. While taking these informal pictures, I supposed that the Santa Claus hat might be appropriate with the little girl, and Liston grudgingly agreed. After seeing the Polaroids of himself in the Santa hat with the little girl, and seeing that the girl loved them, Liston softened a millimeter. Louis told Liston that the hat looked good on him. I prompted that it made him look important: why don't we try you alone with the hat, just to see if you agree? And so it was done."

Esquire's advertising director had suggested to Hayes that the magazine ought to wait until Saks Fifth Avenue put a black Santa in its stores before putting one on its cover, much less "the baddest motherfucker ever kissed by fame" as George Lois, the cover's creator had called Liston. Lois acknowledged that "many advertisers don't like to buy ad pages from niggerlovers"; I use that quote only because Lois was just stating the obvious back then. *Sports Illustrated* later wrote that Sonny was the last man on earth that America wanted to see coming down its chimney and they seem to have been right. But to Hayes, Sonny's black Santa was the perfect magazine cover for America at the time.

When *Newsweek* ran a full page story about *Esquire's* cover in its December 16 issue, it said Fischer's photo was "at first glance, simple and pleasant. Then it turns savage. It is the face, uncaptioned but unmistakable, of the heavyweight champion of the world, Sonny Liston." Of course, it was *Newsweek* that described Liston with the words, "viciousness and everything that is evil," less than 15 months earlier. If you take a good look at Carl Fischer's cover, I don't think you'll see a single negative thing about it, unless you're afraid of blacks.

The cover won an international award as the Finest Front Cover of a men's magazine in 1963, and a professor or art history termed it "one of the greatest social statements of the plastic arts since Picasso's Guernica." That was the good news. The bad news was quantifiable. Both the magazine's editor and advertising director estimated that the cover cost *Esquire* at least $750,000 in pulled advertising revenue, which back then was a lot of money. The advertising director believed the loss was even greater since at least one of its major advertisers abandoned the magazine for ten years.

Sonny's Santa was *Esquire*'s most controversial cover until 1970 when Carl photographed Lieutenant William Calley Jr. with four small Asian children. Calley had been convicted of murdering civilians at My Lai in Vietnam. The heavyweight champion of the world had worn a red Santa's cap. Two brilliant covers but only one should have been controversial.

SONNY LISTON
PHOTO GALLERY

I believe this was the proudest moment of Charles Liston's life. More than 1,500 people greeted him upon his return to Denver, July 24, 1963 after he defended his title against Floyd Patterson. "I'll cut Clay in half, like this cake," Sonny told a group of invited guests in the airport's VIP lounge. (*Denver Post*)

You can see Sonny's smiling face in the middle of a throng of youthful fans. The soon-to-be-champ had just delivered a speech on street gangs to an overflow crowd at Archie Moore's Gym in Chicago. (Chicago History Museum) (ICHi-65093)

The Listons move into their new Chicago house in December, 1962. Geraldine had great taste and their homes were always beautifully furnished. (Chicago History Museum) (ICHi-65092)

Sonny and Geraldine with their son Bobby, one of several children Liston fathered out-of-wedlock. Little Bobby would become a central figure at Sonny's 1965 rematch with Muhammad Ali in Lewiston, Maine. (*Denver Post*)

If not for three-year-old Dana Resnick, Carl Fischer's iconic 1963 *Esquire* "Black Santa" cover might never have happened. Sonny wanted nothing to do with the photo shoot but posing with Ash Resnick's daughter softened the champ's mood. (Courtesy of Carl Fischer)

America's favorite villain shops for toys in a non-staged pose that belies Sonny's reputation as the world's meanest man. No child was ever frightened in the presence of the guy they affectionately called Uncle Charles. (*Denver Post*)

Sonny and his trainer, Willie Reddish, had a great time shopping for kids' Christmas presents in December, 1963. Liston was always very generous with his family, friends, and other people's children. (*Denver Post*)

Sonny and the great light heavyweight champ, Archie Moore, show off their impressive fists during a press luncheon at Fritzels in Chicago. Both men were denied their title shots for far too long. (Chicago History Museum) (ICHi-65094)

Liston and his manager, Jack Nilon, have a laugh at Cassius Clay's expense. The fighters had just signed the contracts for their first fight. *(Denver Post)*

Sonny and Geraldine Liston enjoy their lunch that day and Clay gets ready to do the same. *(Denver Post)*

On Christmas Day 1964, Sonny was arrested for drunk driving even though he wasn't behind the wheel at the time of the arrest. The impeccably dressed ex-champ was acquitted at a January trial during which the prosecution took an astounding 10 hours to present its case. (*Denver Post*)

Sonny's sister, Alcora. Sonny's generosity helped Alcora's family survive some very tough times. (Helen Long)

Alcora's oldest daughter, Helen Jean, was named after her grandmother. Helen was her Uncle Charles' favorite niece and she inherited his huge hands. (Paul Gallender)

Liston's son, William Wingate (right), seen here with Tommy Manning. Tommy and Sonny were close friends when the Listons lived in Philadelphia, and Manning always thought of Sonny's wife Geraldine as the mother he never had. (Paul Gallender)

Sonny Liston's final resting place is in Las Vegas.

PART TWO

IT WAS BEAUTY KILLED THE BEAST

CHAPTER SEVEN

A PERFECT SETUP

Boxing's two greatest heavyweights were born into different generations and socio-economic classes. They approached their places in the world in very different ways, and their paths to the title had almost nothing in common.

Cassius was the eldest of two sons in a middle-class family, and people who had seen him in his cradle told him he looked like Joe Louis. "The first thing he said was 'Gee-gee,' and that's what people in the family still call him: Gee," said his mother, Odessa. "Later he said that Gee-gee stood for Golden Gloves, which he was going to win."

Clay's father was a sign painter who always tried to surround his children with good people and avoid the ones that would get them into trouble. "I dressed them up as good as I could afford and kept them in pretty good clothes," said Cassius Clay Sr. "They didn't come out of no ghetto. I raised them on the best street I could." That street was in the west end of Louisville, Kentucky, which, though segregated, was clean and peaceful and wasn't at all like the Deep South.

Cassius religiously avoided street fighting for the same reason that most people do. "You can get hurt, killed, fighting with rocks and sticks," he said. "We'd have these fights on the way home from school. I was afraid of a lot of those kids, the ones that was a little bigger." Cassius couldn't remember ever getting into a real fight when he was a kid. He wouldn't play tackle football because he thought it was too rough, but once he discovered boxing he'd constantly ask his brother to throw rocks at him. "I thought he was crazy, but he'd stand back and dodge every one of them. I could never hit him," said Rudolph.

The only time Cassius got into trouble was when he hit a teacher with a snowball. After apologizing to the disciplinary board he told them he was going to be the heavyweight champion of the world. Cassius wasn't a bright student, didn't particularly like to read, and ranked 376 in a high school graduating class of 391 with a D-minus average. Though he bragged he was the greatest, Cassius said he never claimed he was the smartest.

There was nothing even remotely middle class about Liston's family and upbringing. He was raised in abject poverty in the deepest part of the South. The son of an Arkansas sharecropper, Sonny lived in a cardboard-lined shack with more siblings than he could count, got his first pair of shoes around the age of ten, and didn't learn to read or write. He grew up on his own, ran around without any kind of supervision, and never went to school.

Fist fights were a fact of life for Sonny as far back as he could remember. Having absorbed regular and painful beatings from his abusive father, he wasn't about to let anyone else treat him that way. He grew so big so fast that older kids quickly learned he was the wrong guy to mess with. By the time he turned 12 Sonny was a physically imposing young man. Whereas Sonny was born into a fighter's body, Muhammad Ali had to grow into the role.

At age 12 the 89-pound Cassius was anything but imposing. When someone stole his new bicycle, a policeman named Joe Martin suggested to him that he learn how to fight before trying to beat up the guy who took it. "If boxers were paid bonuses on their potential like ballplayers are, I don't know if he would have received one," said Martin. "He was just ordinary, and I doubt any scout would have thought much of him in his first year." Martin remembered that Cassius's hands shook when he laced on his gloves. "He was emotionally wild before a fight," said Joe. "He'd build himself up into a regular frenzy, letting that fear out by tormenting his opponent."

Odessa Clay always believed her son when he told her he would be a world champion someday, mostly because of his wealth of self-confidence. "But not as a heavyweight!" she exclaimed. "For the longest time, he was *so* skinny." Clay weighed just 178 pounds when he won the light-heavyweight gold medal at the 1960 Olympic Games at the age of 18.

Like every modern heavyweight champion before him, save for Liston, Ali benefitted from fighting in the ring where rules governed a combatant's conduct. Liston was the only heavyweight champion in history who was the toughest guy on the block, in or out of the ring. In a street fight, Sonny was unbeatable. In the ring, wearing eight-ounce gloves and subject to Marquess of Queensberry rules, he was only slightly less so.

When Ali was facing jail time in 1968 after being convicted of draft evasion, a reporter asked Sonny how his former adversary might fare in jail. "He's always saying how pretty he is, so slim and pretty," laughed Sonny. "If they put him with a couple of lifers they'll show him how pretty he is." Liston knew Ali would have been overmatched and overpowered outside of the ring where speed, skill, and finesse are far less important than brute strength and roughhouse tactics. Ali knew it as well.

Gene Kilroy was as close to Ali as anybody and he wasn't afraid to argue with him. During one such argument, Ali challenged Kilroy to a fight and Gene accepted. "How you gonna beat me?" Ali asked him. "I'm a three-time champion!" Kilroy said he'd kick him in the groin and gouge his eyes out. When Ali told Gene he couldn't do that, Gene told him yes he could. "That's why I've never been in street fights," replied Muhammad.

The public personalities of Liston and Clay appeared to be polar opposites. Liston's had been cultivated over a lifetime of hard knocks and he shunned the spotlight because being the center of attention brought him only bad things. He let his silence speak for him whenever possible and the strength of his personality allowed him to do that. As good looking and likable as Clay was, he had to make people pay attention to him. Cassius first learned how to draw a crowd in grade school where he noticed that most people liked to watch somebody who acted differently than everyone else. After he started fighting he found out that grown people at his bouts acted just like those schoolkids.

The boxing persona Clay presented as a young professional took him about three years to cultivate. "Where do you think I would be next week if I didn't know how to holler and make the public sit up and take notice?" he told reporters before becoming champ. "I would be poor, for one thing, and I would probably be down in Louisville, Kentucky, my hometown, washing windows or running an elevator."

Archie Moore was one of two sports figures that helped Cassius create the persona that prompted millions of new young fans, including me, to follow his exploits. Watching the way Moore talked confirmed something that Clay already knew, namely that talking was a lot easier than fighting. He also correctly surmised that running his mouth could be a big help in rising through the rankings, and an awful lot of photos of Clay were taken with his mouth wide open. "The big difference between the old man and me is I'm bigger and louder and better," Ali said about Moore. "He believed in whispering something to reporters for them to print—but I believe in yelling."

If you met Moore at a state dinner, you'd think he was the most refined and educated man in the room. He spoke eloquently and he always thought before he spoke. He was unimpressed by the way Cassius ran his mouth prior to their 1962 fight and compared him to a man who could write beautifully but didn't know how to punctuate. "Really, I don't see how you can stand yourself," Moore told Clay. "I'm a speaker, not a rabble-rouser. I'm a conversationalist, you're a shouter." Archie thought Cassius simply wanted to be the center of everyone's attention. "There's a bitterness in him somewhere," said Moore. "He wants to show off, regardless of whose feet he's stepping on."

Of course, Cassius was just a 20-year-old kid at the time, albeit a very talented and charismatic one. Like most guys that age, he thought about girls and the material things that would impress them. He imagined driving a Cadillac down Walnut Street in Louisville on Derby Day where all the people would point and say, "There goes Cassius Clay." He'd have $500 in the pockets of his black mohair suit, his white shirt would be starched, his bow tie would be black, and he'd look great in his alligator shoes. He admitted that while girls were looking at him longingly, they didn't know that he wanted them more than they wanted him.

An even bigger shaper of Clay's new-found persona was the famous white wrestler and entertainer Gorgeous George. The two met in Las Vegas in 1961 when promoter Mel Greb arranged for them to appear together on a radio talk show to hype their respective bouts. Clay's pro career was less than a year old and while not subdued that day, he was far from loud. George was anything but. "I'll kill him!" shouted George, referring to his opponent. "If this bum beats me, I'll crawl across the ring and cut off my hair, but its not gonna happen because I'm the greatest wrestler in the world."

After the show, George told Cassius he needed to be a lot more outspoken if he wanted to get anywhere. Clay went to see George's bout and found 15,000 screaming people who had apparently come for the express purpose of seeing him get beat. "This is a gooood idea!" Cassius thought to himself, realizing that talking and acting in a way that got people to root against you was actually pretty smart. "I started off slow because I was feeling my way," Cassius said later, "but pretty soon I caught on to what reporters liked to hear and what would make the public pay attention." He would be affectionately and somewhat mockingly known as the Louisville Lip.

Clay quickly decided that George's nickname of "The Greatest" suited him better than it did the wrestler. There were times when he appropriated George's act lock, stock, and barrel, like the day before he signed to fight Sonny. "When I fight Liston, I'm going to have five of the prettiest girls in the world in my corner. I'll have one to take off my crown, one to hand me my robe, one to spray the corners of the ring with perfume, one to give me a rubdown, and one to comb my hair." The press ate this stuff up, laughing both with Clay and at him. But a lot of sports fans became boxing fans because it was hard not to like him. The way he looked, the way he moved, his above-it-all attitude, and his sheer gall compelled you to follow and root for him.

If they were fighting today, neither Ali nor Liston would have a diamond in his ear or a tattoo anywhere on his body. Because they had great pride and admiration for their god-given bodies, and were also scared to death of needles, neither would have taken steroids, nor could steroids have benefited either one of them. Ali's body suited him perfectly and spectacularly, and nothing could have made Liston more formidable or stronger than he already was. The thought of Sonny Liston on steroids is too frightening to contemplate.

Neither man liked fighting as an occupation. "I don't like earning my living getting hurt," said Sonny. "If I could do something else I would." He knew there wasn't anything else he could have done that could make him financially comfortable for the rest of his life. "I don't really love to fight," echoed Clay shortly before he fought Liston. Boxing was simply a means to an end for both men—and that end was money. Both of them wanted to build expensive homes, drive fine cars, and wine and dine pretty women to their heart's content. By the time they fought each other, Clay had three Cadillacs and Sonny had two. "The fame and pride of doing something real well—like being the world champion—is a pretty nice thing to think about sometimes, but the money I'm making is nice to think about all the time," said Cassius. "I suppose it's the one thing that keeps me going."

However proud Ali would become, the honor and satisfaction of being heavyweight champion of the world would mean a lot more to Liston. Joe Louis had always been his idol, and he wanted to be even better than Joe. On the walls of his training quarters for the first Patterson fight was a black-and-white poster showing all the heavyweight champions since 1730. "When I win the championship, I want my picture right here in the middle," he told his handlers. "I want it bigger than all the others and I want it with stars around it."

Liston learned from his trainers but Ali basically trained himself. In 1960, the Louisville Sponsoring Group sent Clay to work with 46-year-old Archie Moore, who they thought could provide their young fighter with life lessons as well as boxing skills. "I taught him how to slip punches," said Moore. "At one time he was going to leave the training camp because I was too hard on him. I beat him up like his daddy." Clay's insistence on doing things his own way caused Moore to send him home less than two weeks after he arrived. Angelo Dundee ended up training Cassius but his influence on the fighter was also limited. "Dundee gave me the jab but the rest is me," Ali said in 1963. "What changed the most was my own natural ability."

Liston and Clay always fought their own fights, meaning they did what they did best no matter who the opponent or what that opponent did. Neither one of them liked to enter the ring with a detailed battle plan because they both could adjust to the other guy's style and tactics if they had to.

Liston and Ali were the absolute bosses of their training camps and they were often overbearing. Both men had mean streaks and both were intimidators. Liston was mean when he stepped into the ring but not when he left it. He was always intent on destroying his opponent but emerged from his victories respecting the courage of the man he had just beaten, unless that man ran. For Sonny, boxing was all business.

In contrast, Ali was rarely mean in the ring but when he was, it was personal and vicious. Shortly after winning the title, Ali said fighting was just a game to him. "But Patterson I would want to beat to the floor for the way he rushed out of hiding after his last whipping (by Liston), announcing that he wanted to fight me because no Muslim deserved to be the champ. I never had no concern about his having the Catholic religion." Floyd had infuriated Ali by publicly describing the Nation of Islam as a black Ku Klux Klan and for failing to call him by his chosen name. "I won't even call Patterson a man or a fighter. He's a sissy," Ali said to a bunch of stunned writers in September 1964. "I hate him so much I'd kill him. I'd kill him." By the time he fought Floyd in late 1965, Ali was still seething. "Watch closely," he told reporters at ringside. "I'm gonna show you real punishment."

Ernie Terrell had also infuriated Ali prior to their 1967 fight when he called him Clay. "I'm going to give him the Patterson treatment, only it's gonna be worse."

Ali said. "I'm gonna make him suffer, make him call me by my name." Actually, Ali did a lot more than that when he deliberately thumbed Terrell in the second round. "He pushed the bone in my eye, and the soft tissue behind the eye became damaged. My eye muscles jammed," said Ernie. Later, Ali grabbed Terrell's head and rubbed his injured eye against the top rope, choked him in some clinches, and spat at his feet. Ernie didn't expect Ali to fight dirty and was surprised that the referee did nothing to stop it.

Ali despised Patterson and Terrell just as much when he left the ring as when he entered it. They had demeaned his religion and that's something he wouldn't tolerate from an opponent or a friend. But when Ali fought angry he kept his poise and seemed even more focused on the task at hand. Unlike Muhammad, Sonny simply could not fight his own fight when he was angry. Outside of the ring an angry Liston would have been a more formidable fighter but inside the ring the opposite was true.

Mark Kram was present when Cassius met Sonny close-up for the first time in November 1962. The young fighter had just beaten Archie Moore and was standing in front of a mirror applying rouge to his face. "I keep lookin' like an angel 'stead of a fighter," said Cassius, not realizing that Sonny had entered the room. Liston put a hand on his shoulder and said, "Take care, kid. I'm gonna need you. But I'm gonna have to beat you like I'm your daddy." The usually loquacious Clay was speechless; veteran trainer Willie Ketchum thought Cassius looked at Sonny as though he were holding a gun to his head. "Don't let anybody tell ya that Clay wasn't scared to death of Liston," said Ketchum.

Clay knew Liston was the world's best heavyweight long before Sonny won the title from Patterson. "He was everything they said he was, a mass of muscles, power, force," Clay said after watching Sonny train early in 1961. "He can hit a guy on the elbow and just about break his arm. After my first feeling of awe and fear wore off, I watched him in the gym with keener eyes." The fact was that Cassius didn't want any part of Liston for quite some time. Instead, he thought a lot about Sonny's actions outside of the ring and spent many nights trying to figure out how his mind worked. "Liston's got one of them bulldog minds," he said. "Once he ever starts to thinking something, he won't let hold of it quick."

After surveying the heavyweight division, which back then was boxing's equivalent of Dresden, Clay figured Liston would embark on a Joe Louis style bum-of-the-month club and correctly assumed that Sonny probably thought he was the biggest bum of them all. "I didn't make no sound that wasn't planned to keep him thinking in that rut. I wanted him thinking that all I was was some clown, and that he never would have to give a second thought to me being able to put up any real fight when we got to the ring," Ali said later. "The more out-of-shape and overconfident I could get him to be, the better."

The Louisville Lip's campaign of psychological warfare would end up being the biggest sting operation in the history of sports. Cassius almost intuitively realized that what he did to Liston outside of the ring might be even more crucial than what he did to Liston inside the ring. Getting the Bear to underestimate him was the most important part. Part two would be to needle, harass, and confuse the champ so badly that Clay would have him beat before he ever faced him in the ring. The most brilliant fight strategy in boxing history was devised by a teenager who had graduated 376 in a high school class of 391.

Sonny chuckled when he talked about Clay and called him his million dollar baby. He told different people he was going along with the Lip's act because it would help build the gate. "So at first I couldn't get him really mad, because he had this idea fixed in his mind," Ali said later. "But I kept right on working on him. A man with Liston's kind of mind is very funny. He ain't what you would call a fast thinker, like I am."

Sonny sincerely believed Clay's best weapon was his mouth and he told boxing historian Jimmy Jacobs to bet his life that Cassius wouldn't last three rounds against him. When he was in a good mood, Liston would tell people a story that indicated how he felt about his young challenger.

> "Clay! Let me tell you a story. Once I was in the country on a very cold day. Very cold. It was snowin', it was snowin' hard. I was out in a field. The snow was about four feet deep. And there was a little bird shiverin' up on a branch in a tree. It was cold, and he had no food. Up above in the sky was a hawk circlin' around. Just circlin'. All of a sudden a big white horse comes along, and he puts some manure under the tree. The little bird sees this, and he flies down from the branch and has himself a good meal. He's so happy! He flies back up to the branch, where he starts singing', 'Tweet, tweet, tweet, tweet.' And the big hawk circlin' up in the sky hears him, and he swoops down and eats him! And the moral of the story is: don't get too frisky when you're full of manure."

On at least one occasion young Cassius got a little too frisky. Prior to the Liston–Patterson rematch, Clay was in Las Vegas for an interview with David Brinkley and he went to a casino where Sonny was shooting craps. Cassius walked up behind the champ, took some of his chips, made several attempts to grab the dice, and told him he didn't know how to play the game. As the story goes, Sonny threw craps, glared at Clay, then picked up the dice and rolled craps again. Clay continued to heckle Liston and culminated his abuse by shooting a water pistol at him.

Like most kids, Cassius probably didn't fully anticipate the consequences of his reckless behavior. "But then very suddenly Liston *froze* me with that look of his," said Clay. In a quiet voice Liston told Clay to follow him to an unoccupied area of the casino. "Listen, you nigger faggot," Sonny said angrily, "if you don't get out of here in ten seconds, I'm gonna pull that big tongue out of your mouth and stick it up your ass." Visibly shaken, Clay quickly left the premises.

"I ain't going to lie," Ali said in a 1964 *Playboy* interview. "This was the only time since I have known Sonny Liston that he really scared me. Anybody tell me about how he has fought cops and beat up tough thugs and all of that. I believe it. I saw that streak in him." Cassius had come oh so close to unleasing one of the most ferocious tempers any man ever had. However, the incident confirmed to him that he had gotten under Liston's skin and he made it his goal that by the time they fought, Liston's anger would cause him to forget everything he knew about boxing.

Sonny began playing into Clay's hands when he hardly trained for the second Patterson match. When that fight turned out to be easier than the first bout, no one in Liston's camp saw any reason to question his training habits. That was fine with Sonny, since the bursitis he experienced in his left elbow while preparing for the Patterson rematch had spread to his shoulder and would not go away. Plus, old fighters look for reasons not to train.

After Liston beat Machen in 1960, there was no one left for him to fight but Patterson. Sonny had two inconsequential fights in 1961 to stay at least somewhat active but he had little incentive to stay in fighting shape. Between March 9, 1961, and February 24, 1964, Liston fought only three times, each of which ended in one-round knockouts. The sum of his ring time was 6 minutes and 14 seconds, which meant that for all practical purposes Sonny was in the midst of a three-year layoff. "A fighter has to fight regularly to be at his best," said Joe Louis. "Jack

Dempsey found that out the hard way and so did I." And so would Sonny.

Archie Moore was right when he said Liston had almost nothing to gain and everything to lose by fighting Clay. Nobody talked about it at the time, but the aging Bear was walking into an ambush. In what has to rank as the stupidest managerial decision in the history of boxing, Sonny's brain trust scheduled what essentially amounted to a comeback fight against a highly gifted, much younger, and rapidly maturing boxer whose chin and heart were first-rate and who possessed the greatest hand and foot speed ever seen in a big man.

Jimmy Jacobs claimed Clay wasn't just the fastest heavyweight ever, but the fastest boxer he'd ever seen, live or on film. "No matter what his opponents heard about him, they didn't realize how fast he was until they got in the ring with him," said Jacobs. Using a synchronizer, Jacobs measured the punches of Clay and Sugar Ray Robinson and found Clay's jab to be about 25 percent faster than Robinson's even though Cassius was 45 - 50 pounds heavier.

"I knew that Liston, overconfident as he was, was never going to train to fight more than two rounds," Ali said later. "Some of his handlers admitted after the fight that this was exactly what he did. He didn't have no respect for me as a fighter. He couldn't see nothing to me at all but mouth. He was a perfect setup." Liston's camp actually thought less of Clay's ability than they did of Patterson's. Sonny said Cassius had the edge in everything but talent.

Most boxing people sincerely feared for the kid's well-being. Not one of the eleven living former heavyweight champions regarded Clay as being ready for Liston. California State Athletic Commissioner Sol Silverman called the proposed fight a dangerous mismatch that could result in grave injury to the young challenger, and even Angelo Dundee admitted that people thought he was leading his fighter to slaughter. Jimmy the Greek insisted it was impossible for Clay to last six rounds. "The only way Liston can lose the title is to get himself killed by some cop," said former light heavyweight champ, Billy Conn.

Clay's style had a lot to do with people's assessment of his fighting ability. "He wasn't a good technician," said trainer Eddie Futch, whose fighters always gave Ali trouble. Futch said the challenger threw a sub-par uppercut, that his left hook was only adequate, and that he wanted no part of inside fighting. "He's not a complete fighter, never was when I worked with him," echoed Ernie Terrell. "He doesn't want a glove near his face. He lives in fear of that face."

Clay had developed an unorthodox and widely criticized habit of keeping his hands by his side almost all of the time. He would avoid punches by pulling straight back instead of ducking, something no trainer would ever teach his fighter to do. With a few near-disastrous exceptions, Clay's speed and constant movement allowed him to avoid being hit with significant punches by inferior opponents. "He can get away with that against a guy who can't reach him," said Willie Pastrano, who like Cassius was also trained by Angelo Dundee. "If he fights like that, pulling away the way he does, Sonny will knock him through the front door," said Joe Louis.

As far as Cassius was concerned, everybody should have just minded their own business. "Leaning away is a faster reflex than ducking, and I'll go on doing it until somebody proves it's a mistake and that somebody has got to be another boxer, not a trainer," said Clay. Conventional wisdom it was not. Archie Moore said Clay's ability to brainwash himself was one of his greatest assets. "Clay keeps telling himself: 'I am the greatest, I am the greatest, I am the greatest,' until he believes it, and this has such an effect upon his subconscious that it makes him a better fighter than perhaps he really is."

"You can't make mistakes against Liston and survive, and Cassius makes too many mistakes with his hands," said Louis. "I guess it's quite hard to tell Clay not to fight this monster now, but I'm sure he'll be more receptive after he's been there with Liston," said Marciano. A year earlier, Billy Conn had advised Clay not to fight Liston for five years. "The longer you stay away from Liston the better. Let that priest take care of him," said Conn. When Cassius asked him what priest he was talking about, Conn replied, "Father Time."

In light of Clay's last four bouts it would have been hard to take exception with all of the dire predictions. Cassius admitted that the 48-year-old Moore had hurt him a couple of times before he stopped Archie in the fourth-round. Against Charlie Powell in early 1963, Clay was hurt in the first and second rounds. "Powell hurt him very badly with a left hook in the first round and in the second round with a right hand to the body," said Powell's trainer, Eddie Futch. Doug Jones hit him so hard that he knew another such punch would have sent him back to Louisville, and Henry Cooper dropped Clay with a left hook to the jaw and hurt him badly.

Clay had also been floored and knocked somewhat senseless by Sonny Banks in 1962. After stopping Banks in the fourth-round, Angelo Dundee asked Cassius what he was thinking when he was down. Harry Markson, the managing director of boxing for Madison Square Garden, was there and remembered Clay asked Dundee how many times he had been down. "He wasn't jesting," said Markson. "It struck me then that he hasn't shown enough to justify the kind of bragging he does."

Clay had several less-lethal options than fighting Liston. The Associated Press reported that Clay had decided to fight once more in 1963 against either Mike DeJohn or George Chuvalo. A rematch against Jones would have drawn well but Cassius felt one fight with Dougie was enough. Cleveland Williams's manager offered Cassius a potentially huge purse of $180,000 for a 15-round fight. Clay would get $10,000 upon signing, $10,000 at the weigh-in, $10,000 for climbing into the ring, and $10,000 for each of the 15 rounds he could survive. He'd also get a new Lincoln Continental if he could name the round in which he would knock out the Big Cat. Clay, however, seemed to be obsessed with fighting Liston and the huge purse it would bring him.

The Army had other plans for Clay. He had been issued a November 1963 call-up date and LSG Chairman William Faversham was doing everything he could to delay his induction until after he fought Liston. "If they take Clay into the Army, I want to go too, so I can protect him," said Sonny. "You put him into the ring with me before the Army gets him, and you can bet any amount of money that the Army wouldn't want 'pretty boy' after I finish him off. I'll do him a big favor." Ultimately, Cassius was able to delay his induction by switching his residence from Louisville to New York City, taking advantage of a Selective Service rule that allowed a draftee a postponement if he had a valid reason. Clay said his many business ventures in New York necessitated the move.

A steady stream of ring deaths provided a disturbing backdrop for this perceived mismatch. Heavyweight Ernie Knox had died of a brain hemorrhage two days after being knocked out in the ninth round by Wayne Bethea. He died for a $243 payday. Knox was the fourth ring fatality in 18 months, following the deaths of Benny "Kid" Paret, Davey Moore, and Alejandro Lavorante. Lavorante had lost to Clay but many boxing people believed it was an earlier beating from Archie Moore that did the damage.

On October 15, Garland Cherry received a call from Gordon Davidson who told him the Louisville Sponsoring Group wanted to reopen negotiations for the fight and were prepared to accept the same terms they had rejected less than two months earlier. Davidson and Faversham arrived in Chester, Pennsylvania, the next day where they met with Cherry, Bob Nilon, and Sonny's manager, Jack Nilon. By late afternoon, Davidson and Faversham were on a plane back to Louisville with a contract for their fighter to sign.

Clay's 22.5 percent guarantee was the largest share ever paid to a challenger and almost double the 12.5 percent that Patterson gave Sonny. Bob Nilon said he wanted to start the negotiations at 15 percent but that Sonny overruled him. "I got 12.5 percent to fight Patterson but that is wrong," he told Nilon. "He gets the challenger's 20 percent share and that is it." Nilon knew that a lot of fighters would have imposed the same financial thrashing on their challengers that they had received before becoming champion but to Sonny's credit, he didn't do that.

When Gordon Davidson negotiated the Liston bout he did so thinking it would be Clay's last big-time fight. The Louisville group told Cassius he needed more experience but Clay blew them off. "I could get killed crossing the street," Cassius said in his own defense. "Or maybe that mean old bear's knee will give away when he's in there with some bum, and then that bum will be champion instead of me. And I was born to be the champ, so why wait?" Davidson said his group concluded that Clay really didn't care about becoming one of the finest heavyweights who ever lived, just the richest. "I thought that he was going to get demolished, which everyone assumed he would, and at least he could get good money," said Davidson. Faversham admitted his group did not want this fight so soon, but when Cassius insisted, they had to give in.

The fight contract was almost identical to the one that Patterson forced on all of his challengers except this one made no mention of a rematch. Without Liston's knowledge, a second contract had been signed and kept secret from the Miami Beach Boxing Commission. It included a provision that paid Clay $50,000 in consideration for which Inter-Continental acquired the right to promote Clay's next fight, to name his opponent, and to select the site if he were to defeat Sonny.

For some reason, the Nilons believed that this fight would not have been sanctioned had the contract included a rematch provision, even though the Miami Beach Boxing Commission had accepted the same provision just a year earlier when it agreed to host the second Patterson-Liston match. In actuality, rematch clauses were so commonplace that you'd probably have to go back to Jack Johnson's title bout against Jess Willard in 1915 to find a heavyweight championship contract that didn't include one. Then again, there always was a different set of rules when it came to Sonny Liston.

Clay was so afraid of airplanes that it took four days to talk him into flying to Rome for the 1960 Olympic Games. He bought a parachute at an army surplus store and had it on his back for the entire flight. "Without that chute, I'd've turned white for sure," said Cassius. Whenever his mother flew with him, it pained her to see her son so frightened, "his eyes so big and red." Clay preferred to travel in Big Red, a 30-passenger 1953 Flexible bus on which his father had painted: *WORLD'S MOST COLORFUL FIGHTER: CASSIUS CLAY* and *SONNY LISTON WILL GO IN EIGHT.*

Clay drove Big Red to Denver for the November 5 contract signing. He arrived shortly after midnight and called some reporters whose phone numbers he'd been given. Trying to sound like a white man, he said the challenger had just driven into town and was getting ready to break into Sonny Liston's house. Minutes after Clay's bus pulled up, the whole neighborhood was awake. Cassius sent his friend and photographer Howard Bingham to pound on Liston's door while someone else kept his hand on the bus horn. Sonny opened the door dressed in short, polka-dot pajamas with a fireplace poker in his hand. Clay was screaming as loud as he could, taunting Liston to come out and protect his home. Within minutes five police cars arrived with sirens blazing.

"You know that look of Liston's you hear so much about," wrote Ali. "Well he sure had it on standing in that door that night. Man, he was tore up. He wanted to come out there after me, but he was already in enough trouble with the police and everything. And you know, if a man figures you're crazy, he'll think twice before he acts, because he figures you're liable to do anything." A police dog was within a foot of Cassius when he was told to leave or be arrested for disturbing the peace. With Sonny standing in his doorway, Clay exited screaming and his entourage laughed all the way to their motel.

Clay demeaned Sonny on a number of occasions but Barney Baker told me this was the incident that tormented him the most. He had been humiliated in front of his neighbors, many of whom were white and not thrilled with his presence in the first place. "You know how them white people felt about that black man just moved in there anyway, and we sure wasn't helping it none," Ali said later. A week after the Listons moved in, 32 houses in Sonny's neighborhood put up For Sale signs. Having Joe Louis as a neighbor may have been acceptable but Sonny Liston was apparently one black heavyweight champ too many.

At the following morning's press conference one reporter likened Clay to a spoiled child showing off in front of his father. Cassius refused to sit next to Sonny and threatened to walk out of the meeting because Liston signed the three-page contract first. Calling Liston a chump and an old man, Clay said he was going to give Sonny boxing *and* talking lessons. "I'm the champ of fightin', but you the champ of talkin'," chuckled Sonny. Gerry was so entertained by Clay that she laughed until she was on the verge of tears. "Oh, he IS funny," she exclaimed. "Boy! You better not believe half the things you say about yourself," Joe Louis told the young challenger. "You better train hard."

Liston gave Clay a lifesize poster of himself in battle pose with the inscription: *Well, Cassius—now that we have signed, I don't want nothin' to happen to you—I am sending my picture along to guard you! Sonny!* When Cassius punched the cardboard-backed poster and failed to dent it, Liston cautioned him not to hurt his hand. Borrowing a line from Gorgeous George, Clay told Liston he'd crawl across the ring and kiss his feet if he lost. Sonny told Cassius he wasn't going to wait around until he was able to crawl. "People love you, Charles," said the challenger. "The fans love you because I'm the villain." Liston smiled and told Cassius he appreciated what he was doing for him. Sonny told reporters he'd start training five days before the fight and said his only worry was how he'd get his fist out of Clay's big mouth. "Otherwise, he means a lot of money to me. I just hope he keeps well and I sure hope he shows up."

Clay shut his act down as soon as the cameras stopped rolling, at which point Sonny began to talk. Cassius was eating his barbecue chicken so fast that Liston told him, "You eat like you're goin' to the 'lectric chair. Tonight ain't fight night… Is that your brother? If he'll fight, we can make it a tag-team match. Both of you in one corner against me." The comment produced a wave of laughter but Cassius said nothing. Then someone in Clay's entourage, ironically named Clay Tyson, faked a few punches at Liston while Cassius and members of his entourage mocked the champion. "Have your fun," Liston cracked. "You ain't goin' to have all them guys with you when that bell rings. You get to come out to see me all by yourself."

Sonny was immediately installed as a 4-1 favorite by New York oddsmakers. Joe Louis said Clay's two possible strategies were 1) to stay away from Liston and 2) to stay away from him as long as he could. Joe gave Clay no chance to win and offered the belief that Liston could beat him without a right hand. "Liston will corner him on the ropes, Clay will make a mistake and that will be it," said Joe.

Apart from a few trainers and fighters, no one believed otherwise.

The Pennsylvania State Athletic Commission had already told Inter-Continental that it wanted the fight to be held in its state and had assured them they'd be granted a license. However, their application was rejected when the district attorney's office ruled that Liston's stock ownership in his promotional company would give him a financial interest in his opponent. Inter-Continental was subsequently told that the fight could still take place in Pennsylvania if they hired a local promoter to make the actual application of record. This was known as the loaned license practice and was something of which Inter-Continental should have already been aware.

Loaned licenses had been a necessary staple of boxing promotions for years, primarily because most states had a very impractical requirement that a promoter had to be a citizen of its state in order to stage a match. Both Patterson-Liston fights were staged using loaned licenses, as were all of Floyd's title bouts. The International Boxing Club had operated this way for years; there was never any attempt by the promoters to be secretive about it. It was simply standard operating procedure in the fight game.

Several other states contacted Bob Nilon and said they had no problem with the loaned license practice. Inter-Continental received offers from Minneapolis, Chicago, Las Vegas, Miami, Denver, and Montreal. At the November 5 signing two huge offers were made by Los Angeles-based groups, both of which believed the match could draw 130,000 people to the Coliseum. Both fighters said they wanted the match staged in Los Angeles and within the week L.A. County's Board of Supervisors voted unanimously to host the bout. Estimates of gross revenues were in the $8 million range, and Sonny figured to make close to $2 million for his second title defense, far and away the largest purse ever earned by any boxer. However, an investigator for the California Athletic Commission said it would reopen its study of Liston's "connections" prior to the granting of a license. When commission members publicly said their thinking on licensing Liston was the same as New York's, the issue became moot.

Inter-Continental never applied to any other state for the right to promote the fight using a local co-promoter. Instead, they accepted the $625,000 offer of Miami Beach promoter William B. MacDonald Jr., who reportedly had a net worth of $10 million. He owned a mortgage company in Puerto Rico, 45 percent of Tropical Park racetrack, a stable of thoroughbred horses, and a minor league baseball team. MacDonald had always wanted to promote a heavyweight title fight and he made his bid for this fight after being assured by his co-promoter, Chris Dundee (Angelo's brother), that he could scale the house to gross over a million dollars. MacDonald was convinced the fight would be the biggest thing that ever happened in boxing.

Garland Cherry and Jack Nilon went to Miami to negotiate with MacDonald and relied on Sonny's wife to communicate the fight details to their fighter. "When Jack called Sonny, he asked Sonny to put Geraldine on the phone and he explained to Geraldine what we were proposing to do," said Cherry, who claimed it was one of many times that Nilon explained things to Geraldine over the phone so she could run them by Sonny.

Inter-Continental had accepted a proposal for far less money than they could have gotten had they shopped it around. Why? Most likely it was because the Nilons were caterers by trade and in over their heads as fight promoters. They were also preoccupied with other business matters. According to ICP's Garland Cherry, the Nilon brothers had purchased an interest in a Florida racetrack, which kept Jim pretty busy, and their recent investment in the Baltimore Civic Auditorium demanded a lot of Bob's time. They were part owners in a New York track that had gone into bankruptcy, and Cherry said that was occupying all of them full-time.

Incredibly, the Nilons had secured the services of the most valuable asset in all of sports—the heavyweight champion of the world—and they were too incompetent to know what to do with it. They finally realized they needed at least $150,000 for upfront expenses; Cherry was apparently the only one who had that kind of money. So Bob and Jim Nilon left it to Cherry and their brother Jack, Liston's manager, to get the job done.

Inter-Continental transferred all of the ancilliary rights to a new corporation called Delaware Advertising & Management Agency, Inc. (DAMA), of which 80 percent was owned by Jack and 20 percent was owned by Cherry. The deal allowed DAMA to sell the rights to the fight's closed-circuit telecasts, radio, foreign viewings, and television replays and pay Inter-Continental 35 percent of the net income from these sources. Cherry claimed Jack hadn't been paid for his work on either Patterson fight and thought it was a way to compensate Nilon for "some of the trouble and bother that he had had." The plan reduced the value of Sonny's 50 percent share of Inter-Continental's stock. He and his attorney were never notified of DAMA's formation, nor would they ever be given a final accounting of any of its distributions.

Earlier in the year, Liston and Vice President Lyndon Johnson were the guests of honor at a Big Brothers banquet in Washington D.C. Sonny spent so much time interacting with the kids at a government-run orphanage that he was late getting to the dinner. Senator Kefauver was quoted as saying he was convinced that Liston had "gotten rid of the tentacles of the underworld" and was "doing much better" with his new management.

Columnist Drew Pearson interviewed the champ at length in front of 800 people and asked him what could be done to curb juvenile delinquency. "Well, I would recommend more playgrounds. More sports and activity," said Sonny. "Give them something to do to keep their minds occupied—where they wouldn't be idle. They had playgrounds in St. Louis but it wasn't enough for all the kids, so they let the good kids go on it and kept us bad kids off." The champ favored spanking, if necessary, to make sure kids wouldn't abuse their teachers and believed parents should know where their children were at all times and give them curfews.

Pearson's favorable account of the event infuriated J. Edgar Hoover, who wrote on a memo, "just how naïve can some of our VPs get?" The FBI Director found it nauseating the way Pearson tried "to present Liston as a clean person." In retrospect, for the closeted homosexual Hoover to deride Sonny Liston as being less than clean was laughable.

According to *Jet Magazine*, Sonny often went to predominantly black functions at a time when other prominent blacks ignored those invitations. The champ also participated in a civil rights march in Denver, though you could only read about it in black publications. He returned to Jeff City, where he dined in the mess hall with prisoners. Liston made trips to military bases in out-of-the-way places like Wyoming and Alaska and visited orphanages and reform schools to offer hope and encouragement. "Kid, I know it's tough for you and it might even get tougher, but don't give up on the world. Good things can happen if you let them," Sonny told the kids. His attempts to show troubled children and adults that rehabilitating oneself was possible won praise from social workers, penal authorities, and the clergy, but not the press. "He has made some solemnly mumbled addresses in reform schools as a foe of juvenile delinquency," wrote Jimmy Cannon.

The public knew nothing of Sonny's good qualities, one of which was a sincere desire to help those less fortunate than himself. Barney Baker told me

Sonny wasn't the type of person who would brag about the good things he did. "Favors aren't special," Liston once said. "You do them from the way you feel in your heart and you don't tell about them. You do a friend a favor, you don't brag… You know, before I won this title, I done some good things that I kept to myself because, well, I done them because I really wanted to and didn't want people to say, 'Look at this guy. He's putting on a show so we'll all think he's a good guy and let him fight for the title.'"

Sonny's first manager, Frank Mitchell, remembered his fighter had a lot of sympathy for the underprivileged almost from the moment he got out of jail. "I saw him give seven- and eight-year old kids $20 back in 1959," said Tommy Manning. Willie Reddish claimed Sonny never passed a beggar of any color on the street without giving him some money. "He didn't do it for effect," said Reddish. "He never knew I even noticed, but I did. I'd watch him out of the corner of my eye." Skinny Davidson said Sonny would give money to any disabled person he saw.

Davey Pearl remembered the time he was driving in heavy traffic when Sonny jumped out and ran over to a legless woman who was selling pencils. "He emptied out all his pockets and just laid it right out," Pearl told me. "Then he jumped in the car and said, 'Let's go.' Never said another word." While co-hosting a sports show, Pearl read a letter from a guy with a bad heart who needed $40 to buy some sharpening tools. Evidently Sonny was watching the program because he ran down to the studio, knocked on the door, and handed Davey $40. "These are the things about Sonny that nobody knew," said Pearl. "I know he had a heart of gold but as far as the public was concerned, he was a big thug."

Sonny gave time and money to a variety of causes and charities. He offered to visit any hospital or participate in any youth event to which he was invited. He auctioned off the gloves he won the title with for $800 and gave the money to United Cerebral Palsy. When Sonny threw his wife a surprise birthday party, he put the leftovers in his car and took them down to skid row for the guys who he said couldn't afford anything. When asked to guest referee a charity fight in another city, Liston would volunteer his services and pay for his own transportation. Sonny was at the Denver airport when two priests learned that their reservations had been cancelled. Without identifying himself, Sonny arranged for the priests' transportation and paid for the tickets in spite of their protests. The priests closest to Sonny had standing invitations to attend his fights and the fighter would always pay their expenses.

Friends were able to get loans from him, most of which became gifts after the fact, but there were outright gifts, too. Sonny set up his sparring partner Foneda Cox in the garage business in Denver, bought a house for his personal assistant Raymond Munson, and gave his assistant trainer Joe Polino money to help him pay his rent when he was broke. "Nobody knew what a nice guy he was," said Polino. "He'd do anything for you," echoed cornerman Milt Bailey. Barner Baker told me that when Liston tried to visit some of the guys he knew who were still in jail in St. Louis and the officials wouldn't allow him in, he'd leave them money to spend in the commissary. In 1960, Sonny donated $448.47 to Jefferson City prison which, given the amount, was probably all the money he had with him at the time of the visit.

Sonny gave money to at least two fighters who had gone blind from boxing and to former champ Johnny Saxton, who came away from the sport with nothing. He discouraged kids and amateur fighters from pursuing a career in boxing and was always sincerely concerned for the well-being of his fellow boxers. When he attended fights and saw one boxer hopelessly dominated, he'd tell the guy's cornermen to stop the bout and would keep insisting until they finally did. Before and after becoming champ, Sonny lobbied that the count should continue if a boxer was down when the bell sounded and that either the referee or a fighter's corner should be allowed to stop a fight at any time. "If a man is down three times in any round, that should be it," he said. "Instinct will probably force him to get up, but he should be sent back to his corner. Accidents happen this way."

Ash Resnick insisted Liston was a great guy. "Most people think of Sonny as a big brute, a hard-hearted arrogant guy, a troublemaker and things like that," said Ash. "He actually was as friendly as could be. You just had to know him." As far as Barney Baker was concerned, Sonny was "the sweetest son-of-a-bitch who ever lived. He was a beast, but he was a good beast."

Gerald Astor wrote the best family piece ever done on Liston for *Look Magazine* and interviewed him just before Christmas in 1963. Entitled "Sonny Liston: 'King of the Beasts,'" the article showed him at home in Denver with his wife, mother, and daughters Eleanor and Arletha. He was handsome and well dressed, and you'll never see a happier man than the one in John Vachon's photos. "Charles Liston stood up in his white-on-white living room and catechized his family," wrote Astor. "'Am I the King?' he asked. 'You sure are, you are the king of the beasts,' they responded." Of course, as Muhammad Ali would later say, if you're the greatest, you're just the greatest until proven wrong.

On Christmas Day, Sonny held a party at his house for underprivileged children and he went shopping to make sure that every kid would get a really good gift. His house guest at the time was Peter Keenan Jr., the young Irish son of one of the co-promoters of Liston's European tour. The top of Sonny's massive tree was adorned by Peter, dressed as an angel. Some people in Denver still remember that the Listons had the most beautifully decorated house in town that year. Unfortunately, Sonny would never have another Christmas anywhere near that happy.

CHAPTER EIGHT

BOXING IS A SPORT FOR YOUNG MEN

Until now, the backdrop for this fight was not so much good versus evil as it was David versus Goliath, starring an audacious, entertaining, extremely good looking, seemingless foolish and hopelessly overmatched kid who for reasons most people could not fathom thought he was ready to fight the toughest, strongest, and most menacing man that boxing had ever seen. But that story line was about to change in a big way.

Clay began attending Nation of Islam meetings in 1961 but the first publicity of his interest in Islam came in September 1963 when a Philadelphia newspaper reported his appearance at a Black Muslim rally in that city. Then in late January 1964 Clay left Miami Beach with Malcolm X to speak at a rally in Harlem, where he criticized Liston "for training among white people in Las Vegas." The appearance made the front page of at least one New York newspaper.

Ironically, the FBI's Chicago office had recently investigated rumors linking Liston to the Nation of Islam. The Bureau considered the group to be an all-Negro, antiwhite, semireligious cult that preached hatred of all white men. Their memo concluded that it had no information indicating that Liston was connected with the Muslims in any way.

The truth was that Sonny wanted nothing to do with the Nation. "Those people don't come around me," he said. "If they want to think the way they do, let them. But I don't have anything to do with that type of person." When Liston moved to the South Side of Chicago, Geraldine said Muslims were always putting literature in their mailbox. Whenever they tried to discuss their beliefs with Sonny, Gerry said he told them to shut up and get out of his face.

Clay's father told the *Miami Herald* that his son had joined the Muslims shortly after the 1960 Olympic Games. He said the Muslims called him dead because he didn't believe in their God. "Malcolm X came down here. Cassius paid for everything," said Clay's father. "You should have seen them all; they did everything but bow and kiss his (Malcolm's) feet…They made me so mad I threatened to whip three of them." Clay's father said the Muslims wanted him to change his last name to X. "I laughed at them. I told them that after a person learned to read and write, he don't have to use any X. That made them angry."

Mr. Clay considered Islam to be a phony religion and he and his wife were concerned with what they called the poison of Elijah Muhammad's teachings. The couple brought their children up in a Baptist church and made sure they always went to Sunday school. "I don't know how in the world they got caught up with these new ideas," said Mrs. Clay. "We have tried to tell Cassius about his mistake. We think it's hurting his image nationally. But he is stubborn."

In Malcolm's autobiography, he told Alex Haley that Cassius invited him and his family to Miami as a sixth anniversary present and picked them up at the airport. The FBI was told about this but considered it so unlikely that they didn't report it until Clay flew to New York for a Temple No. 7 dinner five days later. Malcolm had met Clay in Detroit in 1962 when the fighter and his brother Rudy came into a restaurant near the Detroit Mosque where Elijah Muhammad was scheduled to speak. "I liked him," said Malcolm. "Some contagious quality about him made him one of the very few people I ever invited to my home. Our children were crazy about him."

The day before Liston arrived in Miami, Angelo Dundee learned that Malcolm was at Clay's training camp. When Dundee saw Malcolm he told Cassius that if people learned of his associations he'd be denounced, the fight would be in jeopardy, and his career would be over. What Angelo didn't know at that time was that his fighter's name was Cassius X and that he was already a follower of Elijah Muhammad.

Within an hour MacDonald asked Clay to come to his office. Looking the promoter directly in the eye, Clay admitted that he had defended the Muslims to newsmen and that he had invited Malcolm to Miami. Holding his anger, MacDonald praised Clay as being a fresh breeze in boxing, a natural attraction and everybody's hero. "That's what I was basing this fight on, the good guy versus the bad guy," said the promoter. "Everybody knows Liston's background. He's a thug, the menace, the monster. You would be like Little Red Riding Hood and he would be the wolf. That would be a good money fight. But you as a 'Black Muslim,' they'd pray for the wolf to win. And they'll stay away. That would wreck my promotion."

Actually, ticket sales were so bad that MacDonald would have gladly opted out of the fight if given the opportunity, something Clay and a lot of people already knew. MacDonald implied that the slow ticket sales were a result of the Muslim stories making their way around Miami Beach and that Jews were boycotting the fight because of them. There may have been some truth to that but the poor ticket sales were due in large part to MacDonald's pricing the top ones at an all-time high of $250. Normally, $100 was the top ticket price for a heavyweight title fight but this time $100 only got you the fourth most expensive seat. Sonny joked that he was glad he'd be in the ring because he couldn't afford to sit at ringside. MacDonald had deluded himself into thinking he could sell 1,000 $250 tickets by himself but he never came close to that total. He was about to take a huge bath and he knew it.

MacDonald threatened to cancel the fight unless Clay proved he was a "patriotic, loyal American" by publicly denying that he was a Black Muslim. When Cassius said his religion was more important to him than the fight, the promoter told him the bout was off and instructed his publicist to get the word out. One of the Louisville sponsors pleaded with Cassius to reconsider his decision. "They'll never give you a chance like this again," Worth Bingham said. "The public climate has changed against you. You win the title and things will be different." However, the fighter would not be moved.

"I call my mother and tell her the fight's off and I'm coming home," Ali wrote in his autobiography, *The Greatest*. "I know by her voice she's heartbroken. It's the end of a long, long road for all of us." He helped Bundini lift a heavy footlocker full of boxing gear onto the bus and sat at the wheel reflecting on his career. "I know it might take years before I get another title shot and this time I might have to come back the hard way, fighting the other contenders who are ahead of me: Eddie Machen, Harold Johnson, Cleveland Williams, Zora Folley, good fighters who sometimes can fight with brilliance. It would be just my luck to catch one of them when he was determined not to lose, no matter what."

Clay was ready to start the bus when Chris Dundee drove up honking his horn and pleaded with him to give his people another hour to talk to MacDonald. About 90 minutes later Dundee told Cassius that Harold Conrad had gotten MacDonald to reinstate the fight, provided that Malcolm X would leave town.

Conrad remembered that Malcolm was quiet for some time before agreeing to leave but said he would return for the fight. When he returned home, Malcolm learned that Muslim officials in Chicago were displeased with him because of the newspaper coverage of him being in Clay's camp.

Ali claimed his conversion to Islam cost him $500,000 in commercial contracts. He had no intention of compromising his religious beliefs for the sake of money, no matter the amount. "They wanted me to do something I think is dead wrong: chase white women in films," he said. Ali thought black women were the prettiest women in the world and that "devil" money, as he referred to the offers, would have brainwashed millions of black children into thinking that "white was right." He hadn't always thought that way and admitted that he too had been brainwashed before embracing Islam. "I used to say a Negro woman can't do nothing for me but show me which way the white women went," he told Jack Olsen.

Now the fight had two bad guys and in some circles, Liston was the more sympathetic of the two. Sonny didn't give a damn about that but he wanted the fight very badly. "I hope he hasn't blown the fight because when I get him in the ring I'll kill him," said Liston, whose rage had been building for quite some time.

When Liston landed in Miami to resume training, he left the plane smiling. "They were making such a big thing of his arriving, you would have thought the Cubans was landing," said Clay. He had been waiting 30 minutes to welcome Liston with his own special greeting and he changed Sonny's upbeat mood to anger in a matter of seconds. "I'm the champ! You're the chump! Let's fight right now. I want my title!" screamed Cassius as several handlers hung onto his arms with explicit instructions not to let go. "Look, this clowning, it's not cute, and I'm not joking," Sonny said sternly, trying to make Clay realize that he was messing with the wrong man.

Liston and a bodyguard took a cart to the airport's VIP lounge as Clay and his friends sprinted after them. Clay almost caught up with Liston inside the terminal but stopped abruptly when he realized his five bodyguards were too far behind to protect him. The police guarded the doors of the lounge while Clay banged on them with his cane, screaming he'd fight Liston for free. Sonny sat glaring at the door for 10 minutes as Clay banged it and shouted insults. "If they ever let me in the ring with him, I'm liable to get put away for murder," said Sonny.

Liston's wife got caught up in the shoving, and Willie Reddish pulled her to safety. "Thanks," she said, "I got bopped in the head by his cane." If Sonny had heard this he may have killed Clay on the spot. Liston was already close to his breaking point and this incident might have pushed his temper past the point of no return. If that had happened, the history of heavyweight boxing might very well have turned on how fast the 22-year-old challenger could have run. Asked if Clay's antics upset him, Sonny said, "You know, even iron wears out. You can get enough of anything."

The fight was briefly upstaged by The Beatles, whose second of three appearances on the *Ed Sullivan Show* was in Miami Beach nine days before the bout. Liston was in the audience and Sullivan introduced the heavyweight champion of the world before bringing on the band. Harold Conrad remembered that halfway through the group's first song, Sonny turned to him and said, "For Christ sake, is them bums what all this fuss is about? Shit, man, my dog plays better drums than that kid with the big nose."

The Beatles wanted to meet and be photographed with Sonny but he didn't think "those little sissies" were worth his time and he blew them off. Instead, the photographer took the unsuspecting Beatles to Clay's training site where John Lennon said, "No, we don't want this one. He's gonna be beaten. Get us the other one. We want to be with a champion."

There was no letup to Clay's psychological war on Liston. Sonny had rented a house in a white neighborhood of Coral Gables and it wasn't long before Clay visited and made a very public scene similar to the one he made at Sonny's home in Denver. Clay supported the Nation of Islam premise that the only way there would be peace between the races was for them to live separately. He claimed white people felt the same way. "I believe the important thing is knowing where you belong and where you don't belong," said Cassius. "He's heavyweight champ and he's catching hell cause because he wants to integrate. I want to be with my people, and I'm catching more hell than he is." Many people thought Cassius was naïve when it came to Islam; *Sports Illustrated* actually wrote that he understood virtually nothing about the religion.

Sonny didn't care about any of that but he was really pissed. "I don't like his talking about my personal life," he told reporters. "Where the hell does he get off talking that way? Why doesn't he mind his own business? I'll straighten out his thinking. I'll put him out of his misery." Liston's anger was beginning to consume him, and fueling that anger was the challenger's No. 1 goal. "This is an angry man and he can't afford to be angry fighting Clay," said Joe Louis.

Clay's relentless tormenting of the champ stemmed from a simple belief that guided all of his pre-fight behavior. "Liston is tough," Cassius would say. "He just doesn't think good." People from Clay's camp went into Liston's gym and watched him train until the champ stopped to personally order them out. When the challenger spread the rumor that he was going to raid Liston's camp, Sonny got so mad that reporters would plead with Cassius to stop angering Liston or the champ would surely kill him. Liston's close friend and sparring partner, Jesse Bowdry, had known the champ for most of his life and truly believed Clay was playing with fire. "Cassius should call Sonny, Mr Liston, and say, 'Yes sir and no sir' to him. Cassius sure ought to show Sonny more respect."

All of this was music to Clay's ears. "It meant if he was that mad, he had lost all sense of reasoning. If he wasn't thinking nothing but killing me, he wasn't thinking fighting. And you got to think to fight." Cassius may have taken his cue from Eddie Machen, whose strategy of angering Sonny in their 1960 fight made Sonny abandon his game plan. Machen had suggested to reporters that Clay could do this by kissing Liston on the neck. "That's what I did and it really works," said Eddie. "He came raging in wide open. That's what Clay has to do, make Liston sore. He isn't used to being called names and no one can calm him down either. I cursed him every time I got a chance. It kept him confused. It kept him from concentrating."

Gaining a psychological advantage in advance of his bouts was something Ali did throughout his career. "He starts a fight early," Ernie Terrell told Mark Kram. "Tries to get under your skin. Maybe that's his best talent." Ali's longtime friend and business manager, Gene Kilroy, believes there has never been a smarter fighter between the four posts. Gene remembers being with Ali in New York to promote his 1974 fight with champion George Foreman. They were sitting with Jack Dempsey in his restaurant when George walked in and tried to intimidate Muhammad with the most menacing glare he could summon. "Excuse me, Mr. Dempsey," said Ali. "I need to straighten this out."

Muhammad walked up to George and with their noses almost touching, berated him. "Sonny Liston pulled this shit when you were just a little bitty boy. Do you think I'm scared of you? I could beat your ass right here. Do you hear me?" A stunned Foreman said nothing and Ali returned to his seat to resume his conversation. "I'm sorry, Mr. Dempsey," he said, "but I just won round one."

Three weeks before the fight Clay decided to picket Liston's gym. Cassius had bought 300 signs that read "Bear Hunting," "March on Liston's Camp," and

"Too Pretty to be a Fighter," only to be told that a city ordinance prevented the carrying of signs. Undaunted, Clay's handlers, all of whom wore jackets with "Bear-Hunting" stitched across the back, taped some of the signs on Big Red, loaded it with screaming teenage girls, and drove to Liston's camp. Clay's entourage created such a commotion that people stopped watching Liston train to see what was going on. One of Sonny's people pulled a knife on photographer Howard Bingham before Joe Louis asked him what the hell he was doing. "We have a championship fight coming up and this kid is talking about psychological warfare," said an exasperated Jack Nilon.

Clay was disappointed he hadn't been able to confront Liston personally and said he'd get him at the weigh-in. When Sonny boxed three rounds that afternoon, one of his handlers said it was the worst he'd looked since coming to Miami. Ali believed that was the day Liston lost the fight.

The public persona the challenger had so carefully cultivated made it very easy for people to discount Clay's words as nothing more than hype. However, when he said, "float like a butterfly, sting like a bee," over and over and over again, he was telling everybody exactly how he intended to fight the champion. But nobody caught on and they continued to treat everything Clay said as theater. His mouth had overshadowed his ability, but Cassius said he always knew the time would come when he'd have to put up or shut up.

Liston truly thought that Clay's best weapon was his mouth. "I don't think he's a good challenger," Sonny said in a fit on anger. "And I don't have any respect for him." Most of Sonny's handlers shared his contempt for the challenger's talent; seeing who could ridicule Clay the most became a running joke at Liston's training quarters. Even other fighters came in and belittled the challenger. "I listened and didn't take him serious," admitted Liston.

"Nobody ever could have conned me the way I did him," Ali said later. "I'd sit down and give his actions careful examination. Liston didn't never even think about doing that. Neither did nobody around him." And that was one of the most amazing things about the runup to this fight. Most of the people in Liston's camp had spent their lives in the sport but none of them seemed to have the slightest idea of what the challenger was doing and how good of a boxer he really was.

Instead, this fight became a primer on how not to prepare for a heavyweight title defense. Judging by the number of guests at Liston's house, his victory party started two or three weeks before the actual bout. Sonny wiled away many evenings eating hot dogs, drinking beer, and dealing blackjack, and a couple of people claimed he was being supplied with prostitutes by members of his entourage. "He was dogging it. I think he sold the boy cheap and I told him so," said Jack Nilon. When Nilon told Liston that Clay was fast and needed to be taken seriously, Sonny reminded him that Henry Cooper was as slow as Christmas and he caught Clay and knocked him down. "Sonny and I were at odds in Miami. We were feuding continuously," said Nilon, who had already decided to resign as Sonny's manager after the fight.

As far as the rest of his entourage was concerned, except for Joe Louis and Ash Resnick, the thought of telling Sonny what he didn't want to hear was something nobody would have relished doing, even if they were on to Clay's game.

Sonny hated the hot, humid Miami weather and would have preferred to stay in Denver until just before the fight. In the mornings, Sonny ran one mile instead of the usual five. He trained in a 15-foot ring rather than the conventional 20-footer but it would have been better to train in a 25-foot ring because everyone, including Sonny, knew that Clay was going to run. His handlers also kept working his midsection even though Cassius rarely threw a body punch.

"I swear to god, I think the way they trained Sonny was wrong," Resnick told me. "You train a 22-year-old that way, not an older fighter. They were killing him with that fucking medicine ball." Almost all of Sonny's sparring partners were light-heavyweights and since they were also friends of his, he went easy on them. Ash tried to get Sonny to hire fighters who would better prepare him for a fight against a big, fast, young heavyweight like Clay. "What does it matter who I take as a sparring partner, Ash?" replied Sonny. "It ain't gonna matter." Cassius, however, knew that it would. "He'll be in there with a big man on the night of February 25, me, and I'm faster than his light heavyweights."

Louis did his best to lessen Liston's contempt for Clay by talking about his own near-disastrous outing against light-heavyweight Billy Conn. Joe won that fight with a 13th round knockout after being behind in points through the first 12. He emphasized Clay's size and reach but Liston said, "The distance to the canvas is the same, Joe," and everybody laughed. Reflecting back on his own career and the problems he had with younger, faster opponents Joe said the years had a way of taking things away from you. Age, of course, robs all athletes of their skills but it takes its greatest toll on boxers. "When you get old, any fight is dangerous," said trainer Eddie Futch.

Sonny was training for a two-or three-round fight and simply couldn't imagine that it would be anything other than a quick one. The challenger had leaked word to Liston's camp that he was scared to death, and Sonny found that easy to believe. "When the bell sounds, I'm expectin' for Clay to jump out of the ring," said Liston. "If he decides to fight, I figure I don't have to use much smartness with him. I'll just corner him and clobber him."

Sonny was so intent on destroying his opponent that he somehow managed to forget a boxing maxim so fundamental that even a 22-year-old fighter like Clay knew it well. "I don't care who a fighter is. He has got to stay in shape," said Cassius. "While I was fighting Jones and Cooper, Liston was up to his neck in all of that rich, fat ritual of the champion. I'd nearly clap my hands every time I read or heard about him at some big function or ceremony, up half the night and drinking and all that."

Ironically, Ali would also forget that same boxing maxim 13 years later when he defended his title against lightly regarded Leon Spinks. "No, he didn't train for the fight," said Gene Kilroy, a very knowledgable boxing man who believes the importance of training can be reduced to seven words. "Failing to prepare is preparing to fail," he told me. "We'd be going to do road work and Spinks would be coming in with two old white ladies. Ali said, 'Look at this guy. Why should I train and punish myself?'" Kilroy even brought in Kris Kristofferson to run with Ali but Muhammad didn't think he needed to do roadwork. "He *had* to train," said Gene, who remembers that the 36-year-old Ali got tired just walking from his hotel room to the arena on the night of the first Spinks fight. "He said, 'This is a long walk. I'm tired.'"

When Kilroy told me this story I thought of three things. First, I had always wondered if Ali might have wanted to lose to Spinks so he could become the first heavyweight in history to win the title three times. After all, Leon had been a pro for just 13 months and had only seven fights under his belt. Second, it's likely that Liston thought even less of Clay's ability than Ali thought of Spinks', and third, Leon's skills were not even remotely near those of Clay's when he fought Sonny for the title.

Sonny also knew that a fighter's mental condition was as crucial as his physical condition. "If you're not in mental shape you're going to lose the fight," he once said. "It is going to cut your physical shape in half." Unfortunately, he managed to ignore that maxim too. Since Sonny's physical condition was nothing close to what it should have been and because he viewed his opponent with utter contempt, he would essentially be fighting Clay solely on emotion.

In contrast, Clay's fight preparations were as good as Sonny's were bad. Angelo Dundee had people film all of Liston's workouts, which he and Cassius studied each night. Dundee told Clay that the way to beat Liston was to "surround his jab." Against sparring partners similar in size to Liston, Cassius did that by moving to his left, away from Sonny's powerful left hand. Sugar Ray Robinson had shown Cassius the film of one of his fights against Jake LaMotta and suggested he use the same circling and retreating tactics against Liston, wearing him down like a matador would a bull, provided of course that Liston would comply by fighting like one. Clay studied that film for three months, along with films of Liston's fights against Williams, Folley, and Machen. Watching those films, he noticed Sonny's eyes seemed to flicker when he was getting ready to throw a big punch, something no one ever noticed before.

When Clay circled the ring, he was the spitting image of Sugar Ray. The young fighter obviously had two role models, Robinson and Jack Johnson. Cassius later said he was like Jack Johnson, without the white women. Like Johnson, Clay would play with his overmatched opponents because it was important to Cassius not only that he was in complete control of the ring but also that everybody knew it. The combination of his considerable physical skills against much lesser foes had enabled him to get away with it, at least until now.

Clay was shrewd enough to make sure that nobody but his own people saw his serious workouts. He worried that some boxing writers might quit praising Sonny long enough to see what his strategy was and that someone in Liston's camp might be able to make the champ believe it. It never happened and Clay was grateful. "Them newspaper people couldn't have been working no better for me if I had been paying them," said the challenger.

Looking back on the fight, Bob Nilon said the quantity of publicity was great but the quality was horrible, primarily because almost all of the reporters considered Clay a farce. "Any serious thought that Clay can lick Liston must be rejected," wrote Shirley Povich. "It's widely believed there are more people in the world who understand Einstein's Theory than think Cassius Clay has a chance," wrote Jim Murray. Cassius actually leveled with Arthur Daley and told him he hadn't revealed half his ability in training. Predictably, Daley ignored the comment and wrote that Clay looked dreadful in his final preparations. Jimmy Cannon called the bout the most grotesque sporting event since women wrestled in ice cream filled rings and said he knew of no one who thought Cassius could win.

A lot of sportswriters intensely disliked both fighters because they thought one had no ability and the other had way too much. Cannon and Daley derided Clay's boxing skill because they were too blind to see it and they slandered Liston's character because they wouldn't allow themselves to believe that he had any. "Cassius Clay belongs with the biggest phonies to appear on the American scene," wrote Cannon. In the same article he said, "Surly as Liston is, nasty in a gangster's way as he can get, he is a prize fighter, and a champion although he hasn't the class of one."

Shortly before the fight, Clay admitted he respected Liston and even expressed doubts about winning. He had already asked Jack Nilon for a $10,000 advance because he wanted Big Red fully stocked and ready to leave in case he lost. "If I don't win the fight, and 'if' is a big word, I still think I will have given Liston a good fight and there is bound to be a rematch." He also said he'd be on the sidewalk the very next day hollering that no man ever beat him twice.

"Folks ask me what I'll do if I win and what I'll do if I don't win, but I don't have the answer yet," said Cassius. "I have to go into the Army pretty soon, and after that I don't know. Maybe I'll build a big housing project and get married and settle down and think about being rich. But I'm not too worried. I think I can make it in something else the same way I've made it in boxing. If things go wrong in the fight, I'll just wait a while. Summertime comes, flowers start blooming, little birds start flying and you wake up, get up, and get out. You change with the times."

The doubts were gone two days later when Clay said it was prophesized for him to be successful. His newly restored confidence was the result of his friendship with Malcolm X. "Cassius was just about hysterical with apprehension of Sonny Liston," recalled Malcolm's widow, Betty Shabazz. "When he arrived in Miami he was very nervous and wondered why he had selected boxing as a career and Sonny Liston as an opponent at this particular time…My husband reminded Clay that David slew Goliath, and told him that God would not allow someone who believed in him to fail, regardless of how powerful the opponent was."

Nation of Islam leader Elijah Muhammad had cautioned Malcolm not to align himself too closely to Clay, fearing that the Muslims would be embarrassed by the fight's outcome. According to Shabazz, Muhammad told Malcolm to offer his support to Cassius as a private person only. "You will not in any way be representing us, because it's impossible for Cassius Clay to win," said the Nation's leader. Days after the fight at a Savior's Day really in Chicago, Elijah was saying something quite different. "White people wanted Liston to beat up and probably kill poor little Clay. But Allah and myself said no. This assured his victory."

Given his size, youth, and speed, Clay should have been no more than a 3-1 underdog against Liston. Cassius was a bold fighter whose highly unorthodox style presented an opponent with a set of circumstances for which it was nearly impossible to prepare, primarily because no sparring partner could come close to imitating him. And what nobody knew at the time, and what nobody talks about to this day, is that Ali always fought only as hard as he had to. Because he had revealed so little of his abilities in his bouts and training sessions, most people greatly underestimated his remarkable talent prior to the Liston fight.

Other boxers had survived against Sonny by crowding him so he couldn't extend his arms but Clay had never fought that way and it would have been foolish for him to start now. For one thing, that strategy had only allowed opponents to last a few more rounds against Liston and they absorbed a lot of punishment in the process. More important, Cassius wasn't tough enough to do it and it also would have negated his greatest strengths, which were his speed and movement.

Though most sportswriters didn't know enough about boxing to correctly handicap this fight, some veterans of the sport did. "Clay is a good fighter," said former Olympic boxing coach Pete Mello. "Don't undersell him. He can punch and box." Trainer Whitey Bimstein said Liston "has to be in top-notch shape and fight his usual style. Liston cannot afford to be lax, otherwise he may be in for a few surprises." Former three-time champ Henry Armstrong said Clay's best path to victory was to exhaust Sonny. Bimstein said he'd tell Clay to run like hell. "He has to bob and weave. He must not stand straight up. That would be the worst mistake he could make," said Whitey. As Eddie Machen put it, "if you stand back from (Liston), it's his meat."

Angelo Dundee was right when he said that the guy who could beat Liston was someone like Cassius. "It takes a rangy guy who can move, who can make Liston move," said Dundee. "Moving and sticking will definitely wear Liston out, a man that huge. You've got to nullify his left hand—move to the outside of his hook and hit him with jabs. And Clay's got the speed and the range."

Sonny, however, was not just a puncher. One of the many facts lost over the years is that Liston was also a very good boxer. Jesse Bowdry said Sonny had the grace of a ballet dancer. "His legs are perfect for a fighter," said Rocky Marciano. "By just looking at them you know they can carry him through 15 fast, tough rounds. There's nothing more important to a fighter than his legs." Liston had fast hands and moved forward methodically and relentlessly, all the while punishing an opponent with his powerful jab. Under Reddish, Sonny had improved his footwork and developed a strong defense, a quality that even Liston's arch enemy Cus D'Amato was forced to acknowledge. Sonny was adept at blocking punches with his hands and arms and was always setting his opponent up for the kill. His balance was nearly perfect.

"He's smart too. He doesn't move too much, but his long reach makes up for it," said Reddish, who marveled at Sonny's ability to adapt himself to an opponent's style. Former welterweight champ Barney Ross noticed the same thing. He had closely watched Liston's sparring sessions and was impressed by his approach in the ring. Ross said Liston didn't let his fist fly until he was ready to throw a real punch to a definite spot and noted that the big man moved his body only just enough to avoid a punch.

"I have the reach on him," said Sonny. "Nobody can fight you standing way back. He's got to come in at me. What else can he do? He's got to hit me with his hands, don't he?" Cassius would need to come within arm's length of Sonny every time he hit him because the champ's 84-inch reach was three or four inches longer than the challenger's. Sonny was a devastating finisher and if he hurt Cassus, it's unlikely that the kid could have survived. Clay simply couldn't afford to make a mistake against the champ and since just three minutes could feel like a lifetime against Liston, the thought of going 15 rounds with him would have seemed like an eternity.

On the morning of the fight Clay awoke shortly after 8 a.m. and had his usual breakfast of five poached eggs, rye toast, and tea with lemon. At 10:30 he climaxed his psychological war against Liston at what one writer called the most entertaining weigh-in since challenger Max Baer pulled hairs off Primo Carnera's chest while saying, "He loves me, he loves me not."

Because of the ineptitude of the Miami Beach Boxing Commission, Clay was able to stage a bizarre spectacle never before seen at a championship weigh-in. By conducting his examination next to the scales, the commission doctor kept Liston and Clay together much longer than necessary and allowed Cassius to turn a routine event into a circus. One of Clay's backers likened the event to a Roman carnival with 500 people, including vendors, crowded into one room. Marty Marshall walked around the room offering people the chance to shake the hand that broke Sonny Liston's jaw.

Clay arrived in his Cadillac convertible surrounded by pretty girls who carried signs that read, "Mommy, Can We Go To The Fight?" Flanked by Sugar Ray Robinson and Bundini Brown, Clay entered the building wearing his blue denim bear-hunting outfit as his entire entourage chanted they were ready to rumble. As Clay waited for his introduction, Robinson tried to impress upon the challenger the seriousness of a championship weigh-in. Cassius agreed to everything Ray told him about the need to act proper and be respectful. Then he entered the hall screaming. Clay and Brown kept walking around the room shouting, "rumble, young man rumble" until somebody escorted them to the dressing room. William Faversham was covered with sweat when he learned that both fighters were refusing to leave their dressing rooms until the other one did. He went to Clay's room and reminded him it was the champion's prerogative to enter last. "I tell you, it was worse than handling Caruso!" remembered Faversham.

Returning to the hall, Cassius and Bundini shouted, "Float like a butterfly, sting like a bee!" The challenger argued loudly with commission officials, who wouldn't allow Sugar Ray to join him on the platform. "This thing can still be cancelled, you know," said Clay, giving new meaning to the word chutzpah. One boxing commissioner said Clay was trying to make jackasses out of all of them.

When Liston entered two minutes later, Clay's outbursts reached a fever pitch. Waving his fists at the champ, Cassius screamed that he'd eat him alive. "Hey chump, you trying to scare me with that look?" shouted Clay. "No boy," responded Sonny, "but I'm going to scare you with this left hook." Clay pretended to lunge at Liston and thinking he was serious, Faversham tried to restrain Cassius by holding him around the waist. Sugar Ray held Clay's right arm while Bundini stood behind the fighter whispering, "float like a butterfly, sting like a bee," into his ear. "For Christ's sake, Drew, shut up!" yelled Faversham. Faversham had a bad heart and his secretary feared the excitement might kill him.

Madison Square Garden's Teddy Brenner said Clay was scared to death and thought he might not show up for the fight. "He's close to dementia now," said Norman Mailer. Arthur Daley suggested it was hysteria; Milton Gross thought it was schizophrenia. Sportswriters were yelling at Cassius to shut up. Commission doctor Alexander Robbins thought Clay was acting like a maniac and tried to get him to calm down. Robbins measured Clay's blood pressure at 200/100 and Clay's pulse at 120 beats per minute, more than double his normal rate of 54. "This is a man who is scared to death," said Robbins. Justifiably alarmed, he announced that Clay was emotionally unbalanced and liable to crack up before he entered the ring. He decreed that the fight would be cancelled if Clay's heart rate and blood pressure were still high at fight time. "No man could have seen Clay that morning at the weigh-in and believed that he could stay on his feet three minutes that night," wrote Murray Kempton.

At the height of Clay's hysterics, he screamed, "You been tricked, chump!" a comment that Liston promptly dismissed. "I'm surprised to see a confused look across his face," Ali said later. "He speaks very low, for no one but me to hear: 'Don't let everyone know what a fool you are.' I'm delighted. He actually believes I'm a fool." The champ made a circular motion with his hand next to his head, then turned to the crowd and held up two fingers, apparently changing his knockout prediction from three rounds to two. When Chairman Morris Klein announced that Clay had been fined $2,500, the press cheered. Clay ranted his way out of the building, climaxing a beautifully orchestrated 35-minute performance.

"You know, fellas, I don't think the kid's all there," Sonny said as he left the stage. "I think he's scrambled in the marbles." Liston seemed calm but he had jumped when Dr. Robbins first reached for his arm to measure his pulse. Another commission doctor said Sonny displayed extreme tension after the weigh-in, when he ordered a photographer to put out his cigar. Things were definitely not going as Sonny had planned. Earlier, he told Harold Conrad that he would "put the evil eye on this faggot at the weigh-in and psych him right out of the fight." Now it seemed that Clay had deflected that look right back at him.

"He just didn't know what to make of the kid," remembered Angelo Dundee, a sentiment confirmed by his counterpart in Liston's camp. "It really got next to him," said Willie Reddish. "I could tell by the expression on his face. Clay was acting like a crazy man." And that was the most important factor about the weigh-in, because as Sonny said in a 1962 *Esquire* interview, the worst person in the world to fight is a crazy person. Geraldine said that was exactly what her husband thought of Clay. "Sonny thinks that boy is crazy! Just out of his cotton-picking mind," she told *SI*'s Mort Sharnik before the fight. "And you never know what to expect from a man like that. You never know what to expect from a madman."

Following the weigh-in the odds in some places rose from 7-1 to as high as

10-1. In Las Vegas, five times more money was wagered on which round Liston would win in than on who would win the fight. Jimmy the Greek said it was impossible for Clay to last six rounds; Joe Louis said he couldn't see how Liston could lose. The rumor that got the most traction was that the commission had called off the fight on the advice of its medical team.

Dr. Ferdie Pacheco had been ordered to go to the challenger's house and monitor his blood pressure. "Angelo, Ali, and I entered the small house now packed with followers of the Fruit of Islam listening to tapes by Malcolm X exhorting them to kill the white devils. It was not a moment I would care to relive. I felt like a Jew at a Nuremberg rally." Clay's blood pressure and pulse were now normal but he was a little worried that he may have used up too much energy "acting the fool" during his self-induced hysteria. When Pacheco asked Cassius why he had acted the way he did, the fighter smiled before answering. "Because Liston thinks I am a nut. He is scared of no man, but he is scared of a nut because he doesn't know what I am going to do. Did I have Liston shook up? I shook him up, didn't I?" Cassius ate his final pre-fight meal of salad, a large steak, vegetables, and tea and napped for the remainder of the afternoon.

Clay's carefully rehearsed routine was probably the most impressive acting performance any athlete ever gave, though he had given a very similar one at the weigh-in prior to his fight against Charlie Powell a year earlier. Apparently nobody remembered that act because the brash 22-year-old challenger had thoroughly convinced Liston, everyone around him, and almost everybody on the planet that he was crazy, scared to death, and incapable of putting up much of a fight. Later that evening reporters waited outside Clay's dressing room to see if he'd actually come out.

It's been widely reported that Clay had a low IQ but it's hard to think of him as anything other than a very smart young man. It took a creative and calculating mind to devise a plan to unnerve a force of nature like Liston and it also took someone with the considerable skills, courage, and discipline needed to carry it out. Of course, having the foolishness of youth on his side probably helped Clay as well.

Nowadays, Muhammad likes to watch some of the interviews he gave way back when, and his wife, Lonnie, says he marvels at some of the outrageous things he used to say. "Sometimes I think he looks at it and say, 'Is that me? Did I really say those things?'" Forty-eight years later, Ali sees himself the way most people saw him back in the day.

Unfortunately for Liston, his health and age were far greater obstacles for him to overcome than was his total disrespect of Clay's ability. For months, Sonny had received cortisone treatments for bursitis in both of his shoulders. Lem Banker was at the Riviera Health Club in Las Vegas when manager Mike Tulane gave Sonny a cortisone shot in his left shoulder. "It definitely helped him," said Banker. Given Liston's legendary fear of needles, he wouldn't have submitted to the shot if he didn't absolutely need it.

In Miami, Sonny sent for Joe Louis's personal physician, Dr. Robert Bennett, because Bennett was the only doctor he trusted. Nobody outside of Liston's camp knew that he had injured his left shoulder so badly during training that it hurt him every time he hit the heavy bag. After every workout, Ash Resnick took Sonny to a health club operated by licensed physiotherapist and boxing referee Barney Felix. "They brought him up the back elevator at night," said Felix. "I gave him hot packs and ultrasonic treatment. He didn't say a word; he was very solemn. This went on every night for two weeks. They said to keep it quiet." Even Liston's good friend Joe Louis didn't know about the visits. Three years later Geraldine told *SI*'s Jack Olsen that her husband sometimes walked the streets of Miami at night because he was in so much pain.

Due to his injury Sonny sparred only 91 rounds in training and by scaling a career-high 218 at the weigh-in he would enter the ring a very heavy 224 or 225 pounds against the fastest heavyweight the boxing world had ever seen. Boxing historian Hank Kaplan maintained that Liston's people went to the boxing commission and asked for a postponement but were turned down. "You're not going to do this again," the commission told Sonny, in reference to his knee injury that cost Miami Beach the rematch against Patterson. Due to their poor opinion of Clay's ability, Jack Nilon said Liston's camp thought they could get away with it.

Sonny's body was beginning to break down and it took a significant turn for the worse during 1963. The knee injury that forced the Patterson postponement was only the beginning. Following the rematch in July, Liston revealed he had injured his left elbow in training and had almost called off the fight. Dr. Bennett said Sonny had suffered from bursitis almost from the time he won the championship in September 1962.

And then there was the matter of Liston's age. The easiest way to make Sonny angry was to question him about his age. "What made him hate writers was all of the writers would make fun of him claiming to be a certain age when we all knew he was older," said Jack Newfield. Whenever Liston was pressed on the matter he'd accuse the person of calling his mother a liar and that would almost always end the conversation. There were at least two times when it didn't.

The first was in 1964 when Mark Kram was a little too inquisitive and found himself being "rocketed" into a Denver snowbank by Sonny. The second was at a 1968 press conference in a San Francisco pub when ABC's Howard Cosell waited until the cameras were off before asking the ex-champ how old he was. "Motherfucker," said Sonny, as he barreled from his chair and advanced toward a guy he absolutely despised. "Howard was so scared he didn't want to come to the fight," said Henry Winston, who witnessed the encounter. "People had to come to Cosell's hotel room and escort him to the San Francisco Cow Palace to do the telecast."

Most boxing people were convinced that Sonny was older than his stated age of 32 at the time of the Clay fight. Liston's 1950 arrest record listed a 1928 birth date and a May 1, 1962, FBI memorandum fixed Liston's year of birth as 1927. Barney Baker told me he thought Sonny was pushing 30 when they first met in 1953, which would have made Liston around 40 at the time of this fight. Clay also believed Liston was pushing 40 before their first fight and insisted Sonny looked old enough to be his father.

Wells Twombly was writing for a Houston newspaper when a little old man came into the sports deparment carrying a scrapbook. "He produced some clippings from the *East St. Louis Journal* of 1934, showing a 17-year-old kid named Charles "Sailor" Liston whose gimmick was a peacoat and a white Navy cap, which he wore into the ring instead of a robe," wrote Twombly. "The face had aged, but the glare was unmistakable." Apart from being a little heavier now, Liston's appearance was almost the same as it was in the early 1950s. When Twombly showed Sonny copies of the clippings he stared at them, mumbled an obscenity, and claimed the guy in the photo was a cousin of his who had boxed and was also named Charles Liston.

"If nothing else, the clippings—if they showed the one and only Charles Liston—would have explained why his career declined so quickly," Twombly wrote a decade later. Sonny's earlier pro boxing career would also help explain why he seemed such a natural talent in his prison days. No matter how good a street fighter one is, and Sonny was the absolute best, proper boxing technique is an acquired skill and one that's very difficult to master.

This prior career would mean that Sonny was actually one of the earlier children of Tobe and Helen Liston, rather than the second youngest as he always maintained. Supporting this notion is the *Encyclopedia Britannica* which lists Sonny's date of birth as May 1917 and a Liston family crest website that pegs Sonny's year of birth as 1919. Even if Liston were only 15 in 1934, it would mean he was 43 when he won the heavyweight title against Patterson and 44 or 45 when he defended it against Clay.

Don Chargin co-promoted three of Liston's later fights and told me guys in the gym were always asking Sonny about his age. The big man took the kidding in a good-natured way without ever answering the question. But one day Liston shocked Chargin and everybody else when he responded to the question by saying, "A lot older than you think." Since boxing people already thought Liston was at least a few years older than he said a was, "A lot older than you think" was a very significant admission from a man who went to great lengths to hide his true age. He was able to maintain that charade because he fought like a man in his prime. But, as boxing historian Jimmy Jacobs said, "No fighter is exempt from the disadvantage of being human. And fighters get older."

Every fighter will tell you that boxing has always been a young man's sport. Louis won the title at the age of 23, Patterson was 21, Ali was 22, and Tyson was 20. "Listen, if you're young and you're willing, it's gonna overcome a guy who's a good fighter and old," Ash Resnick told me. "There's always something missing when you get past 32—nobody's the same." When I asked Ash what he thought Liston's prime was he said, "Jesus Christ, he never really got to his prime. Like before the Patterson fights, to me that was Sonny's prime and he was old then. A fighter doesn't reach his prime when he's 34 or 36 or even 27 or 28. Even that's pretty old."

Consider the skill levels of other famous heavyweights who fought well past their primes. Jack Dempsey was 31 when he lost badly to Gene Tunney in 1926. Looking like a man of 50, Louis had nothing left at 37 when he lost his final bout to Marciano, a fighter who Joe would have quickly dispatched earlier in his career. Even the great Sugar Ray Robinson won just three of 14 fights against top 10 contenders after his 36th birthday.

Joe Frazier was a mediocre fighter after the drubbing he took in beating Ali at the age of 27 and was totally spent at 29 when he was knocked out by George

Foreman. Foreman retired at the age of 28 after absorbing a beating from light-hitting Jimmy Young. Ali lost to Leon Spinks at the age of 36 in the challenger's eighth professional fight. He was also embarrassed by Larry Holmes and Trevor Berbick at the ages of 38 and 39. But no one thinks any less of Ali because of those poor performances against boxers who don't belong in any conversation about the division's all-time greats. And no one thinks any less of Dempsey, Louis, Frazier, Foreman, and Robinson because of their dismal performances late in their careers. The reputation of every one of those former champs has gotten a free ride, but not Liston.

Boxing after the age of 40 puts one's health at risk; only great fighters like Archie Moore and Ray Robinson were able to remain competitive at such an advanced age. Even though Foreman won his second heavyweight title when he was 45, all the money in the world could not have gotten the older George in the ring with the 24-year-old George who destroyed Frazier in 1973. Liston, however, was the only boxer who ever dominated his sport after the age of 40.

I've always wondered how much greater Liston could have been if he were properly managed and trained in his early 20s like Ali, Louis, Foreman, and Tyson were. Unlike Muhammad, Joe, George, and Mike, Sonny was a very old man when he won the heavyweight title and a very old man when he lost it. And, as Ali said, "Don't ever forget that boxing is for young men."

CHAPTER NINE

A LOST-HEAD

At Miami's Hialeah racetrack a three-year-old horse named Cassius won for the first time and paid $19 to win, overcoming odds very similar to the ones his human namesake was facing against the heavyweight champ. If that were an omen of good things to come, most people failed to recognize it. High ticket prices, rain, and the likelihood of a mismatch left a majority of the hall's 16,000 seats empty. The announced crowd of 8,297 was later revised downward by 2,000 and the live gate of $402,000 was less than half of MacDonald's $825,000 break-even point. In the lobby, a large group of FBI and Secret Service agents scanned the crowd for known members of the underworld.

An 1895 Florida law made prize fighting a crime punishable by a $5,000 fine and/or five years in jail. However, the law provided a special exemption for boxing matches held under the auspices of organizations like the Veterans of Foreign Wars. Instead of the usual $20 they got for a fight, the VFW received $500 for this one—along with 38 free tickets.

Few people knew that Sonny made sure there was a provision in every closed-circuit contract that segregation wouldn't be tolerated. "I feel that the color of my people's money is the same as anyone else's," Sonny said. "They should get the same seats. If not, I don't want those places to have the fight." Two New Orleans theaters that had never admitted blacks lost the telecast when they refused to observe the provision. The head of the Congress on Racial Equality (CORE) would congratulate Sonny after the fight for taking that principled stand.

A record 371 locations in the United States and Canada would telecast the bout but little more than half of the 1.1 million seats would be filled. Clay's strategy of looking bad and acting scared had apparently convinced people all over the country that they'd be throwing their money away if they paid to watch. However, 75 million Americans over the age of 12 would be listening to ABC's radio broadcast for free.

"Before the fight the most persistent rumor was that Cassius Clay would not show up," wrote Edwin Pope in the *Miami Herald*. "I really thought Liston was gonna murder him." A radio report said Clay had been seen at the airport buying a ticket to Mexico. Another rumor had him in a hospital wearing a straitjacket; a lot of people wouldn't have been surprised if any of the stories were true. Actually, Clay was standing in the back of the auditorium, wearing a tuxedo, calmly and proudly watching his little brother Rudy win his first professional fight. And then Gee-gee was jolted back to the real world.

Walking to his dressing room Cassius saw 53-year-old former heavyweight contender Kingfish Levinsky, one of many former boxers who had fallen on very hard times after his fighting days. "He's gonna take you, kid. Liston's gonna take you, make you a guy selling ties," Levinsky told him. "Partners with me, kid, you can be partners with me." That's something the challenger really didn't need to hear.

In his dressing room Clay was anything but calm as he awaited his date with destiny. With him were his brother Rudy, Dundee, Pacheco, and assistant trainer Luis Sarria. Pacheco noticed that Clay distrusted everyone except Rudy and ordered his brother not to let anyone touch his water bottle. Clay apparently believed a rumor that the mafia was going to contaminate his water and he checked the bottle several times, taking off the cork, emptying it, and refilling it again. Contaminating a boxer's water used to be a common occurrence in the sport.

"I don't trust you," Clay said to Pacheco. "You want Liston to win. You bet with gangsters." Then the challenger turned to Dundee and said, "I don't trust mafia people. You're a bunch of Italian mafia people." Ferdie believed Cassius was deadly serious when he said those things. "He was very nervous, you could see it," said Pacheco, who believed Clay was just a kid who had no idea if he could really do what he had been saying he could do. "You have to remember one thing," Gene Kilroy told me. "Sonny Liston was a man. At that time, Muhammad Ali was a little boy."

It wasn't just Liston who had the challenger worried. For the past week, Clay had been getting threatening phone calls with warnings like, "Nigger, you'll not win that Sonny Liston fight." On the morning of the fight he got calls saying he'd be lucky just to make it to the ring and if Liston didn't get him, somebody else would. Cassius also prayed a lot, including a silent prayer for Allah's blessings with Malcolm X. Willie Reddish came into Clay's dressing room to witness his hands being wrapped. When the trainer returned to Liston's dressing room Sonny asked him, "You see any Moooslems, you see any guys with bullet heads, dark suits?"

The *New York Times* boxing writer declined to cover the fight so the paper sent feature writer Robert Lipsyte and told him to find the locations of the nearest hospitals so he'd know where to go after Clay got knocked out. "I understood that I should enjoy this week as much as I could because I would never see Cassius Clay again," remembered Lipsyte. Comedian Joe E. Brown said he was putting his money on Cassius "to live." One ringside reporter got a big laugh when he said it was even money Clay wouldn't last past the National Anthem. "Sonny Liston will win in 18 seconds of the first round," joked Jackie Gleason, "and my estimate includes the three seconds Blabber Mouth will bring into the ring with him."

At ringside was a Florida cattleman who had just flown in from Daytona Beach. He had bought ringside seats for the Louis-Schmeling fight in 1936, but didn't bother to attend. "I figured it wouldn't be any use," he said. "You know what happened. Schmeling knocked Louis out. This time I figured if there was an upset, I'd see it for myself."

Of the 58 sportswriters that were polled, 55 picked Liston to win and most of them predicted an early knockout. That well-known tendency of sportswriters to pick the loser in a big fight was about to surface again but this time, who could blame them? As far as most of the world was concerned, this fight figured to be one of the greatest mismatches of all time. "The tension was electric," said Pacheco, "but this tension was more like that of an audience at a hanging. They were here to see this kid get his. When he was going to get it was the only question."

As referee Barney Felix gave the fighters their instructions, Cassius Clay experienced the menacing glare of the toughest and angriest man on the planet. "I won't lie," Ali would later say, "I was scared. Sonny Liston was one of the greatest fighters of all time. He was one of the most scientific boxers who ever lived. He hit hard and he was fixing to kill me. It frightened me, just knowing how hard he hit. But I was there, I didn't have no choice but to go out and fight." Ali felt like Columbus traveling into the unknown. Luis Sarria said his fighter was distraught with fear in the early moments of that first round.

When the bell sounded, Liston's pent up rage caused him to forget most of what he knew about boxing and he chased the fastest heavyweight in history around the ring. "I was trying to knock him out from the first bell," Sonny said after the fight. He was "plum thick" again and this time it would cost him dearly. "Any time you lose your head you're fighting the other guy's fight and you're in trouble," said former featherweight champ, Willie Pep. "Once you get mad, you're going to forget technique and tactics and you'll be wide open for the opponent who stays calm," echoed Jack Dempsey. "You know what I call an angry boxer. I call him a lost-head. He's lost his head and now he's going to lose the match."

"Man, he meant to kill me. I ain't kidding," remembered Ali. Reddish yelled at his fighter to shorten his stance, but Sonny continued to lunge at Clay and punch off-balance with his legs spread wide. A flurry of punches by Clay had the crowd cheering so loudly that the bell rang three times before the fighters finally heard it six or seven seconds after the round ended. In those few seconds, Liston aggravated the injury to his left shoulder that had plagued him throughout training. In all likelihood it happened when Sonny's left hook struck Clay's right glove as it was moving forward to block his punch. The round was the worst of Sonny's career—and his life was about to be turned upside down forever.

You might think that the more experienced Liston would be the one with the fight plan, but that wasn't the case. "All he did was walk in with his face up," laughed Archie Moore. It was Clay who had thoughtfully and deliberately mapped out what he believed to be a winning strategy. He had trained to fight hard for the first two rounds and to protect himself from getting hurt. In doing so, he wanted to prove that he could stand up to Liston and he also wanted to begin to wear the champ out. "You know, a fighter can condition his body to go hard certain rounds, then to coast certain rounds," he said after the fight. "Nobody can fight fifteen rounds."

Keep in mind that the challenger had just turned 22. When Ali fought George Foreman 11 years later, he felt himself getting tired after a brisk first round. "I ain't 22 anymore, I'm 33 and I can't fight like I did 8 to 10 years ago," he said after that fight. "Maybe for a little while, but I can't keep it up… Now I can only do that for 5 or 6, and then I have to slow down and rest for the next 2 or 3 rounds." Ali was a supremely conditioned athlete in both of those fights but he understood the limitations of this most demanding of all sports. Liston, on the other hand, was in his early-to-mid-40s, had trained for a two-or three-round fight, was fighting with an injured left shoulder, and his strategy consisted solely of wanting to kill his opponent as quickly as possible.

Sonny was also feeling the effects of a torn shoulder muscle that was beginning to hemorrhage and returned to his corner complaining of numbness in his left arm. Visibly angry, Sonny refused to sit down between rounds. *Time* wrote that he was trembling with rage. Liston knew he had underestimated Clay, was embarrassed by it, and wanted to destroy him. Such thinking might be fine in a street fight, but not against a highly talented professional like Clay. Across the ring, the challenger was feeling mighty good as Bundini Brown sat on the middle rope giving encouragement to his fighter. Cassius was paying attention to no one but himself. "He was supposed to kill me," he thought to himself. "Well, I'm still alive." As Dundee talked to him, Clay was thinking that Liston would wish he had sat down and rested when he had the chance.

Clay coasted for much of the second round but a more composed Liston got in some good shots while his opponent was on the ropes. "He missed with a right hook that would have hurt me, but that was when he got me with a right to the stomach," said Cassius. Then Sonny landed a long left at the two-minute mark that Clay said rocked him back. "He really staggered me there for a minute. In fact, he did more damage with that than any other punch. But either he didn't realize how good I was hit or he was already getting tired and he didn't press his chance." Whatever the reason, Sonny missed his best opportunity for a knockout. "I sure heard the bell that time," said Clay. "I needed to get to my corner to get my head clear." It appeared that Sonny had established his dominance and the fight was even on all three official scorecards.

Clay taunted Liston at the start of the third round, and the champ obliged him by continuing to fight angry. In the past, Sonny had always been a patient fighter. Even in his first-round knockouts he would wait until his opponent was hurt before going for the kill. But in this fight he looked more like a rank amateur than the killing machine the world had come to fear. A 22-year-old kid had baited a trap—and Sonny had stepped right in it. "There was something missing from the first Clay fight. That wasn't him in there," Ernie Terrell told me. "The fighter I saw that night was not the Sonny Liston that everybody knew." Eddie Machen must have had a big smile as he watched Liston's anger compromise his ability.

Early in the round, a quick left-right combination opened a deep gash under Liston's left eye. Though his nose would often bleed, and it did in the third round, this was the first time Sonny had been cut in a fight. The way the blood spurted out indicated that the cut was a bad one. "My god!" shouted a woman at ringside. "He's human! He bleeds!" At that moment, Clay thought he had a glimpse of how Sonny would look in 20 years. Though the final minute of the round was Liston's best of the match, every spectator knew they had a fight on their hands.

After the round, Marciano turned to his radio partner Howard Cosell and said, "Jesus Christ, Howie, he's become an old man." Ash Resnick told me it looked like Liston had aged ten years right before his eyes. "When I saw Sonny in the third round, I said my God, this isn't Sonny Liston in that ring—this is an old man that can't fight. It even looked to me like Sonny's hair got gray. And you know that happens with black fighters. When they go, they go fast—they really go fast. And it looked like the same thing had happened to Sonny."

By now, the injury to Liston's shoulder made him feel like his glove was filling with water and his left arm felt leaden when he tried to punch with it. He talked about it after every round but his cornermen paid no attention. Even if they had, there was no way to undo the damage or prevent it from escalating. Before the fight, Joe Louis said Sonny could have beaten Clay without his right hand. Joe may have been right but it was Sonny's left that was injured.

Liston overcompensated for the injury by throwing his jab as hard as he could. "He was throwing his left hand so hard that his fist turned when he missed," remembered Angelo Dundee. "When you punch that hard and miss, you wear yourself out." The poorly trained champ was simply making the injury worse. "He strangely threw twisted, turning, sick punches," wrote *SI*'s Gilbert Rogin. "If he jabbed this way he must have hurt his shoulder before the fight or very early in the first round."

One minute into the fourth-round, Liston landed what appeared to be his best left hook of the fight but the punch was of no consequence. Later, two of Sonny's jabs landed flush on Clay's face but the challenger's head barely moved. This was the one and only Sonny Liston throwing the two most devastating punches in the history of boxing but they had absolutely no effect on his opponent. Clay now knew that Liston's arsenal had been severely compromised and he continued to jab at Sonny's cut until it was bleeding worse than before. At no time in the round did Clay give any indication that his eyes were bothering him.

Returning to his corner after the fourth round, Sonny had lost almost all feeling in his left hand and his entire arm had a paralyzed sensation. The tightness of the tape that secured Sonny's glove to his wrist was cutting off circulation to his left hand and preventing him from making a fist. Many of his jabs looked like the awkward shoves of an amateur. "People have scoffed at the shoulder story," said Bill Cayton, who co-managed Mike Tyson, "but if you watch the tapes as I have, you can see Liston never once threw a leveraged left hand. He couldn't throw his left hand at all. He was pushing it." Liston threw more than 80 right hands during the fight, a very high number for a man who always relied disproportionately on his lethal left hand.

The greatest weapon in boxing history had become totally useless and Sonny knew he was in deep, deep trouble. Clay's insistence on going through with this fight because he didn't want to see Sonny suffer an injury against another challenger had been eerily prescient. Jack Nilon could no longer ignore the fact that something was very wrong with Sonny's left arm. He also knew that if a ring doctor were to examine his fighter, the fight would likely be stopped. "I knew it was getting progressively worse," Nilon told a Congressional committee investigating the fight a month later, "but I thought that sooner or later Sonny could beat this boy with one hand. I honestly believed in my heart."

In the history of professional boxing, no one-minute rest period ever found both fighters simultaneously experiencing the type of crises that Liston and Clay faced between the fourth and fifth rounds. A few seconds after Clay returned to his corner he was in a state of panic. "Cut my gloves off. Please, cut them off. I mean it. I'm blind! Dirty work afoot. Dirty work afoot," he screamed at Dundee. "I knew the white man would think of a way to trick us," seethed Bundini. It didn't matter that this was a heavyweight title fight for which Clay had worked so long and hard. "I wasn't going out there and get murdered because I couldn't see," he said after the bout.

Prior to round four, Joe Polino used an astringent solution to stem the flow of blood from the cut below Liston's left eye. Just over a minute into the fourth round, the right side of Clay's forehead was planted firmly on Sonny's cut cheek during one of their rare clinches. "My kid was sweating profusely and it went into both his eyes," said Dundee.

The alcohol and wintergreen combination used on Liston's cut would have hurt Clay's eyes as soon as it came into contact with them but when Cassius sat down between rounds, his eyes were still fine. When Dundee wiped his fighter's brow with a towel in a downward motion, then and only then did Clay begin to complain and panic. Dundee had wiped the brows of his fighters thousands of times in the same way and this had never happened.

There's also a good chance that Clay's eyes were at least somewhat open at the time. It's a little known fact that Clay had cobra vision, an ability to control his eye movement and allow him to keep his eyes open virtually all of the time, even when being punched. "The man simply never closes his eyes, not even for an instant," said sparring partner Dave Bailey. "Not even when you sting him with a jab on the nose. It's uncanny." Jimmy Ellis also sparred with Cassius and confirmed Bailey's comment.

I bring this up because it's long been considered as fact that Liston ordered Polino to apply the astringent to his gloves between the third and fourth rounds, after which Polino supposedly threw the bottle under the ring to avoid detection. The story has been enhanced by rumors that Liston did the same thing to Cleveland Williams and Zora Folley, though I've never found any quote from either of those fighters complaining of such a thing. Moreover, Williams and Folley never had anything but the utmost respect for the man who destroyed them in the ring. And no one has ever claimed to have seen Polino do what he was accused of doing—but the rumor persists to this day.

Dundee threw the sponge and towel away and wiped his fighter with new ones. "I thought your guys were going to kill me," Dundee told Clay after the fight. "They thought I had done something to the water." Dundee said he saved himself by drinking some of the water and rubbing it in his eyes to show them it was safe. Then he turned to the referee and said there must be linament on Sonny's gloves, a move which prompted Barney Felix to walk over to Liston and smell them. "No limament, Angie," Felix told Dundee, all the while keeping his eyes on the challenger. "Clay doesn't want to get off his stool—he's just sitting there rubbing his eyes. Angie pushes him out and says, 'Get out there and fight, you dog.'" Clay raised both of his arms to signal that he wanted to quit, then thought better of it. "Dammit, Clay, get out here!" Felix shouted. Dundee told his fighter to run. After the fight, Clay admitted he wanted to quit and Felix said he was positive there was no linament on Liston's gloves. Felix said Clay came perilously close to being disqualified. "If Clay hadn't moved in a split second, and I mean one second, he would have been finished. I would have been forced to disqualify him."

The challenger attempted to survive the first 90 seconds by backpedaling; Liston's cornermen weren't sure if Clay was acting or not. Cassius tried to keep his left hand on Liston's forehead but was tagged by a left hook to the head, the kind of punch that but for Sonny's injury would have set Clay up for the kill. "Liston was snorting like a horse," Ali remembered. "He was trying to hit me square, and I was just moving every which way, because I knew if he connected right, it could be all over right there." When Clay heard somebody scream, "Beat that nigger's ass, Sonny. Beat that nigger's ass!" the insults made him more determined to hold on.

Sonny landed some punches to Clay's body, and the referee considered stopping the fight and awarding it to Liston on a technical knockout. "Clay ran like a thief, and Liston was swinging and missing," remembered Felix, who had performed physical therapy on Liston's shoulder in the weeks leading up to the fight. "I said to myself, he's going to tear his shoulder to pieces. And he did." Late in the round, Liston threw a hook and when Clay stopped it in mid-air, Sonny felt something happen inside his left shoulder.

As Dundee watched the sixth round unfold, he saw despair written all over Liston's face. Sonny's inability to hold his left arm much above belt level made him an easy target and reduced his own offense to right hand leads. No longer afraid of Sonny's left hand, Cassius stopped circling. The emphatic way that Liston exhaled when the bell sounded was a sign of his exhaustion and demoralized mental state. Robbed of the most devastating jab and hook in boxing history, the poorly trained, poorly handled, 40-something destroyer of men had suddenly joined the ranks of mere mortals. The fight was dead-even on the official scorecards but Liston's championship reign was as good as over.

When Clay sat down, he turned to a television commentator and said he was going to upset the world. As it turned out, he was less than 60 seconds from doing so. "I think Sonny is beginning to worry now," Joe Louis said to the worldwide audience. "At least his corner is beginning to."

Across the ring, Reddish told Liston to start double-jabbing Clay. When Sonny told him he couldn't jab because he couldn't close his fist or lift his arm, Reddish said they'd have to stop the fight. "What can we do?" Liston asked Nilon. "What can we do?" responded the manager. "We will have to stop the fight." Liston told his corner he wanted to keep fighting but when he said his shoulder felt like it was broken, they wouldn't let him continue. Sonny spit out his mouthpiece and cursed his opponent. "I can beat that bastard one-handed," he said, slumped on his stool. *SI*'s Tex Maule saw tears trickling down Sonny's cheeks. "There is no doubt that Liston's arm was damaged," he wrote.

Referee Felix realized something was wrong when Liston's handlers didn't leave the ring at the start of round seven. When he walked to Liston's corner, Nilon and Reddish stepped in front of their fighter and waved Felix off. "No good," said Nilon. "He can't make it. He broke his shoulder." Nilon saw no need to call for a doctor. Clay was watching Sonny's corner closely and erupted with joy. "I just upset Sonny Liston!" he shouted. "I MUST be the greatest!"

Dundee walked over to Liston's corner to offer some sympathetic words, but Sonny wasn't listening. "He was wailing: 'My arm feels like it's full of water,'" said Dundee. Liston's handlers were in a state of shock. Jack Nilon had said on numerous occasions that the only way Sonny could lose was by an act of God. "I thought nobody in the world could beat him. I thought he was like the Titanic, unsinkable," said Reddish, who insisted Sonny wanted to continue. "He never said to me that he wanted to quit. He was too brave a man." Liston left the ring amid boos and cries of "Fix!"

Joe Louis made several inarticulate attempts to explain what he understood to be the nature of Liston's injury. To underscore the enormity of what had taken place, Louis matter-of-factly stated that Clay had just beaten the greatest heavyweight champion in history.

Liston's victory party in the ballroom of the Fountainbleau Hotel was over before it started. Gordon Davidson admitted his group hadn't even thought about a victory party for Clay. That was fine with Cassius since he had already made other plans. After the fight, he drove across Biscayne Bay to Malcolm's motel in the black section of Miami, where he celebrated with some vanilla ice cream and Muslim prayer.

Within minutes, the FBI began to look into the fight's outcome. According to a declassified memorandum, a night supervisor at the FBI's Miami office was told to notify the Bureau at once if any information came to light that might indicate the fight was not legitimate. The Boxing Commission immediately announced it was withholding Liston's purse pending the findings of its medical team.

Geraldine was in her hotel room with a police contingent outside the door. When she was told the news she immediately went to the arena and asked Ash Resnick to go to the hospital with her husband. Sonny was disgusted when he left his dressing room. Sitting next to Liston in the back seat of the limousine was Resnick's four-year old daughter, Dana. "I loved Sonny and all I remember is sitting next to him and seeing him bleeding. I hate fighting and it started then in that limo."

Marilyn Resnick was sitting next to her husband in the limo's front seat. "At the fight I was in shock," she told me. "Ash was like ashen white. I had never seen him like that. If there was only one sure thing in life it was that Sonny could beat this man with one arm tied behind his back. I know Ash lost a lot of money on that fight. He had a habit of biting his lower lip when he had done something like that. That was a giveaway."

Doctors took 12 x-rays of Sonny's left shoulder and arm. The muscle damage had swollen the circumference of his arm by almost four inches and his his fist was swollen as well. Ash remembered that Liston couldn't feel the shot he was given to ease the swelling. Ash stayed at the hospital until Sonny left some four hours later. *Sports Illustrated* writer Mort Sharnik saw Liston at the hospital and said he looked like the loneliest person in the world. One of the eight doctors who treated Sonny described him as being sad and depressed.

Liston told Dr. Bennett he was trying to throw a punch and block one at the same time in the first round when he first felt the injury. Bennett said the pain was so severe that Sonny couldn't get his coat on when he left the hospital. Bennett said he treated Liston's bursitis in Las Vegas in January and was called to Florida two weeks before the fight, where he spent another week treating Sonny. In between those visits he mailed Liston pills from Detroit. "It's no secret," Bennett said. "I'll be glad to explain it to anyone who's interested."

Later, publicist Harold Conrad found Sonny sitting in bed, drinking. "What are they saying about the fight?" Liston asked. "That you took a dive," replied Conrad. "Me? Sell my title? Those dirty bastards!" yelled the ex-champ, shattering his glass against the wall. "You see me, you know what it means to me to hear a kid say, 'Hello, champ'?" Ash Resnick told me Liston got drunk that night and that it was the first time he ever saw him drink.

The following morning, Dr. Robbins announced that the commission's eight person medical team had unanimously concluded that Liston injured the long head to the biceps tendon of the left shoulder. There was tearing of the muscle fibers with some hemorrhaging into the mass of the biceps, numbing the arm and preventing Sonny from using it to defend himself. Robbins said the injury was such that Liston could fight a while before his arm basically went dead. He said Sonny told him he couldn't lift his arm and that it was numb all the way to his fist.

"There is no doubt in my mind this fight should have been stopped," said Robbins. One of the other doctors said Liston's injury was particularly prevalent in older athletes whose bodies tend to deteriorate rapidly under intense physical strain. Based on their examination, all eight doctors concluded that Sonny's true age was between 38 and 41, rather than his stated age of 31. Boxing Commission Chairman Morris Klein announced that the athletic commission was completely satisfied that Liston had suffered an honest injury. Dr. Bennett estimated it would be at least two months before Liston could begin training again but one of the examining physicians said it could be twice that long.

Jack Nilon insisted the decision to stop the fight was made by him alone. "You couldn't send a man out to fight with one hand. Sonny said, 'I'll go on', but I didn't pay any attention to him." Nilon compared his dilemma to that of a jockey on the Kentucky Derby favorite who notices his horse is favoring its left front leg. By letting the horse run, the jockey might be risking permanent injury but by pulling the horse up, he might be able to compete in the Preakness and Belmont Stakes. "That's what I did with Sonny," said Nilon. "He couldn't feel his fingertips. He couldn't hold the arm up to defend himself, and he was slapping, not punching. One doctor thinks his arm is hurt worse than we imagine." Nilon planned to take Liston to the best orthopedic specialist in the country and promised his fighter would be hungry when he returned. "This guy has pride, you can't imagine such pride. This thing is killing him."

Sonny faced the press wearing sunglasses, with his arm in a sling and a small bandage on his cheek. Speaking softly, Sonny said he injured his arm late in the first round when he felt something snap while throwing a punch. "(After that) I just couldn't throw a punch, not the jab anyway. My arm was killing me." The ex-champ said he erred in the first round by swinging with everything he had and trying to knock Clay out. "I threw too many wild punches. That was a big mistake. I should have just been a little patient and stalked him until I got an opening. If I had done that, I would still be heavyweight champion of the world." Sonny said Machen and Folley were better fighters than Clay who, he said, was as scared as a thief and wouldn't be champion for long. "Patterson came to win or lose," said Sonny. "He didn't run or hide like he stole somthin'." When asked about a rematch, Sonny said, "If he wants to fight me I'll take it. If he don't, I imagine I'll forget it."

Joe Louis once said he never thought about losing until he won the title. He knew he might lose it someday but he never picked out a particular fight and thought it might be the one. By all accounts, Sonny never thought the Clay fight would be the one he would lose, either.

Asked how he felt about losing, Liston revealed a depth of character that most people thought him incapable of possessing. "I feel like the people did when President Kennedy got shot," said the ex-champ. When Sonny thanked the reporters and said goodbye, someone called out, "Thank you Mr. President." Sonny received a round of applause from several hundred reporters and photographers and was surprised and touched by the gesture. "Never had he seemed so relaxed, so approachable," wrote *Newsweek*. "In defeat, Liston seemed as never before to have entered the human race."

At his own press conference, Clay showed compassion for the ex-champ. "You'd never think I'd end up feeling sorry for Sonny Liston, but I do," he said. "You built him up too big and now he has such a long way to fall." The speed with which Sonny plummeted to earth was something no one would have imagined.

CHAPTER TEN

IT WAS A VERY BAD YEAR

On their first trip back to Philadelphia, Sonny and Geraldine were invited to dinner again by Willie Reddish's ex-wife. Willie Jr. remembers that the mood that night was understandably somber. Nevertheless, his mother couldn't resist the opportunity to take a dig at her ex-husband by reminding him of something he had bragged about at one of their previous dinners. "Well," she said rather matter-of-factly. "I guess they found that gorilla, didn't they?"

The rewriting of Liston's boxing history began almost immediately. "The reverends of the press have returned to their true gospel and are preaching hellfire and damnation for Sonny Liston, the sports world's favorite sinner," wrote the *Denver Post's* Harry Farrar, one of the few white sportswriters who ever defended the ex-champ. Calling Liston a crude lumbering oaf, Arthur Daley said Sonny's performance "showed unmistakably that he was the biggest hoax since the Cardiff Giant."

A *Sports Illustrated* article said Sonny "quit on his stool for reasons that will be found only in his strangely confused character." Referring to him as "the old hoodlum," Jimmy Cannon said Liston was "as dumb and helpless as a scarecrow on sticks." *Ring Magazine* said Liston was "by nature a lazy man," but stopped short of calling him shiftless. Some people suggested that Sonny should be barred from the ring for life.

Approximately 200 people greeted the Listons when they returned to

Denver, and Sonny was pleased by the welcome. Asked how he felt, he said, "Very fine," but they were the only words he spoke. As the crowd cheered him, Sonny and his wife walked to a taxicab that took them home and into seclusion. "I honestly think Sonny would bust out crying if he tried to talk to you fellows right now," his spokesman told the press. "He feels awfully bad."

Sonny was on the verge of feeling much, much worse. Even his good friend Joe Louis criticized him for letting the fight end the way it did. Louis thought Sonny should have gone to the center of the ring and fought as well as he could and that if anyone was going to stop the fight it should have been the referee or the ring doctor, rather than Liston's manager. Joe thought Sonny looked to be in decent shape but admitted that being in good shape and being in good fighting condition were two different things. "When you've been going only one round and you find yourself in the sixth round, you've got to be in trouble, especially if you're having trouble with your shoulder," said Louis. "The doctors said it was a painful injury. When he got home his shoulder was swollen."

Florida State Attorney Richard Gerstein said Liston's failure to come out for the seventh round left him wondering if what he had seen happen actually did happen. He initiated an investigation of the fight to focus on Liston's injury, for which he enlisted the services of his office's medical/legal adviser and the Dade County Medical Examiner. A Florida state law provided for a prison term of up to ten years for anyone found to have fixed or thrown a boxing match.

The boxing commission in Sonny's home state of Colorado suspended him immediately after the bout. "I'm not gonna look at any medical examination and let that guide me wrongly on account of his being injured," said one commission member. A federal income tax lien of $868,000 was filed against the Listons and two other liens totaling $1.9 million were filed against Inter-Continental and DAMA. Ex-manager George Katz filed a $1.3 million breach of contract suit even though all he was legally entitled to was his 10 percent share of the two Patterson fights, or approximately $50,000.

After a meeting with the IRS, Sonny held an impromptu press conference. He admitted that he was out of shape for the fight and that living the high life of a champion had made him very complacent. Though he knew his left shoulder was injured prior to the fight, he decided to go through with it to avoid the bad publicity a postponement would have brought. After he aggravated the injury late in the first round, he said knocking Clay out was all he thought about. "I knew when the left went dead in the first round that I couldn't punch hard," he said. "He's just an average guy," Sonny told the *Denver Post*, "and most of all, has a lot of luck with him."

Losing his title sent Sonny into a bout of depression. Teddy King said March 9 was the first day he saw Sonny smile. "He came in and told me some jokes," said King. "The trouble with him is he needs something to do. All he does is sit around all day." Sonny's major daily activity had always been his training but his injured shoulder prevented him from doing any kind of physical activity.

Sonny's emotional rebound lasted all of a day. Early on March 10, the Listons were modeling hats at a charity fashion show. Just a few hours later, Sonny was arrested for driving 76 in a 30 mph residential zone and carrying a loaded .22 caliber revolver. The arresting officer was James Snider, who held the city's record of issuing more than 100 tickets in a single day. Sonny was accompanied by a young woman; Snider let drive her away in Liston's car. It took several police officers to put the handcuffs on Sonny, and they just barely fit around his wrists. Snider claimed Liston admitted to drinking half a bottle of vodka but felt Sonny could have passed a breathalyzer test had he agreed to take one. In late May, Liston pleaded no contest to a charge of carrying a revolver and was fined $300 and given a 30-day suspended sentence. He was fined another $300 after pleading guilty to speeding.

Four weeks after the bout, the results of Gerstein's investigation confirmed the findings of the eight doctors who had examined Sonny after the fight. "While Liston's injury is beyond doubt, there is also little doubt that he went into this fight with a sore or lame arm," stated the report. It also noted that none of the pre-fight information was imparted to the Miami Beach Boxing Commission. That means the commission chose not to mention the fact that they had turned down Sonny's request for an injury-related postponement. The investigation revealed no evidence that the fight had been fixed, and Gerstein's office found no fluctuation in the betting odds anywhere in the country. "Unless a substantial betting coup could result, there would seem to be no real motive to fix the outcome of a championship fight," Seymour Gelber wrote in his report to Gerstein.

Ash Resnick was prominently mentioned in Gerstein's report as a well-known gambler and bookmaker who had been barred from every horse racing track in south Florida. Ash claimed his main purpose for being in Florida was to make sure Sonny and his handlers followed an agreement to wear the Thunderbird Hotel's T-shirts. The report said Resnick enjoyed the full run of Liston's training camp, had been present in his dressing room prior to the fight, and had accompanied the ex-champ to the ring where he observed the fight from Sonny's corner.

Miami had been Resnick's holiday destination during most of the 1950s; he stayed at the Gulfstream in a bungalow next to the one rented by J. Edgar Hoover and Clyde Tolson. "I'd sit with him on the beach every day. We were family," said Resnick of Hoover. Several years later, Ash told Pete Hamill that Meyer Lansky was the man who "nailed Hoover." When asked what he meant, Resnick told Hamill that Lansky had pictures of Hoover and Colson having sex. According to Ash, Hoover's homosexuality was his Achilles' heel and the reason why the FBI never bothered any of Lansky's people.

Years later, Ash discussed the fight's outcome with me. He remembered that Sonny had ordered thousands of souvenir paper pads with his picture and signature on it prior to the fight, something a guy wouldn't do if he knew he was going to lose. "I always said if someone's going to throw a fight, it's gonna be for money," said Resnick. "What else is there?" Ash remembered that bookmakers were offering odds as high as 10 to 1 on Sonny by fight time. "They were betting Clay wouldn't show up for the fight. You know, if a fight is fixed, the price would go down. You couldn't bet on Ali. Nobody wanted him."

Ash had called his good friend and bookmaker Lem Banker the night before the fight to place a bet on Sonny. Lem told him that because of Clay's behavior at the weigh-in, the only bet on Liston he could accept was that the fight wouldn't go four rounds. Ash lost $10,000 on that four-round proposition. Lem told me he kept a piece of the bet for himself because he knew Sonny hadn't trained properly and that it would probably take him more than four rounds to catch Clay. Given their close relationship and Ash's connections, if Sonny was going to have thrown the fight, Resnick would have known about it.

Though he'd been cleared of throwing the fight, Sonny's first full month as an ex-champ ended even worse than it began. Michigan Senator Philip Hart's Subcommittee on Antitrust and Monopoly met to determine whether or not boxing should be placed under federal control. Senator Keating of California said it was essential for the committee to determine if Frankie Carbo had managed to place his underlings in both fighters' camps, even though he was in jail at the time. In its coverage of the hearings, *Time* misspelled Sonny's name as Listen—it's hard to believe that it wasn't done intentionally.

"I do not believe," said Senator Keating, "that with the possible exception of deaths in the ring, there has been another single occurrence that has contributed more to bringing professional boxing into widespread public disrepute than the Clay-Liston bout and the antics that both preceded and followed it." Keating was more disturbed by Ali's conversion to Islam than he was by the fight's outcome and he wasn't alone.

The pastor of Kentucky's largest Negro Baptist Church said the new champ was "not helping the soul of America." The president of the Louisville chapter of the NAACP said he hoped "Clay will shake himself out of this delusion, lest he ruin his chance to be a great champion." Senator Richard Russell of Georgia told the Senate that "Clay will now be subject to harassment, humiliation, and insults such as he has never experienced. He will pay for this. He will need a higher degree of courage than when he climbed in the ring with Liston." As far as I can tell, nobody asked Russell to amplify on his comments.

The hearing's first witness was Garland Cherry, Inter-Continental's attorney and corporate secretary. The Nilons had given him 5 percent of the company's stock in exchange for his handling virtually all of the company's business. He was grilled on the secret contract that Inter-Continental had signed with Clay. When the Louisville Sponsoring Group wanted $50,000 in training expenses, Cherry told them that in consideration for the extra money, Inter-Continental wanted the right to promote Clay's next fight. Told that it was a non-negotiable point, Clay's backers agreed to the provision.

"If there was any idea that Clay would actually win the fight, I am sure that $50,000 would have been $250,000," Cherry told the committee. "The remark that I heard from one of the individuals I was negotiating with on behalf of Clay at that time was, "We feel that this is his only day in the sun," indicating, of course, his own belief that he didn't think Clay could beat Liston. We felt the same way."

Cherry said Liston didn't know about the second contract and that Inter-Continental never explained to Sonny that he had no legal right to fight Clay again in the event the challenger won. He admitted that Inter-Continental had never convened a formal meeting of its board of directors and that Liston never sat in on any of the company's negotiations. What meetings they did have were informal, and Sonny and Sal Avena were always given waivers to sign. Cherry said he knew Liston well enough to appreciate that he couldn't understand legal matters and most financial transactions and that he was unable to protect himself in business dealings.

"My first meeting resulted in real confusion in trying to communicate with him," Cherry told Senator McClellan. "After that, Jack Nilon would say, 'Sonny, come over here,' and they'd walk out and go into an office and they would talk. Apparently he could communicate with Sonny." Cherry conceded that Liston's final source of counsel and guidance in his negotiations with Inter-Continental was almost always his manager. McClellan pointed out that meant Sonny looked to the brother of those with whom he was transacting business to get his counsel and protection.

Cherry maintained that he had never asked Jack about his relationship with Liston and said he first learned that Nilon had a contract to manage Sonny when Jack was asked about it at the recent IRS meeting. Bob Nilon would also testify that he didn't know about his brother's contract with Sonny until he heard about it at these hearings. Their statements were ridiculous on their face, and the Senators didn't believe them for a second. "It sounds to me like Liston was fleeced," said McClellan.

The next person to testify was Sonny's close friend Sam Margolis, who was represented by Sal Avena. Sonny had transferred 275 of his 500 shares in Inter-Continental to Margolis who, with Liston's permission, then transferred 50 of the shares to Avena as compensation for the legal help he had given the fighter. Sam's income from his ICP shares figured to be worth about $100,000 after taxes and he also stood to earn 22.5 percent of Inter-Continental's corporate profits for another six years should Liston regain and hold the title. With that in mind, McClellan tried to ascertain what consideration Sam had given Liston in return for his share of the company.

"Sonny and I had a verbal agreement that if I got him anything, half was mine," said Margolis, who claimed his cut of Liston's share in Inter-Continental was in consideration for getting Liston a piece of the promotion. McClellan called it one hell of a finder's fee, especially since Margolis had not helped in putting together the corporation in any way, shape, or form. Given Sam's close relationship with Frankie Carbo and Blinky Palermo, the committee believed that Margolis was merely fronting for one or both of them, a charge that Sam vociferously denied.

By the time Jack Nilon testified, he had already resigned as Liston's manager, though his inability to get along with Sonny was only one of his problems. Two weeks earlier, a New York grand jury had indicted a politician for lying about an attempted bribe. The grand jury said the politician had offered an unnamed state official $100,000 for approval to start a racetrack and that Nilon had given the politician the money to get the concession rights at the new track.

The attorney for Clay's Louisville Sponsoring Group was the next to testify. Gordon Davidson said he had recently proposed to Garland Cherry that they sign a new contract with the same terms, but with Liston's and Margolis' interests eliminated. When asked why he had requested such a change, Davidson said it was because his clients didn't want to appear before this committee again. "I think that in actual fact the way things look now, Clay will not fight Liston as the first challenger," said Davidson, whose group had talked with Inter-Continental that very morning about a fight against Doug Jones and other contenders.

The fight's gross was close to the $4.8 million of the first Liston-Patterson match. After the 50 percent share of the closed-circuit revenues was given to the exhibitors, and TNT took their closed-circuit fee, Inter-Continental's 37.5 percent share would amount to around $875,000. Sonny's 22.5 percent share of ICP's income would have come to about $200,000. Based on Cherry's figures, Liston's 40 percent of the fight revenues was a little over $900,000, out of which Reddish would get his 10 percent trainer's share and Jack Nilon would get the one-third stipulated in his written contract. That would give Liston another $510,000 and make his total earnings a little north of $700,000.

However, Geraldine would later claim and co-promoter Chris Dundee would assert as well that Sonny never received anything from the live gate. A lawsuit filed by ICP to collect the $625,000 guarantee from Bill MacDonald was dismissed following MacDonald's death in 1966. That meant Liston was deprived of a chunk of both his champion's purse and Inter-Continental revenues. Plus, Ali's financially savvy backers would have made sure he was paid his 22.5 percent of the live gate, thus further reducing ICP's take.

The bout had been a fiasco of epic proportions for Sonny. He had been fooled by a boxer young enough to be his own son into thinking that he couldn't possibly lose the fight and he had been manipulated by his manager and business partners into believing that he was getting the best deal any fighter ever got. It was a worst-case scenario for Liston on both counts.

By the end of the hearings several Senators were incensed by what they had learned. They had been provided with what one of them termed a "shocking illustration of how a championship fighter, unversed in the ways of business and finance, can fall prey to the very persons who pretend to be his friends and his intimate advisers." In Liston's case, he had escaped the mob's fire by jumping into the Nilons' frying pan. "All they do is keep the money and send you to the poor house," Sonny said of managers. "Great friends."

This kind of managerial treatment plagued Liston throughout his career. "Sonny always had bad management," Ash Resnick told me. "What the hell, the Nilons just loused him around like most managers did." But it didn't have to be that way. Sonny Liston was a man of principle, integrity, and an unshakable sense of fairness and one need only have treated him with respect to bring out the best in him. My guess is that any manager could have operated on a handshake with Sonny and probably received 20 or 25 percent of his purses without a written agreement, along with Liston's undying respect and loyalty. Even at 25 percent, the manager would have been overpaid.

The traditional manager's share has been one-third of a fighter's earnings, though a 50/50 split has been more common than you can imagine. In truth, you'd be hardpressed to find more than a handful of boxing managers who weren't grossly overpaid for their efforts. Anyone with a grasp of fundamental business principles and a working knowledge of boxing promotion could do as good a job of managing a fighter as someone who spent his entire life in the sport. Managing a champion, particularly a dominant one like Liston, is the easiest job of all because of the leverage that is built into it.

Each month brought more bad news and humiliations. In April, ABC Sports aired the closed circuit telecast of the Liston-Clay fight and 20 million viewers got to relive Sonny's nightmare. Later that month, the government agreed to release the liens against corporations set up by the Nilon brothers and said its tax interest would be protected by the $868,000 lien against the Listons.

Using Sonny's March 10 traffic arrest as a pretext, the World Boxing Association's executive committee voted unanimously to drop Liston from its ratings, the first time in the 45-year history of official ring ratings that a former heavyweight champion had been unranked immediately after losing his title. WBA President Ed Lassman said his group might reinstate Sonny if he "behaved himself" for several months. Lassman also tried, unsuccessfully, to get the executive committee to withdraw recognition of Ali because of his "detrimental" behavior since becoming champion—i.e., his conversion to Islam.

Politics aside, everyone knew that Ali and Liston had to fight again. When Ernie Terrell beat Eddie Machen for the vacant WBA title, the live gate was just

$47,000 and less than 2,000 people at nine theaters across the country attended the closed-circuit telecast. "There are no other worthwhile heavyweights around," wrote *SI*'s Robert H. Boyle. "What fighters Clay has not beaten, Liston has demolished. They have no one but each other."

Inter-Continental entered into another agreement with the Louisville Sponsoring Group and without Sonny's knowledge, paid Ali $90,000 for the right to promote his next fight in the event he beat Liston in the rematch. It meant that Sonny now owned 22.5 percent of a promotional company that was betting he would lose.

At their July convention, the WBA formally voted to strip Ali of his title. "This borders on the ridiculous, to have to take a man's title with a fountain pen," said Archie Moore. "I would say it's almost as hard to come by a title as it is to be President of the United States." One of the many bigoted WBA members said, "Let's put Liston back where he belongs, in the gutter." A delegate from North Carolina said the colored gentleman who worked in the locker room of his country club told him that Liston was a disgrace to his race and he got the man's permission to use the quote at the convention.

In truth, the WBA was a self-appointed joke of an organization. It was basically the old National Boxing Association reconfigured with a few representatives of foreign commissions. Many of the 37 member states were staffed by people who knew nothing about boxing. The WBA was so pathetic that it seriously deliberated the issue of who to pick as heavyweight wrestling champion of the world.

Spokesmen for both fighters said they would stage the rematch with or without WBA approval but the problem was that no city seemed to want the bout. Ash Resnick hoped to promote the rematch in Las Vegas and told the city's 11-member hotel association that Vegas could have the fight if they would each buy a certain amount of tickets to ensure the live gate. At the time, all association votes needed unanimous approval, and two of the hotels objected after considerable pressure was applied to them by Athletic Commission chair Art Lurie. "I haven't seen Liston on any Wheaties boxes, or Mr. Clay either," said Lurie. "I know when I was a kid I could look at a cereal box and see my heroes."

Finally, at the urging of some of the Nilons' most influential friends, Governor Endicott Peabody of Massachusetts said his state would host the bout. However, there would be no $500,000 live-gate guarantee that the promoters had sought. In fact, there would be no live guarantee at all. The bout would be co-promoted with Sam Silverman and would pay each fighter 30 percent of all net revenues. Tickets would sell for $10 to a high of only $50, a far cry from Miami where $50 got you only the fifth most expensive ticket.

On September 14, contracts were signed for a November 16 rematch at the Boston Garden and Ali became the first and only fighter in history to sign a contract using two different names. Throughout the proceedings, Ali criticized the press for continuing to call him by his slave name. "Let's get this understood right now," he told reporters. "My name is Muhammad Ali. It's not Cassius Clay." Still, much of the nation's press would continue to call him Clay for years. They also demeaned him by calling him Cassius XYZ and Gassy Cassy.

Ali's face was puffy from all the weight he had gained. He was also suffering from a bad cold and for once was more subdued than a relaxed and amiable Liston. Before the signing, the two fighters engaged in what may be their longest recorded conversation.

> *Ali*: "If I get beat I'm gonna retire."
> *Liston*: "He says he gonna hang up the gloves? He can start drivin' the nail right now. He should be arrested for impersonatin' a prizefighter."
> *Ali*: "What was he impersonatin' in Miami Beach?"
> *Liston*: "The WBA should be investigated."
> *Ali*: "Who gonna investigate them?"
> *Liston*: "Same people always investigatin' me."
> Sonny was asked why Ali was frowning.
> *Liston*: "He knows what he's in for" (Ali dropped his head to his chest and began to snore.) "He's getting' used to doin' that."
> *Ali*: "No, I don't say I'm the greatest any more. That wouldn't be right. I'm humble. But I'm still the most colorfullest. You gotta call me Muhammad Ali because the messenger of God, Elijah Muhammad, gave me that name."
> *Liston*: "I'm not fightin' no Alla Molly. I met him as Cassius Clay and that's the way I'm gonna leave him."
> *Ali*: "He just don't understand."

If anyone other than Liston had butchered his name like that, Ali would have gone nuclear.

Muhammad expected a much tougher fight but reminded reporters that boxing was a sport for young men. "How old is Liston? Well, I hear he's pushing 40," said the champ. "He ain't physically capable of forcing a body that old through four and a half months of the strong training a fighter would need to meet a young, strong fighter like me." The champ would seem to have been stating the obvious but Archie Moore believed that if Sonny pushed himself in training, the fight wouldn't last more than five rounds. "This man has a depth of fighting potential that is astounding," said Archie. "I would say here and now that Liston has much more to work with than Clay, despite the fact that he lost to Clay. And despite the fact that he is older. You see, Liston has an amazing amount of energy, and Clay has an unusual amazing amount of energy. But Liston is, we'll say, five times more durable than Clay when it comes to absorbing punishment when it is meted out."

The oddsmakers agreed and installed Sonny as a 13-5 favorite, making Ali an even bigger underdog than Patterson was when Floyd defended his title against Liston. The betting community knew Sonny had fought angry and injured in Miami and had hardly trained for the fight. They knew he was a lot older than he said he was, but they also knew what he was capable of doing.

Sonny trained at an American Legion post in a very rough area of Denver called Five Points, where people could watch his workout for 98 cents. Father Murphy said no respectable woman would visit that gym, and a black police officer said, "I would not advise a Caucasion to go down there at night." One local reporter told Mark Kram that as far as the Denver newspapers were concerned, Sonny didn't even exist.

The ex-champ jumped rope to Lionel Hampton's *"Railroad Number One."* *"Night Train"* had been banished, as was almost everything that was associated with the Miami Beach debacle. Ash Resnick said Sonny got rid of almost everybody. Willie Reddish, Teddy King, and Archie Pirolli were all that remained of what had been a large inner circle when he was champ. An important newcomer to his crew was Sergeant Stanley Zimmering, an unpaid friend of Sonny's who held a second degree black belt in judo and was on leave from the Air Force. Liston spent three months at Zimmering's martial arts club in south Denver where they worked on a regimen of conditioning exercises aimed at strengthening and repairing his left shoulder and upper arm. Before he left Denver, Sonny said his left shoulder was now fully healed.

Reddish was threatened by Sonny's relationship with Zimmering, and with good reason. Liston and his wife felt either his trainer or his manager should have gotten the Miami fight postponed because of the shoulder injury. "Willie trained Charles to be a killer and not to pace himself," added Gerry. "Willie wouldn't let anybody else do anything." She said Reddish had trained her husband as though he were the same age as Clay. She would have preferred for Joe Polino to have trained her Charles.

"I don't know what Zimmering is doing," said Willie. "Exercises, walks, I guess it don't do Sonny any harm or any good. He likes Zimmering. He wants Zimmering. I go along with the program… I don't hang around with him. I don't pal with him. I don't want to lose that edge of respect he has for his trainer, so I can tell him what to do. I'm all business with him. But I think about the fight. I always think about the fight. I want that load off me, then I can breathe."

Father Murphy said Sonny would sometimes drop by just to talk but not about Ali or fighting. He found the ex-champ to be a hurt, humiliated, and lonely man and could sense a difference in him and in the way he felt about the rematch. Mark Kram noticed it too and said it "permeated Liston's camp. You could feel it and it made you wonder what kind of man will be facing Clay this second time."

You could tell what losing the title meant to Sonny by the looks he gave Al Braverman whenever he introduced him as *former* heavyweight champion of the world at his public workouts. Right after he became champ Sonny told Reddish he didn't feel any different but that changed after a while. "He realizes now what it meant, and he wants it back," said Reddish. The fact was that Sonny wasn't nearly as happy about winning the title as he was unhappy about losing it. He was bitter but not bitter enough to lose his head as he had in Miami Beach. "When I catch him, you'll know I'm bitter," he said. Sonny had lived with that feeling since losing his title. He said he was taking it out on the world in general and wasn't any good to anybody, including himself and his wife. "It was the lonliness and disappointment," he said.

Strategic planning was now part of Sonny's training routine and it underscored his new-found dedication. He knew he had fought a stupid fight by running after Clay. "I guess I just stopped thinking," he said. Liston trained harder for the rematch than for any of his previous fights. As if doing his roadwork in the high altitude hills of Denver wasn't difficult enough, Sonny did it wearing a backpack filled with bricks. He also spent a week in the woods chopping down trees.

Liston would box more than 170 rounds preparing for this bout, almost twice his total for the first fight. His workouts included 6 rounds of sparring, 6 minutes on the big bag, 9 minutes on the speed bag, and 9 uninterrupted minutes jumping rope. "Ain't no playin' this time," said Sonny. He was being trained for a 15-round fight and Zimmering said he'd be able to go 30 rounds by the time they got to Boston. This time Sonny would fight *his* fight, just as he had against everyone except Machen and Clay. One solid left hook is all it would take to unleash the killer in him, and Ali knew it. "I face reality," Muhammad admitted. "I may not sound human, but behind closed doors I worry and pray."

When Sonny set up camp in Plymouth, Massachusetts, two undercover agents from the Boston DA's office were on hand to watch for any indication that something might be wrong with the upcoming fight. A spokesman for the Plymouth Chamber of Commerce described Liston as a terrific asset for the town. "He's an awfully nice person," said Chamber member, Beverly Barr. "A person can't help but feel a warm rapport with him." The ex-champ welcomed children of all ages to his training quarters, smiling at them before and after his workouts and giving out autographs. There was a noticeable change in Sonny's demeanor; people said his glare was far less intimidating than it used to be.

For the first time, Sonny bared his feelings when asked what was important to him. "Just the title, just that championship, that's all there is in this world. That title—my title—is there and I'm going to get it and I'm going to keep it a long time. And I'm going to like it and with it I won't be lonely…You'll never know what it's like, I hope. One day you are the king. Your friends, or the guys you think are your friends, are all around you. They give you, 'Yes, champ; no, champ; you got no worries, champ. No one in this whole world can beat you, champ.' Then all of a sudden you're not the champ and you are alone. The guys with the big mouths are out talking about you, not to you, and what they say isn't what they said the day before. It's a big price to pay." Sonny smiled and said he looked forward to seeing which guys from the old crowd would have the gall to come around again after he regained the title.

Archie Pirolli referred to Sonny's sparring partners as his shock absorbers. Getting them to come to camp was still a major problem and keeping them was an even bigger one. In exchange for two, three-minute rounds each day, a brave man received $250 a week, all he could eat of some very good food, and a large, comfortable room with a view of Cape Cod Bay. In Miami, Sonny didn't feel the need to prove he could beat up his sparring partners, a mindset he believed had contributed to his defeat. But it was open season on these guys now.

After 35 very tough rounds, Amos Lincoln spit out a tooth and said, "This is a hell of a way to make a living. I wouldn't wanna be Clay." On October 26, Lee Williams became the third to quit in two days and the 10th since Liston began training. His trainers flew in Ed Green from Detroit and flew him back after one round of work—with eight stitches in his mouth. Two weeks prior to the fight, only two sparring partners remained in Liston's camp. Everybody in Liston's camp had grim looks on their faces.

Sonny expected to weigh between 209 and 212 pounds for the bout, which had always been his prime fighting weight. "Clay has to only make that one mistake Sonny needs," said Joe Louis, who knew Ali had a history of making mistakes against lesser opponents. Both Sonny Banks and Henry Cooper had floored him with left hooks. Doug Jones and Billy Daniels repeatedly showed that the young fighter could be tagged with right hand leads and Liston knew that Ali had been knocked down by a short right hand from one of his sparring partners. Amos Lincoln had sparred with Ali two years earlier and told Sonny he patiently waited for an opening and landed some pretty good right hands. "You can't go after him swinging all the time, because that's what he likes," echoed Willie Richardson who sparred with both fighters. "He would move around, dance in, hit you pop, pop, pop, dance out, make you miss...But I used to wait and wait and look for my shot, and I hit him pretty good." Willie was let go by Clay's camp after only four days because they didn't want a sparring partner showing up their fighter.

Sonny had studied the films of the first fight for hours and had seen something that would help him. He wouldn't talk about it but in one sparring session Liston landed three hard, right-hand leads, one of which knocked the helmet off his sparring partner's head. It was the kind of adjustment that Ali wouldn't have expected Sonny to be capable of making. "Liston always was a predictable fighter," said Cus D'Amato. "He isn't now. He's changed."

Zimmering compared Sonny's physical condition to a stick of dynamite that would be lit by the sound of the opening bell. Though never a fan of Sonny's, Howard Cosell said he had never seen him look so formidable and thought he would destroy Ali. *Time* said Sonny was in the best shape of his career and "the toughest looking 40-year-old (or so) around." The old man, as Ali would often call him, was prepared to show the world that he still had it. "He gets his mental attitude into condition, he'll win," said Louis.

The difference in the fighters' workouts was dictated by the huge disparity in their ages. Liston performed a series of exercises like whirling his arms in a circular motion and reversing the rotation, then twisting left and right and touching the floor. Ali warmed up by grabbing the ropes and doing a couple of knee bends. Liston punished the heavy punching bag for several minutes but Ali never even used it. While Sonny endured 20 or 25 medicine ball throws to his midsection, Ali would strengthen his abdominal muscles by lying on the ropes while a sparring partner hit him hundreds of times. Sonny maintained a serious, all-business demeanor throughout his workout and never changed his facial expression, even when sparring. Muhammad never seemed to be very serious while working out and rarely stopped talking, even during the one-minute rest period between rounds. Sonny welcomed children to the workouts, after which he would sign autographs for them with a smile. Youngsters were discouraged from attending Clay's workouts unless they had the $1 admission.

Less than a week before the fight, Sonny weighed 212 and said he could enter the ring at 208 or about 17 pounds less than he was when he entered the ring in Miami. Something quite different from the first fight was taking place. In a stunning turnaround, Liston was the more dedicated gym worker. This time it was Ali who was living the life of a champion and taking his opponent lightly. He had gotten married and gone on an 8,000 mile trip to Africa and the Middle East, where he was given what may have been the warmest reception a visiting American ever received. He had also eaten himself out of shape for the first time in his life and when he looked at his 245-pound body in the mirror, he saw Jackie Gleason. After getting his weight down to 217 Muhammad claimed it had been "health fat." Six months later, Angelo Dundee would readily admit that Ali was in much better shape for the Lewiston fight than he was in November for the originally scheduled rematch in Boston.

Bundini said the champ had grown into a man since the first fight and his main worry was that Ali would try too hard to prove that he was one. "The man apt to take too many chances trying to prove that, and he can't afford no chance-taking." Bundini said Ali had shown only one-quarter of the things he could do in Miami and though he was exaggerating by a factor of at least two, Sonny had displayed absolutely none of his talents in the first fight. Most national sportswriters, though, accepted Sonny's performance in Miami on its face. In Gilbert Rogin's final pre-fight story for *Sports Illustrated,* not a word was devoted to the real reasons behind Sonny's debacle, which were his injured left shoulder, his decision to fight angry, and his unwillingness to train.

Liston's physical was scheduled two hours before Ali's, but Muhammad showed up 30 minutes earlier to resume his campaign of harassment. Dragging a bear trap around, he barely missed being hit by a street car and tied up traffic by stopping drivers to ask if they had seen The Bear. "There's a bear loose and I gotta catch him," Ali told any motorist who would stop to listen. When Liston pulled up to the building, Ali and his entourage surrounded the car, shouting for Sonny to come out and be caught. Sonny was escorted inside by the state police, where one of the examining doctors estimated that Liston's age was "at least 45 no matter what he says." The doctor called Sonny a freak because his reflexes and physical condition were apparently as sharp as Ali's, despite the huge gap in their ages. When Liston drove away, Ali sprinted after his car.

Ali boasted that 1 billion people would be praying for him on the night of the fight, but conceded almost none of them would be in the Boston Garden. Muhammad mocked his opponent by telling reporters he was considering manufacturing Sonny Liston Sit-Down Stools. "They'll sell the canvas off Clay's back," Liston shot back. Ali also worried about a plot to somehow cheat him out of his title and talked of flying in 15 United Nations observers as insurance. "I expect dirty stuff," Ali said. "The referee, the judges, newspapermen, and everybody is against me. If I'm going to lose, it's going to be fair and square. So I'm going to have cameras on everyone and both corners and at ringside."

The two finest heavyweights ever to grace the squared circle were about to meet at a time when their physical and mental conditions were as closely aligned as they would ever be. The much older Liston was in the best fighting shape of his life and had never been hungrier or more motivated than he was for that bout. He was also an 11-9 favorite. Conversely, Ali was more confident than he should have been and much more dismissive of the threat Sonny posed than he could afford to be. But none of these things would matter because this fight would never take place.

By some accounts, Liston was a very superstitious man. He wouldn't train at the Dunes in Las Vegas because five fighters, including Patterson, had trained there and lost. He knocked on wood for luck, conscientiously avoided stepping on sidewalk cracks, and if someone ran around a pole during roadwork, Sonny made him go back to the other side. He would always touch or shake the hand of his trainer just prior to the opening bell, and his friends knew better than to throw a hat on a bed or sit on a trunk. So it's likely that Sonny approached every Friday the 13th with at least some trepidation. However, Friday, November 13, 1964, would be the cruelest day of his life.

Ali wanted to mark the occasion by delivering a sack of black cats to Liston's training camp but was talked out of the idea by his handlers. After running five miles in the morning, he cancelled his afternoon workout and went shopping for a new suit. Back in his hotel room Ali dropped a water glass that shattered on his bathroom floor. "I ain't superstitious," he said to Dundee, "but I wonder if that's a bad omen?" After eating a large meal of steak, spinach, potatoes, and a tossed salad prepared by three Muslim women cooks he had brought from Miami, Ali was watching *Little Caesar* on a projector when he was overcome by nausea and began to vomit. He had suffered an incarcerated inguinal hernia when a loop of his intestines popped through the wall of his abdominal muscles and into his scrotum, raising a lump the size of a lemon on his right groin. Ali had known about the hernia condition for four months and had scheduled an operation after the rematch.

Rudolph covered his brother's face with a towel and he and another man walked Ali's stretcher down the hotel corridor to a service elevator. The police arrived with an ambulance and took Ali to the emergency room of Boston City Hospital. Reporters were limited to the outer hallway of the hospital's fourth floor, where Muslims guarded every door, glaring at intruders. There were no other patients on that floor. "Keep away," said a minister of Boston's Muslim mosque. "Nobody goes through these doors; somebody get hurt if they try." A *Boston Herald* photographer was so intimidated by Ali's bodyguards that he took no pictures. Doctors said if Ali had been in the ring when the hernia occurred, he might have died. They speculated that Ali might be able to return to strenuous activity in three months and be able to fight again in six.

Sonny and Geraldine had just returned from a walk when Reddish and Harold Conrad gave them the news. Geraldine cried and Conrad remembered looking at Sonny and seeing a man get old right in front of his eyes. "I don't believe it," said Sonny. "That faggot. It's another one of his tricks." When the report was verified, Sonny said, "Shit, I worked hard for this fight. What a letdown." Liston said he wished the injury had happened earlier rather than after all the hard work was over. In response to a question, Sonny said he didn't plan to visit Ali before returning to Denver.

Sportsvision's president, Fred Brooks, estimated that $4.6 million in theater tickets would have been sold, and local promoter Sam Silverman said the Boston Garden would have sold out. "We took a bath, a bad bath," said Brooks. Win or lose, it would have been a great payday for Sonny and, as it turned out, almost twice what he would end up earning from the eventual rematch.

Lost to history is the fact that Ali's hernia altered the course of both men's lives and careers in major ways. Given Liston's physical and mental condition, it was better than even money that Ali's championship reign was about to end. Because of the depth of Sonny's bitterness, it may have ended very badly for the young man. Had their rematch taken place as scheduled, by the end of the first round the world would have seen that Sonny wasn't the same guy who stunk up the joint in Miami Beach. By the end of the second round, Ali would have known that he was fighting more for his life than he was for his title—because Liston was fighting for his entire future. It would have been the greatest boxing match of all time.

I'm not saying Ali couldn't have won that fight. What I am saying is that no one could have beaten Liston if he was in physical and mental shape. Sonny would have hurt Muhammad at some point in that 15-round fight and that would have unlocked the gates of boxing hell on this remarkable young man. The rematch in Boston could easily have been Ali's final fight; he was tough enough and young enough to absorb the kind of severe beating from which he may never have recovered.

Ali was one of a kind but Liston was the only one *of* his kind. No one is that tough in his '40s. No one is that tough, period. Unfortunately, the postponement changed everything for Liston, and changed it forever. In retrospect, a congenital defect common to every man started the clock ticking on the final 2,237 days of Sonny's life. It's not that much of a stretch to say that Ali's hernia may have saved his own life and that it probably killed Liston.

◇ ◇ ◇

Just before noon on Christmas Day, Sonny was arrested in Denver for driving under the influence. Three policemen stopped Liston's car outside the drive-in restaurant where Sonny and Richard Zephyr had eaten lunch. The arresting officers would later admit they left the drive-in and waited for Sonny to leave so they could confront him on a public street. Sonny objected to being questioned because he wasn't driving at the time he was stopped but the police claimed to have seen Liston and Zephyr change places in the car after they knew they were being watched.

Officer Donald Smith said Sonny was uncooperative and used abusive language. He and his partner put the fighter in a police car but they radioed for help when Sonny kept getting out. "It's Liston and we can't hold him!" shouted Smith. The call was answered by ten policemen in four cars, and Sonny was irritated by the department's show of force. Liston refused to ride to in a police car, and since all the officers were afraid to ride with him anyway (according to Smith), a patrol wagon arrived to take him to jail. Sonny wouldn't walk the line to measure his sobriety and talked Smith into walking it for him. Five hours after being wrestled into a cell he was released on a personal recognizance bond. "I wasn't drunk," the fighter said later. "They arrested me because I was Sonny Liston."

Geraldine was furious over the arrest. "Charles is no preacher," she said, "but all this to-do was over nothing. People getting killed and shot down and they put Charles' picture on the front page. That's stupid. They ought to be worrying about the world...You know what they said to him? They said, 'We don't want you here.'"

Geraldine told Jack Olsen that she drove Sonny's brown and yellow Cadillac to the drug store one night and by the time she turned the first corner, she noticed she was being followed by a police car. When the cops saw her get out of the car at the store, they immediately drove off. Sonny was rarely if ever out of the sight of Denver's cops; they had been gunning for him almost from the moment he moved there.

Liston's sparring partner Ray Schoeninger estimated that the former champ was stopped 100 times by the police, including 25 straight days. "Same two cops. They thought it was a big joke. It made me ashamed of being a Denver native." When Sonny drove *SI*'s Barbara LaFontaine on a tour of downtown Denver, she was watching the police car that they passed. "It had the good fortune not to climb the curb in spite of the two officers virtually hanging out the window to stare at Sonny," she wrote. At the time Liston was describing the city/county building to her as "the prettiest thing you ever saw when they decorate it at Christmas."

More than 200 spectators packed the courtroom where a jury of three men and three women sat for 12 hours before the prosecution rested its case at 10:15 p.m. Early the next morning Sonny took the stand and admitted to having two cups of eggnog and a bottle of beer three to four hours before being arrested, but denied he'd been driving under the influence of alcohol. He said he lost his temper because he was being arrested for drunk driving and he wasn't driving. He became angrier when the police just stood around talking until the photographers arrived. "The bigger the crowd got, the longer they waited," said Sonny. "Them lights from the camera was in my face."

After deliberating for 90 minutes, the jury found Liston not guilty. Sonny seemed surprised at the verdict and smiled when the jurors walked past him. A reporter asked Liston if the Denver police were trying to harass him in any way. "Like anything else, you can always find a bad apple," he said diplomatically. "I think they're jealous of a man riding around in a fine car." Actually, the criminal record of the Denver police department was a lot worse than Sonny's. A three-year police crime scandal had resulted in the convictions of 43 of 50 indicted officers. SI's Barbara La Fontaine wrote that by 1962 "it was *their* distinction to have been proved the most systematically corrupt police force in the history of this country."

Liston would soon leave Denver because of the continuing police harassment. He said the police really didn't bother him. "They just all want to be Eliot Ness," he said. Counting St. Louis and Philadelphia, Denver was the third major city whose police department had run him out of town, though St. Louis was the only one that threatened to kill him if he didn't leave.

La Fontaine's article on Sonny brought her to Hollywood, where the fighter was filming a scene for the movie *Harlow* in March of 1965. Prior to his shoot, Liston held a press conference arranged by Harold Conrad and La Fontaine saw firsthand the way the mainstream press treated Sonny.

> REPORTER: "You talk about your sparring partners being better."
> LISTON: "I got Amos Lincoln. He's 6 feet 3 and I got another one from Pittsburgh, he's 6 foot 3."
> REPORTER: "So they'll be something like Clay in style?"
> LISTON: "Much better."
> REPORTER: "Lincoln. He says that by the time he gets a chance at you, you'll be in jail."

After a brief silence, the reporter admitted he made the story up. "I didn't think Amos would say that," said Sonny. La Fontaine was particularly impressed by the sparring match Liston had with writers regarding his age. "It is difficult to convey the quality of the maliciousness of the last questions," wrote La Fontaine. "They were baiting Sonny, in a curiously spiteful, effeminate way; the word for it would be catty—if catty were strong enough."

CHAPTER ELEVEN

CAUGHT IN THE CROSSFIRE

The rematch was rescheduled for May 25 at the Boston Garden. To get there, Ali drove Big Red through the rural South to allow country folks an opportunity to see "the greatest man in the world in person." The trip was delayed when an axle on Big Red caught fire in North Carolina. "He's driving, poor boy," said Liston when he heard about the incident. "I hope he doesn't strain himself and get another hernia. I worry about that boy."

Sonny flew into Boston on May 2 accompanied by his wife, father-in-law, accountant, and assistant trainer. "I'm better now," Sonny said when he landed. "I feel better, I think better. I'm in better shape. Nothin's gonna bother me. Just go ahead with my work." When told that the fight was being investigated by Suffolk County District Attorney Garrett Byrne's office, Sonny said, "If they're talkin' about partners and managers, I got them. One person: my wife."

At 2:30 the following morning, somebody in Liston's motel sounded the fire bell. It was a false alarm but nobody could get back to sleep. "Sonny didn't say a thing, but you could see all this harassment was getting him down," said sparring partner Amos Lincoln. Lincoln also said the four days Sonny had been idle while traveling to Boston had thrown off his timing.

The town's police chief was at Sonny's first workout to enforce the law, which prohibited the charging of admission unless all participants were licensed and a doctor was present. When he learned that Liston and two of his sparring partners weren't licensed, and no doctor was there, the chief agreed to let Sonny continue the workout only after he returned the spectators' $1 admission. The chief said he'd check up daily on Liston's camp because he "wouldn't tolerate crime in Dedham."

Two undercover agents from Byrne's office were usually at Sonny's camp. Byrne wanted to enforce a state law that required the licensee to pay 5 percent of the television *and* broadcast rights to the state treasurer 24 hours before the fight, even though the fee had never been collected on any fight that had ever been televised out of Boston. Byrne also insisted that local promoter Sam Silverman had violated the law that forbade the loaning of licenses. Talk about selective prosecution. Byrne had been district attorney since 1952 and hadn't missed a big fight in years. During his term in office, many "foreign" corporations had done business in Massachusetts and every one of them paid a local promoter to run the show under his license. That promoter was often Silverman but Byrne had never made an issue of it until now.

When Byrne announced he would seek a temporary injunction against the fight, closed-circuit director Fred Brooks said the promoters were willing to post a bond of 5 percent of the television and broadcasting revenues 24 hours before the fight. That satisfied the boxing commission but not Byrne, who felt Inter-Continental could probably sue to get its money back after the bout. Byrne also said he could prove that state officials were paid off to bring the fight to Boston. It was now clear that Byrne was determined to run the fight out of Beantown.

Inter-Continental's main concern was the closed-circuit telecast, which would generate 90 percent of the fight's revenues. The president of Sportsvision assured people that the only thing in question was *where* the fight would take place and claimed they were prepared to stage the rematch on a barge in a Florida swamp if necessary. It didn't matter to the promoters whether there were 5,000 people watching in person, or just five, so long as the closed-circuit feed was working.

On May 5 the promoters gave Boston 24 hours to make its decision. In response, the local DA's office presented the court with a ten-page document that called the fight a public nuisance and sought to stop it. At the following day's court hearing, the promotion was represented by nine attorneys, including one for Inter-Continental, one for Silverman, five for Ali, and two for the Boston Garden. The judge instructed opposing counsel to come to court the following day prepared to make their arguments.

Sensing the inevitable, the promoters were faced with the task of finding a state that both wanted the bout and had a building available to stage it on May 25, a mere 20 days away. They flew to Cleveland but when the mayor's staff told them he didn't have time to meet with them, they placed an urgent call to Maine. Sam

Michael had called Inter-Continental a week earlier when he realized Boston was about to lose the fight. He suggested Lewiston, Maine, as a potential site but was told the possibility was remote. All of a sudden Lewiston became the last available option and on May 7, Michael and Inter-Continental met with Maine Boxing Commission officials to work out the details of the fight.

"He had to start at the bottom, really," said Michael's widow. "Everybody was so enthralled with the thing (that) everybody cooperated." Time was such an issue that Michael started selling tickets before they were printed. Inter-Continental guaranteed Sam $15,000 plus expenses in the same kind of borrowed license deal that drove the fight out of Boston. They also promised to let Michael co-promote Sonny's next bout if he regained the title. Without notifying Liston, Inter-Continental paid Ali an additional $50,000 for moving the fight from Boston to Lewiston.

The fight was 18 days away when Governor John Reed officially welcomed it to Maine and said it was one of the finest things that ever happened in his state. Reed had checked with Maine's attorney general and U.S. Attorney and was told that the Justice Department knew of no improprieties regarding the fight. Within 24 hours, even Lewiston's district attorney was asking the promoters if there was anything his office could do to help.

With a population of 41,000, Lewiston was Maine's second largest city owing to the population boom it enjoyed in the 19th century, when the high demand for textiles during the Civil War transformed Lewiston from a small village into a city with a strong industrial base. At one point, Lewiston produced one-fourth of America's textiles, but by the late 1950's its main industry had fallen on hard times. The city was the smallest to host a world heavyweight championship bout since Shelby, Montana, staged the Dempsey/Gibbons match in 1923.

The bout would be held at the Central Maine Civic Center, a small, cement-block hockey rink known as St. Dom's Arena. It would have been difficult to find a more unlikely venue for a heavyweight championship match. "It was just so unthinkable that one of the biggest sporting events ever was coming here," remembered the promoter's son, John Michael. "It was kind of like Disneyland (meets the) Twilight Zone." When Ali visited the site, he called it a disgrace.

Sonny's sparring partners were main event fighters Amos Lincoln and Willie Richardson. They were far better than the lighter ones Liston used for the Miami fight and they made Sonny work hard. In the past this would have been just what he needed but now as age was rapidly eroding his skills and endurance, those daily sessions took a lot out of the ex-champ. Liston admitted he'd never really quit training since the postponement. He actually ran 60 miles more for this fight than he had in preparation for the ill-fated November match. After running five miles in the morning, Sonny often had nothing left for the workout. "Experts in training tell me that nobody at Liston's age can get into tip-top condition twice within six months," said Ali.

Angelo Dundee had someone take pictures of Liston's sparring sessions, something that Ali's camp would never have permitted an opponent to do. Dundee thought that Sonny looked to be in good shape. "I'm just hoping he'll overwork," he said. Nobody in Sonny's camp seemed to understand that they couldn't work an old fighter like they could a young one. Dr. Ferdie Pacheco said the bodies of old fighters couldn't tolerate the rigors of training. "As an old man, your muscles can't take it," said Pacheco. "You overtrain and you're dead."

Some of Sonny's workouts were turned into special occasions. A Mother's Day reception was followed three days later by the Children's Hour, where a little deaf-mute named Kathy ran toward him. The few minutes Sonny held her demonstrated his profound love of children. After the workout, he asked Geraldine, "Where's my girl?" but was disappointed to learn that Kathy and her parents had already left. The onetime toughest man on the planet appeared to be close to tears. "She called me a Tiger," Liston told his wife. "Get her address. I want to see her again."

Sonny's spirits lifted when a 12-year-old came in and said: "Hi, champ. You look wonderful." Sonny returned the greeting, placed his huge hand on the kid's shoulder, and said, "Let's go and see how Betsy is." Betsy was a neighborhood horse; every afternoon all the kids would accompany Sonny to the stable, where they'd talk boxing. Sonny spent early evenings in a drugstore listening to "My Girl," played for him by teenagers who joked with him at the soda fountain. On his last night in Dedham, the teens gave him a gift and a card that read, "Win, lose or draw, you will always be our champ." Geraldine said it would be difficult for Sonny to leave because the locals treated him better than the people back home in Denver did. "He loves children, young animals, and everybody who's been nice to us. He's been so happy with the kids," she said. "But he knows he has to go. There's important things ahead, like getting that championship back. He's lonely and hurt without it. Little kids and those small animals help him get by."

Sonny was ordered to fly to Maine on Saturday, May 15 and accepted the order without complaining. He would have preferred not to change his training site this late in the game, especially after the negative effect the move from Denver to Boston had on his ring sharpness. Ali was given no such order and would come to Maine just two days before the fight, after all the hard training was over.

The Maine State Police escorted Sonny from the Lewiston–Auburn Airport to The Poland Spring Inn, one of the city's two hotels. The Inn was a deteriorating 171-year-old resort, where former heavyweight champs Gene Tunney and Jack Sharkey once trained. Former Presidents William Taft, Teddy Roosevelt, Woodrow Wilson, Warren Harding, and Calvin Coolidge had slept there but until recently no Jews ever had. The view from Sonny's window overlooked a cemetery; Angelo Dundee thought the inn looked like the house on the Munsters' television show.

The inn's owner, Saul Feldman, decided to host Sonny when one of the promoters told him that the ex-champ loved kids. Liston arrived at Poland Spring surrounded by his trainers and armed security guards. He looked so intimidating that nobody approached him until Feldman's daughter-in-law, Tudi, stepped forward to welcome the ex-champ. Sonny was holding a box of chocolates that hid the shock buzzer in his right hand. When Tudi shook Liston's hand she felt the shock, and Sonny laughed. The Feldman family joined the Listons for dinner almost every night. "I loved him," Tudi said later. "He was wonderful. You had to get to know him, though. He didn't let many people get to know him."

The only guests at the 100-room hotel were at Sonny's invitation, and four of them were priests. Jefferson City prison chaplains Father Stevens and Rev. Edward Schlattmann were joined by Father Murphy and Rev. James Moynihan of Denver. All four priests were as devoted to the ex-champ as he was to them. "He's not the kind of man who wants to hurt anybody except in the ring," said Schlattmann. "That's his business. If you knew Sonny as we do, you'd agree he isn't the man he's pictured to be."

When Saul Feldman heard that Ali was planning to raid Liston's camp, he borrowed two black bears from the state's game farm and tied them to posts outside the Poland Spring Inn. A guard was stationed at the front of the hotel at all times—not even close friends could get in without first being approved at the door. From 10 a.m. to 9 p.m. Liston was guarded by four local sheriff's deputies, and his own guards protected him the rest of the time. In the gym was a bird with a broken wing that Sonny found while running one morning. He immediately picked up the bird and cradled it in his hands as he jogged back to his training headquarters, where for the rest of the fighter's stay the bird feasted on worms and Poland Spring's famous, crystal-clear water.

Interacting with the community gave Liston a great deal of pleasure, and Tudi Feldman said he sought no publicity for it. Sonny toured the Androscoggin County Jail and gave autographs to anyone who wanted one. He visited a nursing home, where he talked with a 32-year-old patient who had been bedridden since birth and spent much of that afternoon talking with other patients. Then he addressed the children of the Poland Community School after being personally invited by Saul Feldman's grandson, Mike. Liston made an appearance in every classroom, answered questions, signed autographs, and distributed mimeographed copies of one of his hands to everyone. "Study hard and you'll be successful," Sonny told the kids, smiling all the while. He stressed the importance of being good to parents, teachers, neighbors, and the police, two of whom were with him at all times in Maine. "The police walk right with me, my friends," he said. "In Denver, they follow me all the time. This is the place for me."

Sam Silverman said he had never seen a fighter train harder than Liston. Assistant trainer Joe Polino said Sonny wanted to win more than any fighter he ever knew but worried that he might peak too soon. Sonny said he thought about the first fight during workouts and it motivated him to run farther and jump rope longer. He had played it light in Miami and knew he had no one to blame but himself for losing his title. "It was all my fault," he admitted. "I used the wrong sparring partners. I took time out for fishing instead of roadwork and I made the mistake of listening to some of the people around me who told me, 'Take it easy, Sonny, you can knock him out with your finger.'" The ex-champ said there was no doubt he would win the fight if he was in shape.

Sonny wanted to prove to everyone that the reason he didn't come out for the seventh round was because he was in so much pain that he couldn't throw his left hand. He knew the only way he could convince people of that was to win the rematch. "This time, the only way he will get me out of there is to kill me," he said. "I got to get to him. I let down a lot of people. I never realized how much I could hurt inside doing that."

Championship-caliber fighters rarely climb into the ring thinking they can't win. The exceptions include Michael Spinks, who looked like he knew he was doomed when he fought Tyson. Likewise Patterson, who was scared to death when he finally faced Liston. Three or four days prior to the match, Sonny apparently still believed he was going to win. He called Johnny Tocco and others in Las Vegas and told them to "load up on the fight cause I'm gonna kill that bum this time." Years later Tocco told his friend Tony Davi that Sonny wouldn't have told him to bet on him if the fight were fixed. Then again, timing is everything.

Ordinarily, the excitement of a heavyweight championship fight would be more than enough to produce a highly electric atmosphere, but this time a different kind of tension was building in the little town of Lewiston. UPI reported that Ali was thought to be a prime assassination target by Muslims who wanted to avenge the recent killing of Malcolm X; the story gained credibility every day. Ali had sided with Elijah Muhammad when he drove Malcolm from the Nation of Islam and it was believed by many that Malcolm's murder was carried out by supporters of the Nation's leader.

During Ali's first week in training camp, five FBI agents came to his hotel and told him they believed there was some truth to the rumors. They posted a 24-hour guard around him using a 12-man detail from the Chicopee, Massachusetts, police department. Two police cars followed Ali to the track each morning and wouldn't let him run until five officers checked the field to make sure no one was waiting to ambush him. "Every five or six hundred feet I saw a policeman with a rifle hiding in the bushes," said Ali. "When I went to the gym, plainclothesmen circulated through the crowd."

Four days before the fight, a group of police officers rushed to Ali's training camp after the NYPD told them that a group of Malcolm X's followers were "missing from their usual haunts" and could be on their way to Lewiston. Twelve policemen and plainclothes detectives were positioned throughout the audience at his workouts. Two New York detectives who had investigated Malcolm's death were assigned to Ali's camp and they carried pictures of several black nationalists. All black spectators were searched before being allowed to enter the gym. "I don't want Lewiston to go down in history as the place where the heavyweight champion was killed," said Joseph Farrand, Lewiston's chief of police.

Ali tried to mask his anxiety by saying he was afraid only of W.D. Fard, who founded the Muslim movement, and Elijah Muhammad, who led it. But he seemed genuinely worried when he asked reporters why the police hadn't already arrested the men. "Why not go and get them? It only takes three hours to get here from New York. The detectives around here got their names—they showed them to me. Why don't they hurry up and get them."

Realizing he had shown fear, Ali quickly said, "The hell with Malcolm's boys, whoever they are... I fear no one but Allah and he will protect me... If they shoot, the gun will explode in their hands, the bullets will turn. Allah will protect me." Banging the table as he talked, Ali told reporters he would walk to Maine to show that he feared no man. Ali was supposed to travel there by bus two days before the fight, but Dundee snuck his fighter out of town in the champ's new Cadillac a day earlier.

Ali was scared and some people thought he was as afraid of the Muslims as Liston was. Hours after Malcolm's death, Ali and his wife, Sonji, were having dinner at a restaurant when a fire broke out in their Chicago apartment. Firefighters said it was an accident but some people, including Sonji, thought the Muslims had sent a message designed to keep her husband in line. "The night of the day Malcolm X was murdered! It was too coincidental," she said.

Sugar Ray Robinson got a glimpse of Ali's fear of Muslims when the fighter was about to be drafted into the Army. "Elijah Muhammad told me that I can't go," he told Robinson. "I'm afraid, Ray, I'm really afraid." Sugar Ray asked Ali if he was afraid of going to jail or of what the Muslims might do to him if he didn't obey them, but he never got an answer to his question. "The kid was terrified," Robinson told Mark Kram. "I left him with tears in his eyes. If you ask me, he wasn't afraid of jail. He was scared of being killed by the Muslims. But I don't know for sure."

In Lewiston, Ali's bodyguards were everywhere. When Ali did his roadwork less than a quarter mile from the Maine Turnpike, a state trooper ordered him to stop. Ali handled the situation well but a short time later he responded angrily to a white reporter's question about the need for police protection. "The Negro has the fear put in him by your people," he said. "That's our biggest problem. But you people run the country and you should go out on the highway and stop anybody coming after me."

Sonny had armed guards around him at all times, and one of the guys on his staff was responsible for tasting his food. Like Ali, Liston also tried to hide his concern. "What's there for me to worry about?" he said to a reporter. "It's his life they're threatening, not mine." A couple of days later, though, you could see the toll the story was taking on Sonny when he asked *New York Times* writer Robert Lipsyte, "They're comin' to get him, not me, right?" Lipsyte believed Sonny was terrified by all of the rumors and it's likely that he was. Liston once said he was afraid only of crazy men, and Norman Mailer thought he was afraid of the Muslims because he couldn't understand them. But Sonny understood violence and knew from personal experience that crazy people could be counted on to do crazy things. Lewiston would be one drawn-out nightmare for the former champ.

Trying to be funny, the head of the closed-circuit firm said he could sell a million tickets if he could assure people of an assassination. His firm took out a three-day, $1 million life insurance policy on Ali to magnify the rumors. Jimmy Cannon's columns repeatedly referred to Muslims in the crowd at Liston's camp and, according to Cosell, the stories had murder-by-implication hanging in the air. The sports editor of the *Boston Globe* took out additional insurance on the lives of the paper's five reporters who would be ringside.

Ali tried to exploit Liston's fears while diverting attention from his own. "He's gonna be scared by this," he told *Newsday*'s Steve Cady. "It might be smoky in that arena and you couldn't see good. I'm gonna say, 'Sonny, I'm fast and you're slow. You might catch one of them bullets. Lemme knock you out so we can both get out of here.'" It was the kind of logic that would make a lot of sense to Liston. In truth, the two greatest heavyweights of all time were afraid for their lives.

Ali was also concerned that the mob might try to involve itself in the fight's outcome. He said he'd have five cameras taking pictures and several writers as witnesses just in case the mob tried something. "Talkin' about it, maybe I can prevent something from happening," said Ali. "But the game could get crooked… And I have lawmen as well as yours. That'll be the hottest arena ever, hotter than hell if anything happens to me." Nobody asked Ali who his lawmen were or what kind of hell he had in mind.

Three days before the fight, Jimmy Ellis landed a right cross to Ali's ribcage that stopped him in his tracks. "I know something is deeply bruised, if not broken," Ali said later. Since he had already boxed eight rounds, nobody thought anything was wrong when he said he was through for the day. Later, he rubbed alcohol and wintergreen on his ribs, which were so painful that it made him cry out when he pushed on them but he decided to keep the injury a secret to avoid another postponement. However, news of the incident quickly made its way to Liston's gym, where Sonny dismissed it as another one of Ali's tricks, primarily because he didn't think Ellis, a bulked-up middleweight, could hit very hard.

Later that day two Nation of Islam members had a brief conversation with Liston at his headquarters. Afterward, Sonny looked catatonic and became robotic in his sparring sessions. When Angelo Dundee went to watch Sonny train that day, he saw him get his feet tangled up when he tried to jump rope. The man once described as menace personified when he jumped rope now lacked the coordination to do the simplest and most repetitive of training exercises. Sonny was so unimpressive while sparring that a spectator turned to his friend and asked which of the two boxers Liston was. Sonny was miserable and had fallen into the kind of mood where he couldn't be reached by anyone. "It was very disappointing," his wife remembered. "The training was bad. It was wet. It was damp. And the little place where they were going to fight was terrible, you know, so Sonny was very disappointed and I guess he was just to the point that he'd say, 'Well, win or lose, forget it, you know.' He was in a very low spirit."

No one could remember such an absence of malice in Liston this close to a fight, and that should have been a tip-off of impending doom. Sonny's training regimen had always been timed to make sure he entered the ring at his physical and mental peak. He once said that he got so mean and short-tempered before a fight that sometimes he didn't even like himself. Before the second Cleveland Williams fight, he told a reporter, "I just came here to kill him. That's the way I feel when I get in the ring." This time, though, Liston's temperament lacked the malevolence that always used to accompany him into the ring.

Following his final workout, Sonny told reporters he wanted to work with kids when he retired from boxing. With an uncustomary display of emotion, he talked of setting up a nonprofit foundation to finance a sports center for kids in Denver. The sports center had been a dream of Sonny's since he visited there in 1961, and he talked about it a lot as the bout drew closer. "I want to build a skating rink with facilities for basketball and boxing. I'd give out trophies and things and help get the Golden Gloves back to its feet. Used to be a big thing, for kids, was the Golden Gloves. It seems to be dying out now…If I could work out a way to fight and give the proceeds to the thing I want to build, I'd do it. Trouble is, the government don't allow too much deduction and you got to have enough to live on. When I retire from boxing, I'd like to work with kids." When Sonny called his lawyer C. J. Murphy up to the table and asked him to comment on the plan, Murphy said it was feasible and they were working on it.

The day before the fight Sonny was served with a restraining order that would put a hold on his share of the live gate. The court order was sought by the Associated Booking Corp. of New York City, which claimed it was owed almost $70,000 because Liston failed to make four scheduled appearances in Great Britain when he cut short his European tour the previous fall. His sparring partner Amos Lincoln said was Sonny was quite upset about it.

Ash Resnick was in New York when Liston invited him to Maine and he arrived the day before the fight. Resnick took his dear friend Joe Louis aside and asked him how Sonny looked and if he should bet on him. "Ash, if you bet on Sonny, you're throwing your money away. They killed him in training. They worked him so hard, Ash, they killed him. He can't fight at all," Louis said in despair. Resnick bet on Sonny anyway and Ash's daughter, Dana, wasn't surprised that he did. "Loyalty was my dad's big thing and because Sonny was his friend, I can see him betting on Sonny even though Joe told him not to."

Joe Polino's fears that Sonny would peak too early had been confirmed. "Liston had been ready last week. He was at a fine edge, but he would not relax," said Joe. "I tried to hold him back, but he wouldn't listen. He kept going all out." Sonny was in his mid-40s, had trained continuously for almost a year, and though he tried mightily he couldn't get back into fighting shape following the November postponement.

"Anyone that old has to get moldy," said Bundini Brown. "We just get fresher. The wait for this fight gotta hurt Liston more than the champ." Bundini's sentiment was widely shared by people in the boxing community including Al Bolan, whose company handled the closed-circuit productions for several championship bouts. Bolan had discussed this point with many knowledgeable boxing people and he said they all agreed that Liston lost his chance to regain the championship when the match was postponed. Ali felt the same way.

"I have to circle him, taunt him, make him miss, get him tired," the champ told *Ring Magazine*. "I have to see that, not for a second, do I present a stationary target. I am not playing this bear man for a sucker. I am not going to forget the tactics which made me the champion… Another thing I learned at Miami Beach, Liston was not in shape. He figured he would belt me out fast and snided his training. I was in fine condition when I beat The Bear and I will be in similar shape when I beat him again. Granted that he got into great shape for the fight last (November.) Can he do it again?"

At Monday's noon weigh-in, police were positioned in and around the ring, in the aisles, at every entrance, outside the building, and at most of the roads leading to town. Because the Dominican Fathers (who owned the arena) would not allow working on Sunday, dozens of workers were still getting the arena ready for the following day's bout. Liston walked up the aisle toward the scales and was greeted with raucous cheers. AP writer Murray Rose thought Sonny looked to be at least 50 years old. Rose saw the same look in Liston's eyes that Jersey Joe Walcott had at the weigh-in of his second fight with Rocky Marciano, the one that Walcott was widely believed to have thrown in the first round. After waiting five minutes for Ali, Liston went back to his dressing room without ever changing his expression.

Ali finally arrived 20 minutes later to a chorus of boos from the 2,000 people who paid a dollar each to watch what they hoped would be another spectacle. Ali told Liston he had five guys outside waiting to take care of him. When Sonny said, "I'll take care of you myself," he appeared to be the intimidating, confident fighter that he always was. Ali leaned over Liston as he got off the scale and Sonny shoved him away and called him Clay. "Don't call me Clay!" snapped an angry Ali.

Both fighters assumed fighting stances and Liston smiled when the crowd yelled for him to hit Ali. His reaction was odd because Sonny never smiled at weigh-ins. It was standard operating procedure for Liston to put the fear of God into his opponent whenever they were face-to-face. Moreover, this was the kind of smile that one would use while joking around with friends. But this was the day of a heavyweight championship fight and Sonny never, *ever*, smiled at someone who he was going to destroy in a few hours. He might smile after a fight, but never before. Sonny was definitely out of sorts but if any of the writers noticed, they didn't think it was important enough to mention in their stories.

Ali left the building while his Muslim security team yelled at the crowd not to touch him. After the six-minute weigh-in, the arena was cleared and thoroughly searched from top to bottom by a New York City bomb squad.

How quickly and dramatically things had changed since the second Patterson fight just 22 months earlier. Back then Liston had every reason to believe that he would rule the sports world for as long as he chose to. Now, on his way back to his Poland Spring headquarters he must have been wondering how it could have all gone so terribly wrong. Losing his title and a lot of the respect he had so richly earned had tormented him and now he found himself in the middle of a dangerous situation over which he had absolutely no control. The assassination rumors surrounding Ali put the ex-champ in a state of despair unlike anything he had ever experienced. And it was about to get worse.

Around 3:00 p.m. on the day of the fight, Sonny sat down to eat his final pre-fight meal, at which time he received a phone call that ended with him slamming the phone down in anger. He pushed his plate away and when his handlers asked him what was wrong, Sonny just waved them off. His people knew something was up because Sonny let someone tape his hands, even though he had taped his own hands almost from the beginning of his career. The worst 15 months of his life were about to be punctuated by the worst hand any fighter was ever dealt.

◇ ◇ ◇

Ring Magazine's pre-fight editorial underscored the importance of this match. "It has got to be a hard, clean fight. It must not leave behind any unpleasant aromas," wrote Nat Fleischer. "The result of this fight must, most emphatically, merit the confidence and approbation of the public." If the rematch had taken place in November as planned, boxing would have gotten just what it needed—and a whole lot more. Because of Ali's hernia it didn't, and nobody could have possibly imagined what was in store for the already-damaged sport.

The mostly white crowd of 2,434 was the smallest live gate ever to witness a heavyweight championship bout. In spite of several hundred teenagers who got in with free tickets, there may have been more people outside of the arena than in it. Each fighter was expected to earn $550,000, which was $400,000 less than the pre-hernia estimates. The fact that Liston was a 7-5 favorite at fight time was an indication that his reputation was still intact.

Radio broadcasts took the fight into Australia, New Zealand, South America, Great Britain, Germany, Austria, and other countries in their native languages. For the first time, a major American sporting event was being telecast live in Britain, beginning at 3:30 a.m. via the new Early Bird satellite, and in Paris, where tickets sold for 60 cents each. After the fight, kinescopes and video tapes would be flown all over the world to be shown the next day in the Philippines, Kuwait, Nigeria, Sweden, and other countries. More people would see this fight than any bout in history.

Surrounded by state policemen, Ali entered the arena through a rear door singing "Let's Dance" at the top of his voice. A short time later Sonny arrived in jeans and a hooded sweatshirt, saying nothing and staring straight ahead.

Time reported a security force of 300, a ratio of one lawman for approximately every eight paying spectators. Police Chief Joseph Farrand announced he had nearly tripled his force for the fight. Supplementing the 72-man Lewiston police presence were State Police, State Parks Police, off-duty members of the Lewiston Fire Department, inspectors from the Maine Liquor Enforcement Commission, Sheriff's Deputies from various counties, police from nearby Auburn, the county's civil defense reserve unit, and members of the Shore Patrol. Each man was assigned to a detail and had a specific job.

The police guarded every door in the arena and law enforcement officials scanned the incoming crowd, as did Muslims from Boston and New York. Chief Farrand had 47 men stationed around the ring and permitted no one near it unless they had a special permit. He also set up an interrogation room on the premises in case anyone was arrested. As Farrand was explaining the list of precautions to a reporter, William Faversham emerged from the champion's dressing room and ran outside the arena. When he got back he was asked why he left and replied that Ali saw someone he didn't like.

Muslims took pictures of the policemen who were searching handbags, packages, and suitcases for concealed weapons. The mother of Lewiston's 24-year-old mayor was among those who were stopped and searched. Men were not being frisked but a Lewiston police officer said another detail was making checks on anyone who had suspicious bulges. The death threats against Ali had created a tension in St. Dom's Arena that was palpable and inescapable, and some boxing writers positioned bulletproof shields behind their ringside seats. "By fight time we had written ourselves into a high quiver," Robert Lipsyte remembered.

The arena was wholly unsuitable for an event of this magnitude. The sound check earlier in the day revealed that the acoustics were terrible. When Canadian-born Robert Goulet was rehearsing the "Star Spangled Banner" with the organist, the music couldn't be heard 20 feet away in an empty and quiet hall. That meant it would be extremely difficult if not impossible to hear a count, but nothing was done to fix the problem. The arena reminded Ruby Goldstein of the many times he had refereed bouts in small fight clubs where there were no amplification systems and the referee had to read the lips of the knockdown timekeeper. "It's not as easy as it sounds," said Goldstein.

The knockdown timekeeper was a 63-year-old retired printer who was inexperienced in this job, lacked a microphone, and sat in a position so cramped that he was unable to stand without difficulty. He and the official timekeeper had agreed to squeeze in a bit to give *Ring Magazine*'s Nat Fleischer enough of a surface to sit down because nobody had set up a chair for the Grand Old Man of boxing.

The fights on the undercard pitted the sparring partners from the fighters' camps. Only two sets of gloves were on hand, so when one bout ended, the fighters in the next match had to wait until the gloves were taken off and new laces put in so they could be used again. Huge klieg lights had been installed for the sake of the closed-circuit telecast, raising the ringside temperature to an oppressive 100 degrees. "It was so hot, it was just unbearable," Ash Resnick told me. He and Teddy Brenner walked away from ringside and sat in an an unfilled section in the balcony during the preliminary bouts.

Police officers surrounded the fighters as they made their way to the ring. Liston was accompanied by Willie Reddish, Teddy King, and Ash, and was greeted by a huge roar. The cigar smoke in the poorly ventilated building was suffocating—and there was nothing in the world that Sonny hated more than cigar smoke. As he waited for Ali, sweat dripped off his head and the blank expression on his face was startling for its absence of focus and malice.

"We're both villains," Ali had said. "So naturally, when we get in the ring, the people, they would prefer if it could happen for it to end in a double knockout because they don't want either one of us to win." Sure enough, the champ entered the ring greeted by cat-calls and boos. The crowd's reaction caused promoter Sam Michael to tell Jim Murray that he wouldn't have believed it possible that "this bum (Ali) has managed to make that bum (Liston) into a public hero."

Ali had replaced Liston as boxing's bad guy, something no one would have thought possible before the Miami fight. Actually, people didn't think any more highly of Sonny, they just considered him to be the lesser of two Negro evils. Ali believed he'd never get another shot at the title or perhaps even another fight if he lost. "I know the majority of the people—the press and the fans—want to see me get beat," he had said earlier. "I can feel it when I talk to them. They want to see how I'll look on the canvas."

Goulet had agreed to sing the national anthems of America and Canada but he had never sung the "Star Spangled Banner" before and only agreed to do it because he wanted to see the fight. Goulet and his wife, Carol Lawrence, flew to Maine with Ash and Marilyn Resnick and he told Marilyn how nervous he was, showing her the note cards on which he had written the lyrics. Marilyn tried to calm him by reminding him that he was a great singer and that this was just another performance. Goulet did his rehearsing the night before the fight, when he excused himself from Governor Reed's dinner table three times to practice on the porch. He lost his written lyrics somewhere between his car and the ring, which he entered in a near panic. "The fight lasted a minute and a half," Goulet said years after he screwed up the lyrics. "They blamed me, and I walked out of town a bum."

The third man in the ring was former heavyweight champ Jersey Joe Walcott, who was selected over several experienced and respected referees. Currently employed as the assistant director of Public Safety for the city of Camden, New Jersey, Walcott had been criticized for his failure to pick up the timekeeper's count when he refereed the 1961 Patterson-McNeeley fight. The truth was that Walcott had refereed far more matches involving wrestlers than boxers and his ineptitude was about to be exposed to the world. This would be the first heavyweight title fight in modern times in which the referee kept no scorecard.

Liston stood quietly and Ali shadow-boxed as the Maine Boxing Commission cleared the ring. "When I looked at that crowd around the ring, that big, dark crowd, it was on my mind that somebody might be out there aiming a rifle at me," Ali remembered. Young fans on one side of the arena began to yell at Ali. "You'd better bring your pillow, Clay," said one. "Who is the greatest? Sonny Liston!" yelled another.

When the weak-sounding bell rang, Ali rushed across the ring and landed a right to Sonny's head. For approximately 90 seconds, Liston tried to jab Ali, who backpedalled clockwise to stay away from Sonny's left hand. Ali never used his jab, even though Dundee told him it was the most important thing for him to do. As in the first fight, Liston was off-balance when he threw his punches. It looked as if he was in the middle of a sparring session and was simply going through the motions just to get in some work.

Halfway through the round, Liston threw a lazy left jab. He was inviting Ali to counter with a right hand and the champ obliged with a punch to Sonny's left cheekbone that appeared to travel five or six inches. The toughest man in the world tumbled to the canvas as if he were giving a safety demonstration on how to fall without hurting oneself. Liston landed on his gloves and knees and lurched forward. Then, in what looked like a separate motion, Sonny rolled onto his back. People started hollering "Fake" as soon as he hit the floor. "Get up. Get up and fight, you yellow bum. Nobody will believe this!" screamed Ali, who at that moment believed Sonny was making a fool out of him.

Frank McDonough started the count as soon as Liston went down, rather than waiting for Ali to go to a neutral corner as timekeepers are required to do.

"Walcott was looking at the crowd, not at me," McDonough said later. "What was wrong with him?" Jersey Joe had made the mistake of not locating where McDonough was sitting before the fight started, and since McDonough was a small man, he was difficult to spot over the ring apron. Ali refused to go to a neutral corner and Walcott's attempts at pulling him away from the center of the ring were painfully unassertive. When Ali began storming around the ring, Liston rolled onto his stomach, quickly lifted himself up to one knee, then keeled over as though he'd had too much to drink. He was a great fighter but a very, very bad actor.

McDonough kept counting until he reached 22, at which point Walcott, drawn by the voice of Nat Fleischer, came over to the timekeeper. "The bum is out. The fight is over. The fight is over!" shouted Fleischer. "The knockdown timekeeper has counted Liston out." Only the referee could count a fighter out but Walcott never even began the count. Fleischer knew this but was so appalled at what had happened that he took it upon himself to illegally stop the fight. Walcott was so flummoxed that he acquiesced. Worse still, he had turned his back on the combatants.

"The poor referee, Walcott, was so confused he did not even know the fight was over," said Jack Dempsey who, judging from his other comments, seemed to have been confused as well. Fleischer would later insist that he only called Walcott over because the timekeeper couldn't get his attention. "If that bum Clay had gone to a neutral corner instead of running around like a maniac, all the trouble would have been avoided," McDonough said, trying to cover his ass.

Ali had resumed fighting and Sonny was protecting his head with his arms when Walcott rejoined the proceedings. He pulled Ali away and raised his arm. The ex-champ dropped his hands to his sides and stood impassively, staring at the canvas. In his corner, Ali told his handlers, "He laid down," convinced that his short righthand punch could not possibly have knocked Liston down.

As Reddish cut off Liston's gloves, Sonny stared straight ahead, looking at no one. None of his cornermen said a word. They knew this was the end of the line and they couldn't get out of the ring fast enough. Cheered when he entered the ring, Sonny was jeered out of the arena, and Cosell saw a look of "absolute relief" on Liston's face. As for Ali, the crowd booed him even louder when he left the ring than when he had entered it. Many of the teenagers who had climbed in through the windows made their way to ringside and kept up a chant of "Fake, Fix" for 15 minutes following the fight.

The official time was announced as exactly one minute even though the fight was stopped at 2:11. For some reason, Maine officials adamantly refused to change the official time until several days later.

Barney Felix, Arthur Mercante, and Ruby Goldstein had been given ringside seats when they weren't chosen to referee the fight. All three had substantial championship experience and each insisted that the chaos in the ring would not have happened with an experienced referee. Goldstein liked Walcott and felt sorry for him but said he was against celebrity referees. "They don't work often enough, maybe once or twice a year. The big sin, of course, was Walcott's failure to get Clay to a neutral corner. I cannot imagine why Jersey Joe found this requisite beyond his ability."

Walcott said his major concern was that Ali might kick Liston in the head. "Clay was standing over Liston saying, 'C'mon, get up, get up.' The kid was all hepped-up and bouncing and jiggling and yelling at Sonny to get up. I can appreciate the guy's excitement. Few people ever experience it. I never did count. Guess I was a little excited, too. Sure, I could have manhandled him and got him to the corner quicker, but he's a temperamental type of guy, and I knew the pressure he was under. I was trying to get him back gently." When the Listons' attorney bumped into Jersey Joe on an elevator several months later, Walcott said he felt very badly about the whole thing.

Thinking he had hit Liston with a left jab and right cross, Ali joked that he hit so fast he missed the punch himself. Then he changed his story and said it was Jack Johnson's secret anchor punch that actor Stepin Fetchit had taught him. "It's a chop, so fast you can't see it," said Ali. "It's karate. It's got a twist to it. Just one does the job." Describing the punch as thunder and lightning from the heavens, Ali nevertheless admitted he didn't think he hit Liston so hard that he couldn't have gotten up. When asked why he didn't go to a neutral corner after Liston went down, Ali said, "I never have. I'm not used to going to a neutral corner."

Later that evening Ali called it a phantom punch. After the fight, Ali said the blow had the impact of two cars colliding at 50 miles an hour. A year later, Ali would say that the whole world blinked at the same second. By that time, Ali may have been the only person in America who felt the need to justify the fight's outcome.

Boxers will tell you that they know when they've delivered a telling blow because they can feel it. "I felt enough of him under my glove on that last hook to know it was a good enough punch to put any man down hard," Liston said after he knocked out Patterson to win the title. When Sonny knocked Albert Westphal cold with a right in 1961, he told reporters he knew the guy wouldn't get up the moment the punch landed. Ali experienced no such epiphany in Lewiston because as great a fighter as Muhammad was, he was never a puncher. He punched fast and accurately and though he could hurt you, the damage he inflicted was from the cumulative effect of raining punches on his opponent. "Ali would rub you out," Floyd Patterson told me. "He'd hit you 14,000 times and he wouldn't knock you out, he'd rub you out."

Ali's only other first-round knockout came in his fourth professional fight against a guy named Jimmy Robinson, so it's not surprising that a lot of boxing people had their doubts about the fight's outcome. "People have gone cross-eyed looking for that punch on film," wrote Mark Kram in *Ghosts of Manila*. "There is none unless you, in the interest of Ali's legend, desparately want to see one." Or, unless you want to look at Liston in the worst possible light.

"Give me a break!" said veteran trainer Eddie Futch. "Liston had taken the best punch that Cleveland Williams could throw, right on the chin, and nothing happened. Now, I can't see Ali knocking Liston down with anything. I saw it and I said, boy they got to be kidding. Ali wasn't a puncher. He wasn't a puncher, please believe me!" Ali validated Futch's statement six months later when he was accused of 'carrying' Patterson before stopping him in the 12th round. "Carrying him?" said Ali. "He took my best punches. My hands are swollen."

At ringside, Joe Louis conceded that Clay had landed a right "but it wasn't no good" and compared it to throwing corn flakes at a battleship. Though he was in the ring when it happened, Walcott said he couldn't visualize Liston being knocked out by a single punch. Henry Cooper said the punch was little more than a wrist movement; that Ali was off-balance when he threw it. "Clay was on his toes," echoed Louis. "You don't get that much power on your toes." Former heavyweight champ Jack Sharkey said the punch couldn't have cracked an egg and wouldn't have knocked out his grandson. *Time* wrote that Liston had been "pole-axed, or so it seemed, by a blow that Shirley Temple, in her prime, could have parried with a lollipop."

Patterson said Sonny had slipped badly since he fought him. "It's hard to believe that a man could go back so far so fast," said Floyd. Gene Tunney termed it the most offensive debasement of boxing he'd ever seen, and Jack Dempsey said a federally appointed commissoner was the only thing that could save the sport. "I said boxing was dead," lamented Rocky Marciano. "And I guess it's true." Because the hockey rink was owned by St. Dominic's Church, Jimmy Breslin joked that boxing had gotten itself a Catholic burial.

"Never before did I hear such anger, revulsion, and resentment expressed against any boxing contest," said Boston promoter Sam Silverman. Calling the bout shameful, a closed-circuit operator in San Antonio apologized to the attendees and donated the night's proceeds to a boys club.

Thirty minutes after the fight, Liston faced the press sitting on a training table wearing jeans, a sweat shirt, and work boots. "I didn't think he could hit that hard," said Sonny. "I couldn't pick up the count. I could have continued if I had picked up the count." He said he fell down because he was stunned and didn't get up because "I just lost my balance, I guess." Sonny pointed to his left cheekbone to show people where he got hit. When he said he'd like to fight Ali again, many in the press laughed derisively.

"I have to fight once more. I've got to build that gym," an emotional Sonny said a short time later. "I don't know how I'll do it, but I will. How can I explain it to the kids? I don't want a cent of the purse for me or my handlers. I want to build that gym so I can work with those kids who are in trouble and supposed to be no good. Who can teach them better?"

Geraldine was crying in a corner of the room when Sonny returned to his training quarters. "I'm glad you didn't get hurt," she said. "We've gone through 15 years of this. I've had enough of it." As tough as those 15 years were for Gerry, the last 15 hours had been sheer hell for her.

The following morning Robert Lipsyte found Liston in a friendly mood as he prepared to leave Lewiston. Only one photographer came to see him off, and Sonny obliged him by kissing his wife. Geraldine was savvy enough to know what the fight had done to his career and his legacy. "This one fight washed out all your victories and what you did," she said. "But you're still my champ."

Liston's trainer, Willie Reddish, flew home later that day and a sportswriter named Jim Hunt was sitting directly behind him. Hunt said he overheard Reddish talking to his traveling companion. "I knew the big bum wasn't going to fight much," Reddish reportedly said, "but I thought he'd have the decency not to go down the first time he got hit." After Sonny died, Amos Lincoln told Lem Banker that Liston wasn't hurt by the punch that knocked him down. "He definitely threw that fight," said Lem. "He never told me as much but I'm sure he did."

Nobody involved in boxing sincerely believed that a six-inch punch from Ali could fell a pillar of strength like Sonny Liston. Everyone knew Sonny threw the fight but nobody has ever known why. Nothing in the betting patterns indicated that the fight had been fixed. In Las Vegas, the only two bookmakers who took bets on the fight said there wasn't much action. "Nobody was interested in the fight. I didn't even go see it on TV," said one of the bookies, who claimed the betting odds moved only slightly during the final week. Ash Resnick said there was a little betting but not the kind of money that would affect the price.

"I don't think anybody could give Sonny money and say go in the tank," Ash said. "I think he was just too proud to do that." Liston's Teamsters friend Barney Baker was even more emphatic on that point. "If you ever dared approach him about fixing a fight, I think your burial would be the next day, baby. You better name your pallbearers." Given how well Baker and Resnick knew Liston, something extraordinary would have had to have taken place in order for Sonny to give the fight away.

A week before the fight, Sonny's motivation to win was strong because of his regret at having let so many people down in Miami. However, Sonny was always at his best when he entered the ring in a vicious mood, but that necessary edge on the night of the fight was conspicuous only by its absence. Ali insisted that if the fight had been fixed Liston would have waited more than one round to make it look good. That makes perfect sense but only if Sonny had thrown the fight for the traditional reasons of betting lines and money. Even then, Liston would have tried to give a more convincing performance than the one he delivered, so as to not bring heat on the person or persons who initiated the fix. But judging by the way Sonny went down and stayed down, he didn't care how it looked.

"Nobody really believed that it was a fair knockout—nobody did," Las Vegas casino mogul Morris Shenker told me. "For the life of me, I couldn't understand why he lost that second fight. He was so strong that it just didn't make sense." Shenker thought Sonny was either on drugs or had been intentionally drugged. "I always suspected that they doped him up ahead of time, and I've seen nothing since then that would change my mind." Shenker remembered there was suspicion at the time that Sonny might have been betrayed by one of his handlers, perhaps by contaminating his water bottle. "You know, it's very simple for your own cornermen to set you up and I don't think you have any loyalty there."

Barney Baker also believed drugs played a role in the fight's outcome. He said Sonny's bursitis had worsened significantly over the years and that he had been numbed by the drugs he constantly took to ease the pain in his left shoulder. "Using that stuff could just make you as weak as a cat," said Barney. "He was so loaded with this shit, a baby could have pushed him over. He carried pain. They never got rid of his problem."

Ali believed that the death threats swirling around him destroyed Liston. "He must have felt that somebody really planned to do some shooting," Ali wrote in his autobiography. "I believe while he was looking around at all those bulletproof shields, he thought if somebody was out to shoot me, I'd be dancing and moving so fast they wouldn't be able to get a target. That they might miss me and hit him."

That view makes sense, particularly when you look at Neil Leifer's photo of Liston on the canvas, lying on his back, arms over his head and knees raised. Liston was staring intently at an uncharacteristically ferocious-looking Ali, who was angry because he knew his punch could not possibly have sent Sonny to the canvas. If someone wanted to shoot Ali, Sonny had given the assassin a clear shot. Ironically, Liston's position on the canvas was very similar to that of Jack Johnson's when he threw his 1915 title fight to Jess Willard.

Assistant trainer Joe Polino claimed that the two Muslims who visited Sonny prior to the fight had threatened to kill him if he didn't take a dive. Sonny's young Irish friend Peter Keenan said Liston later told him the Muslims had pressed a revolver to his temple and told him he better not win the fight. The warring Muslim factions seemed intent on killing someone, and Sonny must have wondered how he had gotten himself into such a dangerous, no-win situation. "I don't have firsthand knowledge that they (Muslims) threatened him," said Bob Sheridan, a veteran television broadcaster, "but I do know firsthand that Sonny Liston was scared to death of them." A man who was in jail with Liston in the 1950s remembered that Sonny avoided Nation of Islam members even then.

Marilyn Resnick remembers being unable to contact Geraldine on the afternoon of the fight and told Martha Louis she was worried. "Don't you know why you haven't seen her?" said Joe's wife. "It's the Black Muslims. They have her and the boy. Sonny won't see them again if he doesn't lay down." The boy was Sonny's son, Bobby. "Maybe the Muslims were in the hotel room with Gerry and wouldn't let her answer the phone. I just couldn't get in touch with her," Marilyn told me. Geraldine was allowed to leave her room prior to the fight, but Bobby wasn't. "Gerry's attitude and demeanor had changed very noticeably, and Ash was worried," said Marilyn. "When I saw her, she looked like she had turned white."

Sonny's personal photographer, Paul Abdoo, was standing outside of Liston's dressing room prior to the bout when he saw two white gangster types walk in for a brief visit. "My father was under the impression that Sonny was coerced into not winning that fight," said Paul Abdoo Jr. Trainer Johnny Tocco was once quoted as saying that a day before the fight, St. Louis mobster John Vitale told him that the bout was going to last one round. Years later Tocco told his friend Tony Davi that he had confronted Sonny when he returned to Vegas. "What happened, Sonny? You didn't even get hit hard," said Tocco. "I threw it," replied Liston. "They made me throw it. They kidnapped the kid." Tocco told the same story to Gary Bates in a little greater detail. Bates was the best man at Tocco's second wedding and a pallbearer at his funeral. "Whatever Johnny Tocco said is the gospel," Bates told me, and most Las Vegas boxing people feel the same way. "Johnny said Liston was told, 'If Ali sits down, you lay on the mat. If Ali lies on the mat, you roll out of the ring.'"

It may have been that the mob knew about the kidnapping but didn't actually commit it, or that they were co-conspirators with the Muslims, who also wanted to make sure Ali's victory wouldn't be in doubt. The mob would have done it for the sake of betting; the Muslims would have done it to make sure Ali could not possibly lose his title. Threatening Sonny's kid was a sure-fire way to ensure his cooperation and silence. To this day Marilyn Resnick feels very bad about what happened to Liston and his family. "Sonny had his pride and for him to be swallowed up by people like that who took advantage of him and his wife and his children was horrible. He must have been burning inside and knew just how bad and how rotten they could be. He must have had a lot of torment in him."

Mark Kram was the only writer with whom Sonny ever talked about the outcome of the fight in Lewiston, and he did so on two occasions. "There weren't no fix up in Maine," Liston told Kram in the first of those conversations. "That phantom punch, it stun, that's all. I coulda got up. I just didn't want to…That guy (Ali) was crazy. I didn't want anything to do with him. And the Muslims were coming up. Who needed that? So I went down. I wasn't hit." Kram's second conversation about Lewiston took place in a Las Vegas casino shortly before Liston died. "Sheeeet, man," Sonny told Kram, "yeah, I sit down for that one. It weren't Clay. It was *them*. The Moooslems. I got word, inside stuff, they were going to kill me."

After the fight, Sonny visited his sister Alcora. Her oldest daughter, Helen, told me that she was standing close enough to hear their conversation. "What happened, Charles? He hardly hit you," said Alcora. "I can't tell you about it," he replied. Sonny saw no reason to tell the mother of 14 of his nieces and nephews that his son had been kidnapped. As far as Liston was concerned, the fewer people that knew about that, the better.

If sportswriters tell you that the fight in Lewiston was a legitimate knockout, it's because they want to remember Sonny in the worst possible light. If they sincerely believe it was a knockout, they're delusional.

Bills to ban boxing were immediately introduced in New York, Pennsylvania, California, and Massachusetts. In Washington, Senator John Tower of Texas called Sonny the nadir of boxing and said Congress had both the jurisdiction and the obligation to conduct an investigation of the sport. Five different Congressmen proposed legislation to put professional boxing under federal control and another round of Congressional hearings was held to consider the establishment of a Federal Boxing Commission. Among those who testified during the three days of hearings were seven Congressmen, five state boxing commissioners, four representatives of the Federal Communications Commission, two former heavyweight champs, and the son of a third.

The FBI investigated the fight for several months and instituted "discreet inquiries of highly confidential sources" in several large cities to determine if the bout had been fixed. Early in 1966 Hoover sent a confidential memo to FBI field offices in Denver, Boston, Chicago, Las Vegas, and New York. Though no evidence of a fix had been uncovered, Hoover directed the offices to continue contacting sources referenced in previous communications. He also turned down the Denver office's request to interview Liston personally. The FBI didn't officially end the investigation until June 27, 1966, more than 13 months after the fight. Most people had stopped thinking about it long before then.

When Sonny returned to Denver after defending his title in 1963 he was greeted by thousands of cheering fans and said it was the nicest thing that ever happened to him. This time the reception in Denver was non-existent and only a few reporters and television cameramen were on hand to witness his arrival. "Wife is Only Fan Liston Has Left" was the headline of one local newspaper. Sonny was disappointed at the turnout. "Everybody loves a winner," he said to Geraldine. "Ain't nobody got time for a loser."

Asked about the fight, Sonny said Ali's punch had connected, but singled out the timekeeper for not doing his job properly. He said he'd fight Ali again if given the opportunity, but admitted he'd take what he could get as far as fights were concerned. "I just have to take the bitter with the sweet," he said. "And I've had the sweet, too."

A reporter asked the Listons if they intended to stay in Denver, and Geraldine, holding her husband's hand close, answered. "Of course, we'll stay in Denver," she said indignantly. "Where else should we go? Someone wins and someone loses. Just because a man loses, that don't mean he's got to quit." As he carried his own luggage out of the airport, Sonny made one final heartfelt statement. "Let me say something for the record. I'm real sorry I lost. I'm very sorry I let down Denver and the people who believed in me." Sonny got a lot of nasty letters from people who were mad because they had bet on him. Geraldine answered every letter with a letter of her own and reminded people about the money they had won on Sonny's earlier fights.

Sonny endured an enormous amount of humiliation after the fight. "The very people who had been terrified of him now goaded and teased him from a safe distance," wrote Jack Olsen. Sportswriters were only too happy to accept the legitimacy of the outcome. They shredded Liston's character and reputation, and the tone of their stories was nothing short of venomous. It was as if every bad thing that was ever thought, said, or written about Sonny had suddenly been confirmed and the good things could finally be ignored, denied, or forgotten. If that big, ugly bear could be knocked out by a flick of the wrist from a man not known for his punching ability, they offered, then how good could that pathetic old sonny boy have been in the first place?

"It would appear that Boxing wants Liston to say goodbye and hide his gloves in a trunk," said *Ring Magazine*. Calling him Charley Boy, *Ring* claimed Liston never did boxing an iota of good and said he should be persona non grata as far as the sport was concerned. "At least the boxing racket is completely rid of the deflated orge, the unsavory Sonny Liston. That alone makes the Lewiston charade worthwhile," wrote Arthur Daley. "I believe it was a clean knockout of a man grown old and shaky," wrote Bud Collins in the *Boston Globe*, "but I cannot dismiss the possibility that once down, Sonny liked it there." *Newsweek* liked Collins' sarcasm so much that they used his quote to caption a picture in their post-fight story. They also quoted the *L.A. Herald-Examiner*'s sports editor Mel Durslag, who said Liston had succumbed "either from fright or from the natural ravages of age." *Time* called Sonny an overrated bum and a woozy old stiff. Mel Allen called the fight the worst mess in the history of sports.

Rather than covering the fight with one of its fine boxing writers like Mark Kram, Jack Olsen, Gilbert Rogin, or Robert Boyle, *Sports Illustrated* sent Tex Maule, a man often vilified by his colleagues for his mean-spiritedness. More people read *Sports Illustrated*'s account of the Lewiston match than any other publication; Maule took the opportunity to write Sonny's boxing obituary. Ali knocked out Liston "with a perfectly valid, stunning right-hand to the side of the head, and he won without benefit of a fix," wrote Tex in his opening sentence. He concluded his second sentence with "there is no shred of evidence or plausibility to support the suggestion that this was anything but an honest fight, as was the previous Clay-Liston fight." Near the end of his brief article he decreed that "the myth of the invincible Liston is thoroughly exploded now."

A month after the fight, Boston District Attorney Byrne was telling people that the stench of the contest still dilated his nostrils. In Maine, however, Governor John Reed defended the match as a legal knockout. With a straight face, he said one of his friends had seen the punch through his binoculars and thought it was a good one. Maine's attorney general and U.S. attorney said they had no plans to investigate the outcome of the fight.

The company that handled the closed-circuit telecast sold the film rights to ABC for its *Wide World of Sports* program. ABC ran the tape of the fight several times using stop-action and slow-motion techniques that highlighted the critical points in the bout. A superimposed clock revealed that Liston spent 17 1/3 seconds on the canvas and the program concluded that Liston had suffered a clean knockout. "We (*Sports Illustrated*) took the position that Clay really hit you," Olsen told Sonny two years later.

Liston was finished as a title contender after Lewiston, due less to his diminished skills than the fact that the boxing world wanted nothing more to do with him. When asked about the prospects of another Ali/Liston fight, Sportsvision's Fred Brooks said, "I think that is so remote that I haven't given it any thought. Unless Sonny Liston did something to redeem himself as a fighter, and I can't imagine what it would be, I can't see a third fight being very much of an attraction."

Properly motivated and trained, Sonny was still better than everyone except

Ali. Sonny said he was willing to fight anyone to get another shot at Ali, but the WBA suspended him and his license was revoked in every state in the country. The ex-champ now found himself in the position of having to leave the country if he wanted to fight. When Patterson lost his title to Liston, *Sports Illustrated* wrote that "the events of two minutes six seconds should not spell oblivion for any fighter, no matter how poor his showing." Neither *SI* nor anyone else felt the same way about Sonny.

Just before Thanksgiving, Liston filed suit against Inter-Continental—the corporation of which he was once President. He sought approximately $80,000 in monies owed him, including a $20,000 dividend that was paid to all ICP stockholders but him.

The 1965 holiday season was a very cruel one for Liston. One need only look at the previous two Christmases to see the incredible turnaround in his life. In 1963, the heavyweight champion of the world held a gala holiday party at his house for underprivileged children. In 1964, Sonny spent several hours of Christmas Day in a Denver police cell after being arrested on suspicion of drunk driving, even though he wasn't driving. On December 25, 1965, the Listons put their Denver home up for sale.

In stark contrast, Ali had begun an extended victory lap by fighting Patterson, Williams, and Folley (each of whom Liston had absolutely destroyed several years earlier). Apart from Ernie Terrell, Muhammad had inherited a division that had been decimated by the former champ. In light of his competition, Ali had no worries whatsoever, only easy money—and a lot of it. "He way up there now. Like an eagle," Sonny said to Mark Kram. "Where he gonna land, how he gonna land?"

PART THREE

TO LIVE AND DIE IN VEGAS

CHAPTER TWELVE

HOME AT LAST

Sonny visited Las Vegas for the first time in 1960 while trying to arrange a match. He returned two years later as champ and got $4,000 to referee a fight. Back then, Nevada had the highest crime rate in the country, and Las Vegas had a police force three times larger than other communities its size. Juvenile delinquency was two and a half times the national average, and the suicide rate was the highest of any city in the world and more than 15 times the national average. Gambling was such a major part of life in Nevada that the state prison at Carson City operated a casino for its inmates—along with a racing service that posted the odds before each race. Other than gambling, the state's largest income-producing profession was prostitution.

"Our attitude toward life, save under the most urgent provocation, is relaxed, tolerant, and mindful that if others are to go on their way unmolested, a man stands a chance of getting through the world himself with a minimum of irritation," said Governor Grant Sawyer. That philosophy suited Liston perfectly and Las Vegas qualified as an ideal place for Sonny to blend in and call home. Unfortunately, the city was only just beginning to emerge from a racist culture that could rival that of several Southern states.

Most blacks lived on the city's west side behind what they called the "Concrete Curtain," named for the railroad underpass that separated their community from the downtown commercial district. As late as 1962, Las Vegas was still off-limits to blacks except for entertainers and janitors. In the late 1950s Sammy Davis Jr. couldn't enter the Sands Hotel through the front door and couldn't eat in its restaurants. Though some of the hotels on the Strip let black performers stay in their hotels, most were told they weren't welcome in the restaurants or casinos.

Sonny was unhappy with the way blacks were treated in Vegas. "I'm not staying in any big-assed hotels that segregate," he told promoter Mel Greb. "I don't want to be sitting at one table and have my friends sitting at another." Geraldine, however, was bored to tears in Denver and convinced Sonny they should take a chance on Vegas, a place where she was never bored.

Ash Resnick had arranged for the Listons to buy Kirk Kerkorian's split-level, three-bedroom house for $50,000 cash. The house bordered the 16th tee of the Stardust golf course and was almost directly across the fairway from the Resnicks' home. The backyard had a 10x30-foot swimming pool along with a lot of playground equipment that the Kerkorians had installed. Geraldine moved into their new home at the end of March 1966 while her husband was in Anchorage, Alaska, for an April 2 exhibition at an army camp.

"I hadn't done anything in almost a year," he told Jack Olsen. "Hadn't even trained." After Lewiston, there was no reason for Sonny to step into a gym. He had been retired against his will. Even so, he weighed only 230 pounds with his clothes on and he walked as much as 20 or 30 miles a day.

The Listons still owned two houses in Denver. They planned to sell the one they had lived in and give the second one to Sonny's mother. They were renting out their Philadelphia home, and Gerry also owned her mother's house in St. Louis, which she planned on remodeling. The Listons were thinking of buying a couple of homes in Las Vegas and renting them out.

"Geraldine was madly in love with Sonny," said Marilyn Resnick. "After they got the house, I'd go over and she would ask my opinion on how to arrange the furniture and wanted to know how Kerkorian's wife, Jeannie, had furnished the bedrooms. She was thrilled with the house." The Resnicks' neighbors weren't nearly as happy. "Our neighbors started to treat us differently. All the other homeowners got together and held a meeting, upset that Ash had brought the 'first Negro family on this golf course.' They were upset with Ash and I and thought it was going to open the door for black families to move in and that Joe (Louis) would be coming any time. There no longer were the same friendly hellos."

That aside, someone described Las Vegas in the late 1960s as a place full of people who were fond of Sonny Liston. "I don't bother anybody and they don't bother me. It's really nice for us here. I gotta say that," said the ex-champ. Lem Banker said nobody cared about Sonny's past, and the town was lucky to have him.

Ash Resnick said Sonny loved living there and never had one bit of trouble with the police. In Las Vegas, most police officers liked and respected Sonny. "We had no reason to hate him," said a cop who was on the force back then. "Since we've lived here Sonny hasn't had a parking ticket, he hasn't even been stopped and he's never been followed," echoed Geraldine. She said Sonny was just as well behaved in Denver but the police followed him everywhere and harassed him so much that it was impossible for him to live a normal life.

Liston made a lot of great friends in Vegas, and almost everybody liked him and liked having him around. Las Vegas native Gary Bates met Sonny soon after the second Ali fight and became his sparring partner. Gary was a 21-year-old, 193 pound heavyweight at the time and described himself as a middle class, white, working guy. The two spent a lot of time together and when Gary dealt blackjack at the Frontier Hotel, Sonny would gamble at his table. Later on, Bates would be served up to the likes of Ken Norton, Ron Lyle, and Gerry Cooney when those fighters were on their way up. Now 66, Bates has been Senator Harry Reid's bodyguard for 36 years. He's never been a guy you'd want to mess with.

Sonny was often seen in public with a white girlfriend named Barbara Clark. Clark lived in an apartment building across the hall from Bates and his girlfriend. Bates had recently broken up with an ex-showgirl who came knocking on his door. "When I opened the door she stabbed me in the eye with a rat-tail comb and ran away," Gary told me. The comb just missed his eyeball but he bled profusely. Sonny happened to be standing in the hall at the time and brought Gary a towel. "Is she your girlfriend?" asked Sonny. When Gary nodded yes, Liston said, "Well, I'd quit that bitch." Two years later, Bates married her.

Gary later shared an apartment with Johnnie Hicks, the real life Lester Diamond who was Sharon Stone's pimp in the movie *Casino*. Bates once broke up a fight between Hicks and Lefty Rosenthal, the man played by Robert De Niro in that film. Five days after Gary moved out of the apartment, Hicks was murdered. The police department told Bates they had narrowed their investigation to 15 suspects.

Another one of Sonny's best friends in Las Vegas was referee Davey Pearl. Standing only 5 foot 4, Pearl was a no-nonsense guy in and out of the ring and commanded as much respect as any referee in the world. Pearl told me he came to be known as the conscience of Sonny Liston and said his friend never did a bad thing around him. Pearl didn't ask Sonny any questions and thought that was the reason they got along so well. "He was a good man," said Pearl. "I'm telling you, he had a heart of gold."

Davey remembered the time Sonny went to Henderson, Nevada, to guest-referee some boxing matches involving eight-and nine-year-old kids. "Now I'm going to show you how to really referee," Liston told Pearl as he climbed into the ring. At one point Sonny thought one kid was hitting the other kid too hard so he stopped the fight. The kid who lost ripped off one of his gloves and threw it at Liston's face. "Sonny loved kids. I'm telling you, he loved kids," Pearl chuckled. "But he was so hurt by that that, I could never get him back there to referee another fight."

Pearl did roadwork with Liston every morning and he said they never ran less than five miles every day, seven days a week. In the beginning 20 guys ran with them and most of them tried to get something out of Sonny. Generally, these guys would last about two days and never be seen again. Liston was initially suspicious of Pearl too, but soon began to trust him. "Once in a while he'd get hot and say things he shouldn't have said," said Davey. "I never took it from him. I'd walk away and I'd get lost and he'd come after me."

Lem Banker first met Sonny a couple of days before the Patterson rematch at a party at Ash Resnick's house. Sonny started going to Banker's health club, where Lem put him on a conditioning program. Banker became one of Liston's closest friends simply because he never tried to make any money off of him. Sonny got out of line a couple of times around him but he always calmed down fast. Lem said Sonny was really one of the guys and would talk about almost anything, except for the second Ali fight. "Even when you're good friends with someone, you don't ask him about his women troubles or his downfall," said Banker, who occasionally served as Liston's personal rabbi. Lem said whenever a fan asked Sonny about Lewiston, he'd always say three things went wrong—Robert Goulet forgot the words to the National Anthem, Jersey Joe Walcott lost track of the count, and he forgot to get up.

Sonny had learned to take things in stride. "I don't sit around thinkin' a whole lot," he said. "When you sit around and think about things, you get gray-headed. When you worry…I just don't. What's gonna be is gonna be." Sonny's income potential was a small fraction of what it had been and his friends, as he often said, were in his pocket. The problem was that there weren't enough of them, so Sonny agreed to three fights in Sweden for promoter Bertel Knuttsson, one of

Sweden's last promoters before that country banned boxing in 1970.

Sonny's inner circle now consisted of his new chief trainer, Joe Polino, assistant trainer, Nat Richardson, and sparring partner, Slim Jim Robinson. Willie Reddish went back to training amateur fighters with his son. The younger Reddish said his father never told him what precipitated the breakup, but Sonny and Geraldine both felt Willie's training regimen had played a major role in the outcome of the first Ali fight.

When the Listons landed in Sweden, one of Sonny's girlfriends showed up at the airport and told Sonny she had something for him, a three-year old boy named Danielle who he had fathered on his tour of Europe in the fall of 1963. The Listons began the process of adopting Danielle and brought him home to Las Vegas the following year. "They were so excited," Mrs. Resnick remembers. "I think Geraldine felt that getting Danielle would be good for their marriage."

The Listons lived very quietly during their stay and occasionally babysat for Knuttsson's son, Michael. Knuttsson said Sonny arrived in pretty bad shape but worked hard to regain his form. After scoring his second knockout, Sonny ran out of willing opponents and the third fight had to be put off indefinitely. "Nobody wanted to fight Charles," said Gerry. "The managers holler like a pig on a fence. The public say he's through, and they base it all on the Clay fights. But nobody wants to fight him, so he can't be too through." Nevertheless, when Liston returned to Sweden for two more fights in the spring of 1967, his financial situation was so bad that he had to refinance his Cadillac in order to make the trip, and Geraldine went back to work as a hostess.

When Sonny returned home, his prospects were bleak. "Charles got some money for the Lewiston fight but he has not been paid for the Miami Beach fight," said Geraldine. "It's lucky for us that we have been saving. If Charles had been one of those spendthrifts, we would be in a real bad way." According to Liston's tax returns, his adjusted gross income had declined precipitously from $562,651 in 1964, to $205,694 in 1965, to $19,180 in 1966. Less than three years removed from holding the most important and lucrative individual title in all of sports, Sonny Liston couldn't clear $20,000 a year in his chosen profession.

Ironically, Sonny's commercial appeal was greater as a humiliated ex-champ than it was as the heavyweight titleholder. This may have been because his asking price had dropped dramatically or because he was suddenly far more approachable than when he was the fiercest man alive. In the Monkees' first movie, *Head*, Sonny played himself. His scene was shot in the Olympic Auditorium in Los Angeles and he earned $5,000 for three days of work. In another movie, Sonny played a man who wreaked havoc on a gang of bikers. He also had a role on an episode of *Love, American Style* and played straight man to Andy Warhol in a now-famous commercial for Braniff Airlines.

Geraldine felt boxing was for the birds, especially since her husband had to fight so many people outside of the ring. She looked forward to the time when he would become a businessman and work with kids in his spare time. "I'd like to see him do anything he'd be happy at," she said. She claimed Sonny was prepared to go back to working construction or something similar if his comeback failed. Sonny had received a lot of business offers but all of them required him to put up his own money. "See, a name like Stan Musial means something all by itself, because he's a white athlete. And Arnold Palmer, he have it easy," said Geraldine. "But Sonny's name isn't worth anything unless he sweetens it with some money of his own."

By the spring of 1967, the two greatest boxers in the history of the heavyweight division were unable to fight anywhere in the United States. Ali's problem was that he had been convicted of draft evasion and was facing a five-year prison sentence. Sonny's problem was that he had looked really bad in losing a fight two years earlier.

The declining fortunes of Liston and Ali were apparent when radio producer Murray Woroner came up with the idea of having a computer determine the greatest heavyweight of all time. Woroner gathered the opinions of 250 boxing experts and writers to help him select the 16 tournament finalists; Sonny was not among them. The radio show was a commercial success but the results of the tournament were ludicrous.

The NCR-315 computer predicted that James Jeffries, who couldn't fight a lick, would decision Ali over 15 rounds and knock him down in the process. Ali was so incensed by the result that he sued Woroner for $1 million for defamation of character. Muhammad settled for $10,000, which he received by agreeing to participate in a filmed version of a match between Marciano and himself. Retired for 14 years, Rocky lost 50 pounds and wore a toupee for the filming. The computer had Marciano knocking Ali out in the 13th round. Of course, you really couldn't blame the computer because it was fed tainted opinions.

After the Lewiston bout, Liston and Ali saw each other many times. Their meetings weren't by design and were almost always friendly. "(Charles) and Clay will get together and they'll jam it up," said Geraldine in late 1966. She said Ali marveled at the success of the Listons' marriage. "You've been married 15 years, and I couldn't stay married a year," he said.

Publicist Harold Conrad invited Sonny to Houston in early 1967 for Ali's title defense against Ernie Terrell. "He wouldn't go unless I went with him," Lem Banker told me. Sonny and Lem were at the weigh-in when Ali walked over to Liston, hugged him, and said, "This is a REAL man!"

There was one time, though, when Ali and Liston were anything but friendly to each other. "Sonny, Leotis Martin and I were doing roadwork together," said sparring partner Gary Bates. "We were going west on a 10-foot-wide bridle path when we saw Ali and about eight other guys running east. We cross them—they're in the right lane—like two vehicles passing. It was really a tense situation and they wouldn't stop cussing. It was like motherfucker, motherfucker, motherfucker! There was a guy between the two of them and they couldn't get to each other. You could tell that they harbored animosity."

On July 12, 1967, Ali and Liston were both in Sacramento seeking licenses to fight in California. Sonny met boxing's first black promoter, Henry Winston, at those hearings. Winston was trying to organize an exhibition match for Ali at the Oakland Coliseum to raise money for the Southern Christian Leadership Conference (SCLC). Martin Luther King Jr. had already sent Winston a telegram accepting his invitation to appear at the fundraiser. It would have been a huge event, but the State Athletic Commission refused to sanction the bout.

"I had my little events with the athletic commission," said Winston. "I was the only guy of my complexion in the league at the time." Winston wanted Ali to defend his title against Wilt Chamberlain in the Houston Astrodome and, depending on your age, you may remember seeing Ali, Chamberlain and Howard Cosell talking about it one Saturday afternoon on *Wide World of Sports*. "Ali's manager Herbert Muhammad made it very difficult for me," said Winston. "They cut off my relationship with Ali because Herbert wanted all the control."

Winston used to seal his business deals with a handshake in a sport where you can have trouble even if you have a signed contract. If Winston had wanted to swim with sharks, the image of the black boxing promoter as we know it would be far different from what it is today. The engaging and likeable Henry Winston would have been one of the greatest ambassadors that boxing ever had. To a historian of the sport, his relationships with Liston, Foreman, and Ali are a veritable treasure trove because those guys are Top 5 Heavyweights. Sonny was the only one of the three who didn't treat Winston badly.

After the hearing, Bob Turley, the executive officer for the California Athletic Commission, wrote to the New York Athletic Commission asking for information about Sonny. Before the letter could even be mailed, a telegram arrived from Turley's New York counterpart, Edwin Dooley. "Read where you are considering licensing Liston. We suspended him here some time ago and do not contemplate ever licensing him again for obvious reasons," wrote Dooley. "We are of the opinion that it would be more than a calculated risk to issue Liston a license in this state should he apply for one."

Dooley and people like him were just full of crap. There were apparently two standards that they applied to boxers: one for Liston and one for everybody else. Unfortunately, Sonny had no one in his corner willing to go to bat for him. If he had, he might have prevailed because in those dark days of the late 1960s, Liston's detractors were promoting an indefensible position that they were able to get away with only because nobody challenged them.

Two weeks later, California denied Liston a license based solely on the information in New York's 1962 report on him. Lacking any current information, the commission stated that Sonny had not produced evidence that he had disassociated himself, financially and otherwise, from persons who had criminal records and reputations as underworld figures. Citing the biased, five-year-old report of another state's commission hardly rose to that level. Acting more like a military tribunal than a regulatory body, California claimed Liston lacked the character and general fitness that would be in the best interests of boxing and the public.

The specter of Sonny's underworld connections had been resurrected and used against him yet again. "Palermo's in (jail) for 15 years, Carbo for 25 or 30. They can see I'm not connected with those guys now," Sonny said angrily. "When they try you for murder, they got to produce a body. But nobody can produce anybody who is managing me except me. This is the only thing I know how to make money." Apart from being grossly unfair, it was absolutely ludicrous to keep bringing up Sonny's past associations. Apparently, it never occured to the commissioners to question why the underworld or any other ne'er do well would be interested in someone who could no longer make any significant money and whose best days were clearly behind him.

In 1968, Liston finally secured boxing licenses in Massachusetts, California, and Nevada, ending a nearly three-year banishment during which he won four bouts, all of which were in Sweden. What made his suspension so hypocritical was that those who punished Liston for appearing to throw the Ali rematch were now telling people they believed the knockout in Lewiston had been legitimate. They wanted to have their cake and to eat it too, and Sonny had nobody around him with the guts or the clout to point out the fallacy and hypocrisy of their stance.

Sonny's first U.S. fight was against Bill McMurray in Reno and while there, Sammy Davis Jr. sent someone over to negotiate a contract with him. Davey Pearl was with the Listons when it happened and remembered that Geraldine exploded at Davis' emissary. "You, what are you gonna do for Sonny Liston? You're gonna try and grab the money!" she said loudly. "Here's a guy who works every day, seven days a week with him, and he's not asking for any contract. Why should we give it to you?" That was the last time the Listons heard from Sammy Davis Jr. Pearl said that all of Sonny's managers jerked him around so badly that he and Geraldine didn't trust anybody, black or white.

Sonny's fall from grace hit him right in the face when he fought in Los Angeles for the first time. The highly respected ring announcer Jimmy Lennon introduced him as Sonny Boy Liston. Lennon may not have realized how derogatory that name was and got such an angry look from the ex-champ that the next time he worked one of his fights, he introduced him as Charles Liston. Sonny Liston, it would seem, no longer existed.

Around this time, 20-year-old George Foreman began training with Sonny. They met in Oakland while Foreman was preparing for the Olympics under the guidance of Henry Winston, who hired his dear friend Dick Sadler to train both fighters. Winston also brought in Archie Moore to serve as his matchmaker and to tutor Foreman.

Foreman seized the opportunity to work full-time with the man he would come to idolize. (When it came to training, Sonny thought George was lazy.) Winston remembered the time when Foreman was getting the best of Liston in a sparring session. "George comes back to the corner and I said, 'George, if this were a world title fight you'd be the champion because you whooped his big ass.'" "Don't say that man," replied Foreman. "Don't say that too loud because he'll kill me!"

George fell in love with Sonny and tried to emulate him. The two often ate dinner together and during their evening walks—Liston always took a long walk after dinner—the ex-champ would sometimes mentor the future champ. When

George said he wanted to become champion, Sonny told him any time he spit on the sidewalk they'd write about it in the papers. Sonny told Foreman a lot of things, and George said it took him a while to realize his idol had given him such great advice because he said things only once and with very few words.

George remembered how bitter Sonny was over the way he had been treated during his career. "When I won the championship from Patterson, everyone acted like I stole it," Liston told him. "When I was champ, I used to hear people say that I didn't deserve the title. Then when I lost to Clay, the same people told me I should have won. I know I should have. I should have. I could have. But they all acted like they didn't want me to."

Liston's July 6 fight against eighth-ranked and California state champion Henry Clark was his first televised appearance since the debacle in Maine three years earlier. A press conference for the fight was held at O'Doul's Irish Pub in San Francisco, at which Clark told the press, "He's old, man. Even his scowl is old." Clark had good reason to feel confident. Sonny had looked so bad six weeks earlier when he stopped Billy Joiner in the eighth round that dissatisfied customers had thrown things into the ring to vent their displeasure. "Liston stunk out the joint," said one promoter who witnessed the fight. "He's had it. No legs, no punch, no nothing."

Sonny battered Clark for seven rounds before the referee stopped the fight. Clark's bravado had gotten the best of him and he cried after the bout. "I tried to beat him with brute force and that was impossible," said Henry. "I became angry at him and I went after him and that was stupid, stupid, stupid. Every time I'd hit him he'd grunt and say, 'That's OK, kid, 'cause now I'm gonna bust you one.'"

Sonny was almost giddy after the fight. "Now bring on the big money," he said with a broad smile. "I sure hope those people put me in the ratings. Nine or ten, maybe. I hope they do." Even questions about his age couldn't darken his mood. "I'm 36," he snickered. "Or is it 39? Or 32?" He was back in the heavyweight picture again and ready to straighten out the division one state at a time, if need be. "I only got 49 to go," he said. "It might take a while, but then it might take (Joe) Frazier and (Jimmy) Ellis a while to let me in with them."

However, it was clear that Sonny's legendary punching power had deserted him. "Liston hit that kid with bombs," said Angelo Dundee. "He should have torn his head off. But nothing happened. We used to worry about him. Now he's just a big, old man." Dundee was right but Liston sincerely felt that everyone other than Ali was just token opposition for him and he resented having to prove himself against what he called a bunch of bums.

"Everyone knows how good I am. I ought to fight Frazier. That would prove that I'm the best fighter, that I'm champion. Frazier, you know, he comes at you. That's what I like. I have no doubt I can beat him," he said, grinning. "We would have knocked Joe's dick off," said Henry Winston, who was unsuccessful in trying to arrange a match with Frazier. Near the end of his life, Joe told me he had once considered sparring with Liston but decided he had nothing to gain and a great deal to lose against the ex-champ.

Nat Fleischer and Don Chargin both maintained that none of the new generation of young heavyweights wanted anything to do with the former champ. "Don't tell me that Sonny is through," echoed Ali. "Sonny can whip any man in the world, exceptin' me." Archie Moore felt the same way but didn't think Frazier or Ellis would ever fight him. "What do either one of them need with Liston?" said Moore. "He'd be too strong for either one of them." Sonny ended 1968 ranked No. 5 in the world by *Ring Magazine*.

Sonny had won all 14 of his comeback fights when he fought his former sparring partner Leotis Martin in a nationally televised bout at the Las Vegas Hilton in December 1969. Liston was in Tucson for a guest appearance on *Love, American Style* when he was offered the fight, which he took on two weeks' notice. Sonny entered the ring as a 3-1 favorite but Lem Banker knew he wasn't in shape for the bout.

Every trainer and fighter will tell you that training takes a lot more out of a boxer than the actual fight does. "It ain't the fight, the fight is easy," Rocky Marciano told Ash Resnick shortly after he retired. "I just can't go through that training of getting in shape again, Ash. I just can't do it." According to Foreman, the last thing Sonny wanted to do was train. "He'd want to party all the time, and sometimes he would do so much he wouldn't even know his name." Liston was screwing every woman he could in Vegas or Houston or Los Angeles or wherever else his travels took him. He didn't want to fight anymore, much less train, but it was the only way he knew how to make a living. So he took the fight.

Martin's game plan was to take advantage of Sonny's age. "He is an old fighter, and old fighters don't go 12 rounds at winning speed," said Leotis. For five rounds, Sonny hurt Martin with his jab and knocked him down with a left hook to the head. After eight rounds, Liston was ahead by three points on two official scorecards, and two points on the third. However, Sonny's nose was bleeding and he had trouble breathing through it, so he spit out his mouthpiece prior to the ninth round. One minute into the round, a right hand by Martin stopped Liston in his tracks. A follow-up left-right combination rendered him unconscious before he hit the canvas. The sight was so stunning that fight announcer Howard Cosell kept his mouth shut for one of the few times in his life. "It was a tough fight," said Ash Resnick. "Sonny didn't have anything, so we knew he was shot." Sonny knew it as well.

The party at Liston's house that night was supposed to have been a victory celebration. Foreman had fought on the undercard and when he went to pay his respects to his idol, it ended up being a condolence call. "The depression hung on Sonny like a strait jacket," wrote George. "He sat in the backyard, staring ahead, a dog in his lap." Foreman brought him a soda and squatted down next to him, but Sonny barely acknowledged him. Later, Geraldine began to sob. "What you guys gotta understand is that sometimes you lose," she said. "You can't win them all. Nobody wins them all. You hear that, George? You lose. Everybody loses. But you can't just die!"

Pearl said Sonny was one of the greatest losers he ever saw. He remembered that Sonny took that loss like a man and didn't say a word. That was consistent with what Liston said in an interview a few days before winning the title in 1962. "Know what I want to tell people?" he told David Condon of the *Chicago Tribune*. "Don't be jealous of the other man. He does better than you, OK, don't be jealous. More power to him, yeah."

Sonny should have hung up the gloves, but he didn't. Pearl helped negotiate a $13,000 bout against Chuck Wepner in New Jersey. It would be the big man's last fight. "The only reason he got that fight was because of me," said Pearl. "Abe Greene was the boxing commissioner there and he licensed Liston on the basis of my reputation."

Pearl, Tocco, and Banker made the trip with Sonny and kept their eyes wide open for any signs of trouble. "The promoters of that fight were trying to build up Wepner for a bigger fight in New York and did all they could to make sure he beat Sonny," said Lem. "They offered to set up training facilities for Sonny in New Jersey and then messed them up so that he couldn't train like he should. They put us up in a crappy little motel outside of Jersey City and told us we could eat there for free. After the first meal we looked for somewhere else to go; if the food wasn't poisoned, it sure was prepared by the world's worst cook."

Tocco was in the motel's coffee shop with Sonny when a couple of guys entered and motioned the fighter to come over. Liston told Tocco he'd be right back but was gone for hours. "When I see him, I ask him who those guys were and he just mumbled something," said Johnny. The following day one of the guys Sonny went off with came up to Tocco, shook his hand, and told him not to feel bad if his friend lost the fight. "Well, I went up to Sonny and I said, 'Hey, who are those guys? If something's goin' on, I want to know about it.'" "Aw, go to sleep," Sonny replied. "I'm gonna knock this guy out."

Banker said Wepner's trainer was one of the crookedest handlers in the business and because Sonny was lacking a third cornerman, Chuck's guy put one of his own men in Liston's corner. British promoter/matchmaker Mickey Duff was in town at the time and told Sonny not to drink from the water bucket between rounds because it would probably be tainted. "We didn't know for sure if Mickey was on to anything, but we got our own water bottle just the same," said Lem.

Ali was among the 4,000 people who watched in horror as it appeared that the fighter known as The Bayonne Bleeder might actually bleed to death. Liston fractured Wepner's nose and left cheekbone in the third round and knocked him down in the fifth, after which Wepner became a veritable punching bag. After the eighth round, the referee wanted to stop the fight but Wepner protested and the referee asked him how many fingers he was holding up. Wepner saw only blurs but when his trainer tapped his shoulder three times, Chuck answered three and the referee let him continue.

"Man, I hate to hit this guy anymore," Sonny told Pearl between the eighth and ninth rounds. Pearl said it was probably was the first time in his life that Sonny ever said that. When referee Barney Felix stopped the fight in the tenth, Wepner's chest and Liston's shoulders and gloves were covered with blood from six major cuts on Wepner's face. Tocco said it was like watching colored water pouring out of a fire hydrant.

Wepner didn't protest the stoppage but his manager threw a major fit. Asked if Wepner was the bravest man he ever knew, Liston said, "No. But his manager is." The cuts would need 72 stitches; Wepner also had trouble regaining his equilibrium. "They iced me down for two straight days," said Chuck. "I was in shock for three days. I really was." After the fight, Ali stopped by Liston's dressing room and the two chatted briefly for the last time.

Pearl was surprised when Sonny asked him to get his purse from the promoter. "I felt he trusted me as a friend, but not that strongly," said Pearl. On the flight home, Sonny took $13,000 in small bills from the brown paper bag that the promoter had given Pearl. He counted out $10,000, which he gave to Banker to cover a bet he had lost several weeks earlier when Jerry Quarry, who was white, beat Mac Foster, who was black. The other $3,000 was for Tocco and Pearl.

Back home in Las Vegas, Geraldine gave Pearl a check for his work on the Wepner fight. Declining to accept it, Davey said whatever he did for Sonny, he did out of friendship. Gerry told him that Sonny wished he had been with him from the beginning of his career, but Pearl had already decided that being around Liston was getting to be too much of a drag. Sonny called Davey a couple of weeks later. "He said, 'Don't be mad at me,' and asked me to get him a couple of fights," said Pearl.

CHAPTER THIRTEEN

AND THAT'S THAT

A few hours after he knocked out Roy Harris in Houston in 1960, Sonny was nodding off in his hotel lobby when someone said to him: "Don't turn aroun', nigger." Sonny heard a gun being cocked and felt its barrel against his head. The man said he had one bullet in his gun and would pull the trigger until Sonny said he was a "no-good, yeller nigger." Liston thought the man was bluffing until he twice pulled the trigger. "Wait!" Sonny said. "I'm a no good nigger." The man told him he had missed a word, and Sonny added the word yellow. Liston was told not to turn around and heard the floor creak as the man walked away.

Sonny told this story to Mark Kram in Las Vegas a few months before he died. "I've heard that creak ever since. I was on my way to bein' finished before I got to Clay in Miami," he admitted. "Folks're violent. It got to be a torture for me... bein' public. Like bein' the only chicken in a bag full of cats."

Sonny's former publicist Harold Conrad was in Las Vegas in November and took the Listons to dinner. Sonny owed Conrad six custom-made shirts from a bet they had made several years earlier. "Listen ya New York bum, you're gonna get them shirts," said Sonny. When Conrad asked when, Liston replied: "When ah owns a shirt factory," slamming the table with his fist and laughing loud enough for everyone in the restaurant to hear. A little later, Conrad told Sonny that Joe Louis was trying to kick a heroin habit. "You-son-of-a-bitch!" Liston told him. "You say that about my man. He wouldn't do a dumb thing like that." When Sonny got confirmation of Joe's drug problem, he called Conrad to apologize.

In mid-November, Sonny flew to L.A. to do some film work and pose for photographs. He attended a fight card at the Olympic Auditorium on the 19th, after which he had dinner with some boxing people. He was returning to the LA airport the day before Thanksgiving when his car was rammed on the driver's side while he made a left turn. His body bent the steering wheel; 20 stitches were needed to close the gash on his head after it smashed the windshield. He was driven to a hospital, where he stayed for three or four days. While there, Sonny watched himself in an episode of *Love, American Style*. In early December, he was admitted to a Las Vegas hospital complaining of chest pains but by December 10 he was working out at Lem Banker's gym again.

Though he was still ranked eighth by *Ring Magazine*, Sonny knew he couldn't go on fighting much longer and was looking for another way to make a living. "If Charles don't make it this year or end of next year, they can have it," said Geraldine. "Because Charles knows he'll be too old. You just cannot fight all your life." She had actually told that to Jack Olsen three years earlier, yet here he was still fighting.

The Listons had tickets for a trip to Japan, where Sonny would guest-referee a couple of bouts. Pearl had arranged fights against Karl Mildenberger of Germany and Jose Urtain of Spain, and a third Patterson bout was apparently being discussed. There was talk of a George Chuvalo fight in March, as well as a match at the International in Las Vegas against hard-hitting Mac Foster who, according to a newpaper article in 1968, had knocked Sonny down and hurt him badly in a sparring session.

Banker tried to get his friend a hosting job at the Sahara Hotel, but it didn't pan out. Sonny had talked about opening a gym to train fighters and also had an idea for a valet car wash service with free pick-up and delivery. He had cut a record entitled, "I'm A Lover," but very few people knew about it. Sonny was still trying to get the money owed him from the first Ali fight; a hearing to recover the money owed him by promoter Bill McDonald's estate was scheduled for January.

Near the end of his life, Liston hung out with a rough bunch of people from the west side of Las Vegas. So many cab drivers got robbed in that area that only one company would even go there. Ash Resnick said Sonny never went to the West Side during the first couple of years he lived in Vegas but started frequenting that part of town in '68 or '69, around the time he and Liston drifted apart. "He was still fighting, and I heard he was fooling with drugs but nobody could prove it by me," said Ash. Promoter Vince Anselmo said he had often seen Liston in the company of drug users. Resnick and Banker both told me that Liston was nearly broke and in desperate need of cash. "He was living on the down low," said Gary Bates. "He was collecting for a loan shark."

Sonny always made sure the people he respected most never saw him indulge in alcohol or drugs, but he was drinking more now, smoking marijuana, and may have been snorting cocaine. Although Sonny had never been busted in Vegas, Mel Greb said it was coming to that because of the people he was keeping company with. Greb said Sonny was loaning money to a guy who was going across the border and coming back with heroin. "That, and a tall junkie cocktail waitress are the two things that messed him up," said Greb.

Three days before Christmas, Liston and his family celebrated the holidays at the homes of close friends Pearl and Banker, something they had done for years. Banker remembers giving his friend a watch but can't recall what Sonny gave him. The following day, Sonny helped Geraldine and Danielle pack for their trip to St. Louis. There were rumors that the Listons were planning to adopt a second child, but the couple had grown apart. Geraldine told a friend that Sonny wasn't coming home for dinner anymore because he didn't trust her "on food and things."

Geraldine and their son, Danny, flew out of Las Vegas on the 24th; she called her husband to tell him they'd arrived safely in the Midwest. On Christmas Day, Sonny phoned Gerry and several other family members. That night he was a guest at Redd Foxx's performance at the International and would party with the comedian and his friends deep into the night. The following day he worked as a floor walker at the International and as a celebrity bodyguard for Foxx. There were reports that he had sold small amounts of cocaine to some hotel guests and employees.

Sonny had breakfast with Davey Pearl on the morning of December 28 where they worked on his 1971 appointment calendar. Then he drove to Los Angeles for a dinner meeting with his booking agent, during which they discussed possible guest appearances on several weekly television shows. He checked out of the Biltmore Hotel at 12:45 a.m. and drove home. He was probably doing 90 mph the whole way.

On the night of December 28, Geraldine had a bad nightmare about Sonny. "I had the worst dream," she told William Nack of *Sports Illustrated*. "He was falling in the shower and calling my name, 'Gerry, Gerry!' I can still see it. So I got real nervous. I told my mother, 'I think something's wrong.' But my mother said, 'Oh, don't think that. He's all right.'"

On that day or the next, Sonny called his old pal Barney Baker in Chicago. "He was gonna come in to see me," Baker told me. "He said, 'Barney, be at the airport because from there I got to go someplace. I got 20 big ones for you.'" Baker said Liston felt he owed him from their days in St. Louis. Barney and Liston's former publicist Ben Bentley went to the airport, but Sonny didn't show up. "I couldn't figure it out. So I forgot about it and several days later I read about it."

When Sonny returned home on December 29, he called Gary Bates and told him Geraldine was gone for the holidays and invited him over. "I went over there to his house on Ottawa with a cocktail waitress from Circus Circus," said Gary. "I knocked on the door a couple times, but nobody answered. Nobody showed up."

In 2007, Bates was picking up a load of sand from a construction site when the security guard noticed some boxing equipment in the front seat of his pickup. When Gary said he had sparred with Sonny Liston in his younger days, the small elderly black man told him Sonny had asked him to score some heroin for the two white junkie hookers who were at his house on the day he died.

Mildred Stevenson was the housekeeper for both the Listons and the Bankers. She had a key to the Liston house and went there on New Year's Eve day. She found Sonny dead in his bedroom, called Lem to give him the news, then locked the door and left. Neither Lem nor Mildred called the police.

Tocco threw a New Year's party at his gym for fighters and other boxing people, and Sonny told him he'd be there. When Sonny didn't show, Tocco called his house at midnight and again at 2 a.m. He knew Geraldine was out of town and was concerned when Sonny didn't answer the phone.

On January 1, Geraldine called Tocco and said she was worried because she hadn't heard from her husband in three days. Johnny went to Sonny's house and found the door locked and his car in the driveway. At that point he called the police, who proceeded to gain entry into the house. The living room furniture was in disarray but the house did not yet smell of death. They found Sonny lying on his bed with a needle sticking out of his arm. Johnny left the house before the police did. Tocco told this story to his good friend Tony Davi a few years before the trainer died in 1999. "Johnny says, 'I'm gonna tell you the real story about Sonny Liston,'" Davi told me. "He sat me down in his office and we talked for about an hour. He told me to keep it under my hat and not tell anybody. Johnny wasn't a braggart. He told me in the strictest confidence, but it was like he wanted to get it off his chest."

The way Tocco saw it was that four or five guys fought with Sonny, tired him out, held him down, and shot him up with enough heroin to kill a horse. Tocco was one of the most respected figures in Las Vegas, where he had lived for more than 40 years after moving from St. Louis. He was close to Sonny in the early 1950s and grew even closer to him during the years they spent together in Vegas. When Sonny would train at his gym, Tocco would tell almost everyone there that they had to leave. "I can't see why Johnny would fabricate the story," Davi told me. "He seemed of sound mind when he told me. He did not seem like he was losing it at all." If Tocco's story were true, it would mean that the Las Vegas police and sheriff's department put Liston's house back in order after Tocco left. Why they would have done it is anybody's guess.

Lem Banker is spearheading an effort to get Tocco into the Boxing Hall of Fame, and you'd be hard pressed to find someone who doesn't think he deserves the honor. "His was the gym you went to. The fact that Sonny Liston trusted and endorsed the guy speaks volumes," said Bruce Trampler, matchmaker for Bob Arum's Top Rank, Inc. Tocco once threw Don King and his stable of fighters out of his gym because King tried to tell him who could train in his gym and who couldn't. That move cost Johnny $5,000 a month, but he wasn't the kind of guy who suffered fools gladly.

When Geraldine returned home from St. Louis on January 5, she found her Charles in their bedroom, lying face-up with his feet on the floor. After phoning Sonny's attorney, Geraldine called his doctor, who arrived shortly before midnight. She called the police two to three hours after she got home. The milk bottles and newspapers that had accumulated at the front door indicated that Sonny had been dead about a week. He most likely died on December 29.

Sergeant Dennis Caputo was in charge of the Criminalistics Bureau of the Clark County Sheriff's Department and was one of the first officers on the scene. "It was colder than shit outside and the smell in the house was horrendous," he told me. Caputo had met Sonny several times at Cleopatra's Barge in Caesars Palace, usually in the presence of Ash Resnick. He remembers that Sonny was drunk the first time he met him. Liston was sullen, stand-offish, and clearly did not like cops, but Caputo didn't take it personally. "It was common knowledge that Sonny was a heroin addict. The whole department knew about it," he said.

Caputo found a quarter-ounce of heroin in a small green balloon in the kitchen and a small bag of marijuana. On Sonny's bedroom dresser was a loaded .38 caliber pistol, a small wooden cross, and a rattlesnake tail. No syringes or needles were found in the house. In the living room was a stuffed bear in an upright position with Sonny's championship belt around its midsection.

"Geraldine was very suspicious. She and her attorney were in the house for at least two hours before we got there," said Dennis. "The big question everyone asked at the time was why she waited so long to call us." The police found a few areas in the backyard where holes had been freshly dug in the flower beds, and several officers speculated that somebody must have been looking for something. Caputo said there was quite a police presence at the Liston house that night; when a celebrity died in Las Vegas, the influx of law enforcement personnel tended to go a bit overboard. A lot of officers knew Sonny was dead before Geraldine returned home.

Caputo believes Sonny died of natural causes. "He was in a peaceful position and there were no signs of a struggle." Dennis said the tri-level house was immaculate and there was absolutely nothing that would indicate foul play. Talking with Caputo, I could tell he had no ax to grind with the former champ, unlike a majority of law enforcement officials back in the day. He has always been saddened by the preoccupation with Liston's death. After his appearance in an HBO special about Sonny in 1995, he got so many calls from people wanting to interview him about Liston's death that he stopped returning their calls.

Liston's body was in such an advanced state of decomposition that the coroner had quite a problem getting his corpse into a body bag, down the stairs, and out of the house. His body came close to splitting when they moved it. Joe Louis arrived as they carried Sonny out. When asked for his reaction, Louis said, "Liston was a much better fighter than a lot of people gave him credit for."

Geraldine demanded an autopsy, and the Coroner found traces of heroin byproducts in Liston's system—but not in amounts large enough to have caused his death. There appeared to be fresh needle marks on one of his arms, but the toxicology report compiled by a private lab in Los Angeles said his body was too decomposed for the tests to be conclusive. Officially, Sonny died of "pulmonary congestion and edema…probable mild coronary insufficiency and myocardial fibrosis…pulmonary emphysema…In Sum: Natural Causes."

The police never investigated Liston's death as a homicide, and there's nothing in their report that mentions the disarray that Tocco said he saw in the living room. "What pisses me off is that nobody seemed to care," said Harold Conrad. He had talked to someone in the sheriff's department who told him that Sonny was a bad nigger who got what was coming to him. "In the case of a victim with no record of drug usage, but who is known to have had criminal associations, police are often satisfied to view the death as good riddance and file it away as a routine OD, without troubling to investigate any further," wrote Philadephia writer Jack McKinney.

"The rumors (about Sonny's death) were so thick in Vegas, you're lucky if you don't trip over one," Bruce Jay Friedman wrote in *Esquire* in 1974. Almost all of the people who knew Sonny believed he was murdered, and that belief continues to this day. Of all the murder rumors, four seem to be the most plausible.

Harold Conrad and others believed that Sonny became deeply involved as a bill collector in a loan-sharking ring in Las Vegas. When Sonny tried to muscle in for a bigger share of the action, Conrad surmised his employers got him very drunk, took him home, and stuck him with a needle.

Lem Banker insists that Sonny was murdered by drug dealers with whom he'd become involved. Two Las Vegas policemen stopped by Tocco's gym and told him that Sonny had been seen at a house that would be the target of a drug raid. The police told Tocco they had watched the house for a week to check on Sonny's comings and goings. Banker had a similar discussion with the police, which would indicate that they were looking to give Sonny a pass. "Sheriff Lamb told me, 'Tell your pal Sonny to stay away from the West Side because we're going to bust the drug dealers.'" Lem later learned that the police told Sonny the same thing to his face—and he took their advice. He apparently was at the house of the drug dealers shortly before they got busted, and because of the suspicious timing, the dealers may have thought Sonny ratted on them and they shot him with a hot dose as retribution.

Liston would have been out of his element if he tried to carve out a place for himself in the drug market. As afraid as he was of the mob and Muslims, Sonny should have been absolutely terrified of heroin dealers. And he may have been, but decided to accept the risk because he needed the money, and drugs were a way to make a lot of it quickly.

The third rumor is shared by quite a few people in the boxing community and has its roots in the second Ali fight. Tocco said the mob promised Sonny some money to throw the fight, but they never paid him. As the years passed and Sonny's financial situation worsened, he got mad and told the mob he'd go public with the story unless they ponied up.

Eddie Futch told me the same thing. "I think Sonny's eventual demise was tied to the performance in Lewiston," said Eddie. When Ali signed to fight Joe Frazier shortly before Sonny died, they were each guaranteed $2.5 million, which was a lot more than Liston made in his entire career. "This is just my theory," said Futch, a man not given to idle speculation. "When Sonny saw the money these guys were making, he went back and said 'I need more money for what I did.' Now, you might get away with that two or three times, but if you keep asking you become a liability."

Finally, there are people who believe Sonny was supposed to have taken a dive when he fought Chuck Wepner in June, and killing him was payback for his unwillingness to go along with the fix.

The common thread in all of the rumors was that if a needle delivered the fatal dose to Sonny's arm, it wasn't self-inflicted. Everyone who knew him well would tell you that Sonny Liston loved his wife and children of all colors, that he was a very funny man, and that he was profoundly afraid of needles. "There isn't a public official in all of Las Vegas who will say he OD'd," wrote Bruce Jay Friedman in 1974.

"He had a deadly fear of needles and he had too much pride in his strength," said Davey Pearl. Sonny's friend Lewis Powell said Liston was as scared of a needle as a goat is of a butcher's knife. His trainer in Jefferson City Prison remembered that Sonny never took a shot, no matter how sick he was. Dr. Nick Ragni was Liston's dentist in Philadelphia and remembered the fighter refused a shot of Novocain under any and all circumstances, even when facing a root canal. "There was nothing Sonny feared more than a needle. I know!" said Ragni. "He was afraid of needles," echoed Father Murphy. "He would do everything to avoid taking shots." According to Willie Reddish, Liston had to cancel a planned tour to Africa in 1963 because he refused to get the required inoculations.

"Sonny Liston hated needles," said Tocco. "He wouldn't even go to a doctor for a checkup, for fear some doctor would want to stick a needle in him." Johnny visited him in the hospital after his car accident and said Sonny was angrier about the shot the doctors gave him than he was about the car wreck, and that he was still complaining about the needle mark a couple of weeks later. When Henry Winston got Liston licensed to fight in California, the fighter balked at the mandatory blood test. "Let his doctor tell you how much trouble we had with the big gorilla just to get him to give blood," said Winston. "He wouldn't do it. I had to walk him down to Jack London Square and we laughed about it. 'You big chump,' I told him."

"We heard it was an overdose, that it was somebody who had given it to him," Ash Resnick told me. Geraldine said if Sonny was killed, she didn't know who would have done it. The idea that Sonny was on junk was the most ridiculous thing that she ever heard, and when Friedman brought it up, he said she just laughed and laughed. "Sonny wasn't on dope," she said. "I know a dopehead when I see one, and Sonny never used drugs. He had high blood pressure and he had been out drinking in late December. As far as I'm concerned, he had a heart attack. Case closed."

All of Sonny's friends scoffed at the idea that he was injecting drugs. "I'd swear in court that he wasn't a drug addict," said Banker. "There's no way the man was a junkie," said Pearl. Tocco insisted Sonny never had anything to do with heroin and said he'd believe that until the day he died. Joe Louis felt the same way. "If heroin was in his veins, somebody other than Liston shot it in. Sonny never dealt with heroin." Since Louis did, he probably knew what he was talking about. "That's what the old man said, too. He said this doesn't sound right," said Willie Reddish Jr.

"Sonny was down on a junkie. He was running away from a junkie," said Tommy Manning, a sentiment confirmed by Jack McKinney. "As a guy who had made more than an average share of mistakes, Liston was generally tolerant of imperfections of others. But the notable exception was his hostility and contempt for drug users," said McKinney. After the news of Liston's death emerged, several of his West Philadelphia friends called local reporters to express their outrage about the drug rumors.

Only one person's name has been publicly linked to Liston's death. In a 1991 *Sports Illustrated* article, William Nack wrote that there were police in Las Vegas who believed that Sonny had been the victim of a hit ordered by Ash Resnick. Once great friends, Ash and Sonny had a falling out in 1968 or 1969, but nobody knows what it was about. The rumor was repeated by Nick Tosches in "The Devil and Sonny Liston," in an HBO documentary on Liston, and in Bob Mee's recent book on the two Liston/Ali fights.

Larry Gandy was one of two Las Vegas policemen who got busted for robbing the homes of drug dealers. While in prison he supposedly told somebody that he knew that Ash had Sonny killed. A man by the name of Martin Dardis, who is now dead, apparently was the one who initiated the rumor when he told *Sports Illustrated* about it. After Gandy got out of jail, Ash's daughter, Dana, talked to him. "He told me he never even knew my dad and that the only connection he had to my family was that his ex-wife worked at a photo shop that my mom had at the old International." Dardis told Dana he had gotten his information from Kent Clifford, a former commander of the Las Vegas Police Department's Intelligence Bureau. Clifford was a junior at UNLV at the time of Sonny's death.

The Resnick family has always considered the rumor to be untrue and preposterous, but there's nothing they can do about it. Legally, it's not a crime to slander a dead person. "Sonny was dead almost 20 years before my dad died, and nobody ever said anything about my dad being involved in Sonny's death until he died," Dana told me. "My dad loved Sonny, and I don't know what the motivation would have been for him to do it." According to promoter Bob Arum, "Ash Resnick would not kill anybody."

There are also rumors linking Sonny's death to people who are still alive and far more famous than Ash. But rumors are about as legitimate as Monopoly money; more than 40 years after Liston's death, the people who initiated them are probably long gone, too. Most boxing fans want to assume that Liston was murdered because it makes for a great, unsolved conspiracy.

What seems most likely is that Sonny suffered a heart attack and died where he fell. He probably was doing heroin but not injecting it. He definitely was adrift and was prepared to do whatever it took to make money. Given the tough life he had lived, Sonny's 50-year-old heart may have just given out.

Many people believe it was inevitable that Liston's life would end badly, and I'm inclined to agree with them. Any chance of it ending well evaporated in Lewiston, Maine, where the second Ali fight sealed his doom. "His past never let go of him," said his good friend Lem Banker. Unfortunately, it still hasn't.

The 400 seats inside Palm Mortuary's chapel were filled, and another 500 or 600 people stood in the back and outside. "He had one heckuva smile, and plenty of wives of hotel executives were sorry to see him check out," said Banker. Among those who attended the service were Ed Sullivan, Doris Day, Ella Fitzgerald, Jack E. Leonard, Jerry Vale, Rosey Grier, and Nipsy Russell. Joe Louis arrived late because he was trying to get some bets down.

"Can you tell me what happened to you, Sonny?" cried Geraldine, who sat in a room behind the closed coffin that held Liston's tuxedo-clad body. "I can't even see his face. Oh, Jesus!" The Checkmates had spent the previous evening reworking the lyrics to their song, "Sunny," which they sang at the service. A North Las Vegas reverend sang "Just a Closer Walk With Thee," and a female friend of the Listons sang "You'll Never Walk Alone."

In attendance were two white 18-year-olds, Peter Keenan and David Shapiro, whom Sonny had been close to for the previous seven or eight years. Shapiro had sent a poem by telegram to Gerry, which was read at the funeral. "His heart would melt at children, His smile would light a darkened room, Out of sight, but not out of mind. There are so many things that could be said, but none so beautiful as the man." Father Murphy delivered the main eulogy and said Sonny had qualities most people didn't know about, including his sense of humor, his love of children, and his many acts of charity. When Murphy got back to Denver, he cried for a very long time.

Sonny had told his wife that he wanted to go down the Strip one last time after he died; thousands of gamblers left the casinos to pay their respects as Liston's funeral procession made its way to the cemetery. "They stopped everything," said Murphy. "They used him all his life. They were still using him on the way to the cemetery, another Las Vegas show. God help us."

As they entered the cemetery, a local police officer saluted Liston's hearse. Louis was in a limo with Banker and he looked at Lem, smiled, and said, "Sonny getting saluted by a cop! He would have gotten a kick out of that." Joe, Lem, Pearl, and Murphy were among the pallbearers. Archie Moore, Sammy Davis Jr., Wilt Chamberlain, Ingemar Johansson, and Godfrey Cambridge were honorary pallbearers.

Geraldine remained in the car during the graveside ceremony, where Sonny's mother, Helen, his brother, J.T., and his adopted son, Danielle, sat with some of the couple's closest friends. Other family members decided not to attend when they learned there wouldn't be an open casket.

Sonny's grave was located directly beneath the flight path of McCarron International Airport; the services were interrupted a couple of times because of the noise. "Geraldine told me Sonny would have liked that because, as she put it, he was always coming or going, and the planes were either taking off or landing over his plot," said Marilyn Resnick.

According to Ali's photographer and close friend Howard Bingham, Ali walked over to Geraldine after the service and whispered something into her ear.

"He was an awful nice fellow, and I liked him a lot," Ali told the press. "But just like any fighter who gets old, he had begun to show signs of age."

Charles "Sonny" Liston
1932—1970
"A Man"

Sonny's gravestone is the smallest offered at Davis Memorial Park. Lifetime maintenance of the gravesite was purchased at the time of his death. A steady stream of people come to see Liston's final resting place every week; visitors from other countries seem to be more interested in making the pilgrimage than do Americans. Lem Banker and Gary Bates are the only Las Vegans who pay their respects on a regular basis. Rick Fabroski takes care of the grounds and watches most people make what he calls the Sonny Walk, slowly but deliberately winding their way through the cemetery. After a while, he asks visitors if they're looking for Liston's stone and points the way. Out of respect for the nearly forgotten champ, Fabroski tidies up the gravesite and polishes the urn that rests above Sonny's grave marker. The cemetery keeps an American flag in the urn at all times. If there are flowers there, too, it's because visitors have brought them.

EPILOGUE

Sonny's mother sold the house her son had given her and moved back to St. Louis when she started getting sick. Helen Jean figures her grandmother knew she had a serious ailment because she made the move in the dead of winter. Big Momma put her stuff in a trailer, and a man she knew drove her to St. Louis, where she stayed with her granddaughter. "We got her into a senior apartment building and she stayed there until she got sick enough where she couldn't do for herself," said Helen. "We'd fix her meals and made sure she had all she needed."

Geraldine moved into an apartment; Davey Pearl helped her sell off many of Sonny's belongings. She gave Pearl her husband's scale, which he donated to the University of Nevada, and she gave Banker her husband's medicine ball. After she sold the house, Geraldine hooked up with a musician who drained all of her savings. She then moved back to St. Louis working as a medical technician for several years. Her Pink Cadillac, the one Sonny had repainted to match her favorite sweater, can still be seen on the streets of Vegas.

What little contact Geraldine had with Sonny's relatives basically ended by the mid-1990s. Her health steadily declined and in 2005 she died. Her body was not yet cold when some neighbors called the police to report a domestic disturbance in her apartment. The responding officer found a group of Geraldine's family members fighting over Sonny's memorabilia. The officer walked through the house, which he described as a veritable shrine to the memory and career of the former champ.

When Jefferson City prison closed, the inmates who were relocated took their pictures of Liston with them and put them up on their new cell walls. Sonny's favorite niece, Helen, has a nephew named Charles Liston who will probably spend the rest of his life in jail for conspiring to kill his girlfriend. "We said that name was a curse—same name—Charles Liston."

For many years, some members of the Liston family held a grudge against Muhammad Ali for ruining the life of their beloved Uncle Charles. "My dad was always anti-Muhammad Ali and I could never figure out why," said Henry Page's daughter, Lee. Helen's daughter Adrienne was four years old when her great uncle Charles died and was beside herself with anger toward Ali when she was eight or nine. On the back of a color photo of Sonny wearing his championship belt, a photo that Sonny gave to Helen when he was champ, the following note is written in pencil so faint that you have to look very closely to see it at all. "The one and only one I will love forever. If I have to die I will kill Muhamali. (sic) When I am grown I will go to Hollywood and Kill Ailee (sic) if I have to go to jail for it I am going to show him he can not mess with Sonny Liston. If it takes me forever I will do it. I would go now if I was a lady. The one I will love forever, Sonny Liston. By Adrienne"

Today, the Liston's old house at 2058 Ottawa in Las Vegas has been red tagged by the sheriff's office. It's dilapidated and is destined to be torn down. The neighborhood that was once home to Johnny Carson, Kirk Kerkorian, Debbie Reynolds, Bobby Darin, and Lefty Rosenthal is not what it once was, but it's still nice. One of the current residents is trying to get it into the historic register to protect it from developers.

Even after he died, Liston's good qualities were redefined to demean and degrade him. Sonny became the world heavyweight champion while living in Philadelphia; this is what the *Philadelphia Inquirer* said about him in its obituary: "Though Liston had never learned to read and write, he had 'mother wit,' a sense of shrewd, animal cunning that enables an uneducated man to cope with the storms and furies of public life." If you consult the dictionary, you'll find mother wit is defined simply as innate intelligence or common sense.

"He was not good for boxing," said New York State Athletic Commission chair Melvin Krulewitch. "He could not be trusted with the world title if he achieved it." Mel's the guy who wouldn't even let Sonny be introduced before a fight at Madison Square Garden.

"Let's be clear on one thing that cannot be up for debate. He was the meanest, rudest, bullying, most unpleasant prick I have ever been around," said little Larry Merchant.

In a 1999 NBC restrospective on Ali, the well-respected journalist Dick Schaap said Sonny was a hit man for the mob. There's only one definition of a hit man, and Sonny never killed anyone. But nobody on the production team had any problem with Schaap's statement.

"In the end, Charles "Sonny" Liston was revealed as nothing more than a bully," said narrator Chris Fowler on *ESPN's* 2001 Sports Century documentary. "His one weakness as a fighter was his lack of heart," said former *New York Sun* reporter, W.C. Heinz. "Once you take his gun away, he turned into a sissy."

"The medical reports on his injured left shoulder were vague," wrote Robert Lipsyte in his biography of Ali. "The press exchanged homemade rumors—the Muslims had threatened to kill Liston if he didn't dump, Liston had bet his purse on Clay at 7-1, Liston had dumped because a return-bout clause in the contract assured him a rematch and second payday with Clay." I get the feeling that Lipsyte didn't care a whit about what took place in that Miami Beach fight because every statement in that paragraph was pure drivel. "Poor dumb messed-over Sonny," wrote Lipsyte.

Neil Leifer, who took the famous Lewiston photo, later critiqued the photos he shot at the first Liston/Clay fight in Miami. His contempt for the former champ is apparent when he refers to "big, bad Sonny Liston before the eighth round...I look over at him after the seventh round and I knew that even if he got up, he was going to get knocked down again." Neil was mistaken on two counts. First, the fight was stopped after the sixth round and second, Liston was never down in this fight. Apparently *Life Magazine*, which ran the spot, felt no need to check the facts.

Describing his photo of the weigh-in at the Lewiston fight, Neil said Ali had "in boxing terms, a huge height and reach advantage." For the record, Ali was no more than two and a half inches taller than Liston, and Sonny's reach was four-to-six inches longer than Muhammad's, depending on which stat sheet you're looking at.

Apparently, in order to revere Muhammad Ali, you need to vilify Sonny Liston. And if you stand up for Sonny, you are somehow insulting Muhammad. I'll bet that Ali doesn't feel that way and that his opinion of Liston's talent is very close to mine.

In his second *Playboy* interview in 1975, Ali was asked if he thought he'd be remembered as being the greatest. "I'll tell you how I'd like to be remembered," said Muhammad. "As a black man who won the heavyweight title and who was humorous and who treated everyone right. As a man who never looked down on those who looked up to him and who helped as many of his people as he could—financially and also in their fight for freedom, justice, and equality... And if that's asking too much, then I guess I'd settle for being remembered only as a great boxing champion who became a preacher and a champion of his people." Apart from being a preacher, Sonny's answer to that question probably would have been very similar to Ali's.

"He did come from nowhere to get where he was. He was a good husband and a good man, and that's how I'd like the world to remember him," said Geraldine Liston. Sonny's family and friends feel the same way.

NOTES

INTRODUCTION

Sport Magazine, July, 1964
Liston-Clay closed-circuit telecast, February 25, 1964
Today Show, 1999
Sports Illustrated, November 16, 1964
Time, August 2, 1963
U.S. Senate Hearings, June, 1965
Sports Illustrated, May 13, 1968
Helen Long interview
Ferdie Pacheco, *Muhammad Ali—A View From the Corner*, 1992
Jan Philipp Reemstsma, *More Than a Champion*, 1998
The Sporting News, "Chronicle of 20th Century Sport," 2000
A.S. "Doc" Young, *The Champ Nobody Wanted*, 1963

CHAPTER ONE

Young, *The Champ Nobody Wanted*, 1963
Gary Bates interview
Muhammad Ali, *The Greatest*, 1975
New York Times, September 26, 1962
Life Magazine, March 23, 1962
Esquire Magazine, October, 1962
Young, *The Champ Nobody Wanted*, 1963
Gary Bates interview
Newsweek, July 22, 1963
Sports Illustrated, September 17, 1962
Miami Herald, October 6, 1958
Time, August 17, 1960
Sports Illustrated, September 24, 1962
Boxing Illustrated, August, 1959
Chicago American, September 2, 1962
Sports Illustrated, February 24, 1964
Sacramento Bee, July 3, 1983
Liston-Clay, Fight of the Century, 1964
Cavalier Magazine, September, 1961
Young, *The Champ Nobody Wanted*, 1963
Art Lurie interview
Rolling Stone, October, 1962
Esquire, October, 1962
Liston-Clay, Fight of the Century, 1964
Angelo Dundee & Burt Sugar, *My View From The Corner*, 2009
Sports Illustrated, September, 24, 1962
Gary Bates interview
Sports Illustrated, February 24, 1964
New York Times, February 24, 1964
Denver Post, July 19, 1960
Ring Magazine, October, 1962
Barney Baker interview
Eastside Boxing, interview with Geoffrey Ciani
Newsweek, May 21, 1962
Mark Kram, *Ghosts of Manila*, 2001
Don Atyeo & Felix Dennis, *Muhammad Ali, The Holy Warrior*, 1975
New York Times, February 24, 1964
Ring Magazine, 2003
Don Chargin interview
Newsweek, December 18, 1961
Davey Pearl interview
Time, August 10, 1967
Sports Illustrated, July 17, 1961
Ash Resnick interview
Boxing Annual, 1964
Esquire, February, 1963
George Foreman interview
Miami Herald, February 15, 1964

Life Magazine, February 23, 1962
Sports Illustrated, August 1, 1960
Sacramento Bee, July 3, 1983
Cavalier, September, 1961
New York Times, November 6 1964
Miami Herald, January 30, 1964
New York Times, February 25, 1964
Sports Illustrated, February, 24, 1964
Joyce Carol Oates, *On Boxing*, 1987
Life Magazine, February 23, 1962
Paul Abdoo Jr. interview
Boston Globe, May, 1965
Sports Illustrated, February 10, 1964
Henry Winston interview
Boston Globe, May 21, 1965
Sports Illustrated, September 9, 1960
True Magazine Boxing Yearbook, 1964
Sports Illustrated, February 14, 1991
Harold Conrad, *Dear Muffo*, 1982
Bob Mee, *Liston & Ali*, 2010
Esquire, October, 1962
Don Chargin interview
Young, *The Champ Nobody Wanted*, 1963
Gary Bates interview
Sports Illustrated, September 24, 1962
ESPN's Sports Century 2001
Playboy, October, 1964
BoxRec, Archie Moore
Playboy, April, 1964
Esquire, March, 1962
Helen Long interview
Nick Tosches, *The Devil and Sonny Liston*, 2000
Young, *The Champ Nobody Wanted*, 1963
Liston–Clay—Fight of the Century, 1964
Philadelphia Inquirer, September 27, 1962

Sports Illustrated, July 17, 1961
Deseret News, September 11, 2010
St. Louis Post Dispatch, June 3, 2009
Boston Globe, May 24, 1964
Kram, *Ghosts of Manila*, 2001
Conrad, *Dear Muffo*, 1982
Cavalier Magazine, September, 1961
Newsweek, July 22, 1963
U.S. Senate Hearings, December, 1960
Miami Herald, October 6, 1958
Sports Illustrated, September 19, 1960
David Remnick, *King of the World*, 1998
Young, *The Champ Nobody Wanted*, 1963
ESPN Sport Century 2001
Saturday Evening Post, August 13, 1960
Sports Illustrated, July 17, 1961

CHAPTER TWO

Truman Gibson Interview
Jeffrey T. Sammons, *Beyond the Ring*, 1990
Barney Nagler, *James Norris and the Decline of Boxing*, 1964
Cavalier, September, 1961
Mickey Cohen, *In My Own Words*, 1975
Budd Schulberg, *Sparring With Hemingway*, 1995
Esquire, January, 1974
Willie Reddish Jr. interview
Sport Magazine, July, 1964
Luca De Franco, *The Sweet Science*, October 18, 2005
Sammons, *Beyond the Ring*, 1990
Nagler, *James Norris and the Decline of Boxing*, 1964

Truman Gibson, *Knocking Down Barriers*, 2005
New York Times, January 2, 2006
Sports Illustrated, December 13, 1954
Sports Illustrated, January 31, 1955
Truman Gibson interview
U.S. Senate Hearings, December, 1960
Denver Post, November 7, 1963
St. Louis Globe-Democrat, February 12, 1953
Sports Illustrated, July 17, 1961
Barney Baker interview
Young, *The Champ Nobody Wanted*, 1963
Nick Tosches, *The Devil and Sonny Liston*, 2000
Don Chargin interview
Philadelphia Inquirer, September 26, 1962
St. Louis Globe-Democrat, February 12, 1953
Boxing Illustrated, September, 1962
Eddie Futch interview
Life Magazine, February, 23, 1962
Sports Illustrated, July 17, 1961
Helen Long interview
Barney Baker interview
Robert F. Kennedy, *The Enemy Within*, 1960
Cavalier, September 1961
Time, September 1, 1958
House of Representative Subcommittee on JFK Assassination, May 23, 1978
Barney Baker interview
Sports Illustrated, July 17, 1961
Lem Banker interview
Young, *The Champ Nobody Wanted*, 1963
Helen Long interview

Truman Gibson interview
Rob Steen, *Sonny Liston–His Life, Strife and the Phantom Punch*, 2003
Morris Shenker interview
San Diego Reader.com
Newsweek, July 22, 1963
Young, *The Champ Nobody Wanted*, 1963
Cavalier, September, 1961
Don Chargin interview

CHAPTER THREE

Saturday Evening Post, September 22, 1962
Cavalier, September, 1961
Chicago Sun-Times, August 14, 1963
FBI Memo
U.S. Senate Hearings, December, 1960
Willie Reddish Jr. interview
Mightygloves.com
Tommy Manning interview
Lewiston Evening Journal, May 21, 1965
The Sunday Herald, April 30, 2000
U.S. Senate Hearings, April, 1964
Schulberg, *Sparring With Hemingway*, 1995
Ira Berkow, *Red, A Biography of Red Smith*, 1987
Nagler, *James Norris and the Decline of Boxing*, 1964
Cavalier, September, 1961
Truman Gibson interview
Eddie Futch interview
Chicago Sun-Times, August 7, 1958
Peter Heller, *In This Corner*, 1973
Miami Herald, March 13, 1961
Willie Reddish Jr. interview
Sports Illustrated, May 26, 1958

St. Louis Globe-Democrat, October 24, 1958
Boxingmemorabilia.com
Thomas Hauser, *Muhammad Ali—His Life and Times*, 1991
ESPN Documentary, 2006
New York Times, September 5, 1999
Don Chargin interview
Miami Herald, April 16, 1959
Chicago Sun-Times, August 14, 1963
Time, April, 1959
Boxing Illustrated, August, 1959
U.S. Senate Hearings, December, 1960
St. Louis Globe-Democrat, August 13, 1959
Sports Illustrated, September 19, 1960
Ernie Terrell interview
Seattle Post-Intelligencer, September 4, 1960
Seattle Post-Intelligencer, September 8, 1960
Ring Magazine, December, 1960
Sports Illustrated, August 29, 1960
Boxing Illustrated, June, 1961
U. S. Senate Hearings, 1960
Playboy, October, 1964
Cavalier Magazine, September, 1961
John Cottrell, *Many of Destiny: The Story of Muhammad Ali*, 1973
CyberBoxingZone
Young, *The Champ Nobody Wanted*, 1963

CHAPTER FOUR

Young, *The Champ Nobody Wanted*, 1963
Jack Olsen Tapes, University of Oregon
Look Magazine, June 5, 1962
New York Times, February 25, 1964
Lewiston Review Journal, May 26, 1965
Boxing Illustrated, June, 1961
Ali, *The Greatest*, 1975
Howard Cosell, *Cosell by Cosell*, 1973
New Yorker, October 6, 1962
Young, *The Champ Nobody Wanted*, 1963
Mee, *Liston & Ali*, 2010
Schulberg, *Sparring With Hemingway*, 1995
Sports Illustrated, May 13, 1968
Ring Magazine, 1961
Kram, *Ghosts of Manila*, 2001
MightyGloves.com, 2007
New York Times, July 24, 1963
Willie Reddish Jr. interview
Angelo Dundee, *I Only Talk Winning*, 1983
Newsday.com, January 31, 2009
Ernie Terrell Interview
New York Times, July 28, 1963
Young, *The Champ Nobody Wanted*, 1963
Lewiston Review Journal, May 22, 1965
Life Magazine, February 23, 1962
Sports Illustrated, September 19, 1960
Sports Illustrated, April 26, 1965
Tosches, *The Devil and Sonny Liston*, 2000
George Foreman, *The Autobiography of George Foreman: By George*, 1995
Time, March 23, 1962
Philadelphia Inquirer/Daily News, March 15, 1989
Heller, *In This Corner*, 1972
Tommy Manning interview
Sports Illustrated, February 14, 1991
Young, *The Champ Nobody Wanted*, 1963

Henry Winston interview
Sports Illustrated, April 26, 1965.
Chicago Tribune, September 20, 1062
MightyGloves.com, 2007
Helen long interview
Esquire, January, 1974
Willie Reddish Jr. interview
Tommy Manning interview
Ernie Terrell interview
Lewiston Review Journal, May 22, 1965
Boston Globe, October 23, 1964
Lem Banker interview
Young, *The Champ Nobody Wanted*, 1963
Sports Illustrated, July 17, 1961
Mee, *Liston & Ali*, 2010
Lewiston Review Journal, May 22, 1965
Sports Illustrated, May 13, 1968
Sports Illustrated, April 26, 1965
Jack Olsen tapes, University of Oregon
Lem Banker interview
Londen Evening News, March 21, 1962
Kram, *Ghosts of Manila*, 2001
Helen Long interview
William Wingate interview
New York Times, May 16, 1965
Sports Illustrated, July, 29, 1963
The Sunday Herald, April 30, 2000
Young, *The Champ Nobody Wanted*, 1963
The *Philadelphia Inquirer*, April 15, 1961
Sports Illustrated, January 20, 1964
U.S. Senate Hearings, April, 1964
Philadelphia Inquirer, May 13, 1961
Sports Illustrated, July 17, 1961
Look Magazine, June 5, 1962
Philadelphia Inquirer, July 15, 1961
Associated Press, April 7, 1961

Willie Reddish Jr. interview
New York Mirror, June 13, 1961
Young, *The Champ Nobody Wanted*, 1963
Denver Post, July 20, 1961
Life Magazine, February 23, 1962
Jimmy Cannon, *Nobody Asked Me, But*, 1978
Las Vegas Sun, January 10, 1971
Esquire, January, 1974
Tosches, *The Devil and Sonny Liston*, 2000
Tommy Manning interview
Henry Page interview
St. Louis Today
Truman Gibson interview
Lem Banker interview
Davey Pearl interview
Ash Resnick interview
Philadelphia Inquirer, July 18, 1961
Philadelphia Inquirer, September 29, 1961
Look Magazine, June 5, 1962
Liberator, February, 1963
Esquire, October, 1962
Philadelphia Inquirer, July 22, 1963
Sports Illustrated, September 11, 1961
Life Magazine, February 23, 1962
Jimmy Jacobs interview
Ring Magazine, February, 1962
Sports Illustrated, February 12. 1962
Mee, *Liston & Ali*, 2010
Jimmy Cannon, *Nobody Asked Me, But*, 1978
Sports Illustrated, February 12, 1962
U.S. Senate Hearings, April, 1964
Nagler, *James Norris and the Decline of Boxing*, 1964
Peter Heller, *Good Intentions—The Mike Tyson Story*, 1990
Look Magazine, June 5, 1962

Sports Illustrated, September, 1962
Boxing Illustrated, October, 1961
Sports Illustrated, August 13, 1962
True Boxing Yearbook, 1964 edition
Ring Magazine, March, 1962
Sports Illustrated, March 5, 1962
Lewiston Review-Journal, May 22, 1965
Saturday Evening Post, September, 1963
Philadelphia Inquirer, July 22, 1963
Steen, *Sonny Liston*, 2003
Melvin Kruelwitch, *Now That You Mention It*, 1973
New York State Athletic Commission Memo, April, 1962
Sports Illustrated, September, 17, 1962
Young, *The Champ Nobody Wanted*, 1963
FBI Memo, May 1, 1962
New York Times, May 2, 1962
Conrad, *Dear Muffo*, 1982

CHAPTER FIVE

Newsweek, May 21, 1962
Willie Reddish Jr. interview
Sports Illustrated, August 6, 1962
Newsweek, May 21, 1962
Life Magazine, February 23, 1962
Lewiston-Review Journal, May 22, 1965
Young, *The Champ Nobody Wanted*, 1963
New Yorker, October 6, 1962
New York Times, February 21, 1964
Liston-Clay, Fight of the Century, 1964
Sports Illustrated, September 17, 1962
Washington Post, September 24, 1962
True Boxing Yearbook, 1964
Life Magazine, February, 23, 1962
Esquire, October, 1962

Sports Illustrated, August 27, 1962
New York Times, November 8, 1964
Saturday Evening Post, September 22, 1962
Jet Magazine, October 17, 1973
Mightygloves.com
Chicago American, September 7, 1962
Newsweek, May 21, 1962
Young, *The Champ Nobody Wanted*, 1963
Washington Post, September 24, 1962
Esquire, February, 1963
Conrad, *Dear Muffo*, 1982
Sports Illustrated, July 29, 1963
The Nugget, Septermber 1962
Miami Herald, February 24, 1960
Don Chargin interview
Ring Lardner, *Ali*, 1974
Sports Illustrated, April 26, 1965
Sports Illustrated, September 24, 1962
Conrad, *Dear Muffo*, 1982
Esquire, February, 1963
Philadelphia Inquirer, September 25, 1962
Sports Illustrated, July 17, 1961
Cannon, *Nobody Asked Me, But*, 1978
Tommy Manning interview
Mickey Duff interview
Ash Resnick interview
Henry Winston interview
Sports Illustrated, August 27, 1962
Conrad, *Dear Muffo*, 1982
Sports Illustrated, November 16, 1964
Chicago American, September 19, 1962
Saturday Evening Post, September 22, 1962
Young, *The Champ Nobody Wanted*, 1963
Newsweek, September 24, 1962
Playboy, February, 1983

The Nation, June 29, 1964
New York Times, September 26, 1962
Jet Magazine, September 26, 1962
Barney Baker interview
Chicago Tribune, September 25, 1962
Ring Magazine, October, 1962
Joseph Casciato interview
Saturday Evening Post, August, 1963
Stephen J. Dubner, New York Times blog
Doc Young, *The Champ Nobody Wanted,* 1963
Washington Post, September 26, 1962
Jet Magazine, October 3, 1962
Esquire, February, 1963
Sports Illustrated, October 8, 1962
Time, October 5, 1962
New York Post, September 26, 1962
ESPN Sport Century 2001
Washington Post, September 27, 1962
Washington Post, September 26, 1962
Philadelphia Inquirer, September 26, 1962
Philadelphia Inquirer, September 27, 1962
Miami Herald, February 23, 1964
Young, *The Champ Nobody Wanted,* 1963
New Yorker, October 6, 1962
New York Times, September 27, 1962
Conrad, *Dear Muffo,* 1982
Esquire, February, 1963
Sports Illustrated, September 17, 1962
Jet Magazine, October 3, 1962
Saturday Evening Post, August, 1963
Sunday Mirror, September 1, 1963
Philadelphia Inquirer, September 26, 1962
Philadelphia Inquirer, September 28, 1962

New York Times, September 26, 1962
Philadelphia Inquirer/Daily News, March 15, 1989
ESPN Documentary
Philadelphia Inquirer, September 27, 1962
Willie Reddish Jr. interview

CHAPTER SIX

Liberator, March, 1963
Sports Illustrated, March 25, 1963
Saturday Evening Post, August, 1963
Life Magazine, October 2, 1962
Denver Post, November 20, 1962
Liberator, March, 1963
Jet Magazine, November, 1962
California State Athletic Commission Memo, December 3, 1962
Chicago Daily News, December 5, 1962
Sports Illustrated, July 29, 1963
Willie Reddish Jr. interview
Life Magazine, February, 23, 1962
Ring Magazine, February, 1963
Washington Post, October 5, 1962
Saturday Evening Post, August, 1963
U.S. Senate Hearings, April, 1964
Time, March 22, 1963
True Boxing Yearbook, 1964
Liston-Clay—Fight of the Century, 1964
Sports Illustrated, March 23, 1963
Miami Herald, March 21, 1963
Sports Illustrated, May 26, 1965
Dana Resnick Gentry interview
Marilyn Resnick interview
Jet Magazine, June 7, 1979
Ash Resnick interview
Newsweek, July 22, 1963

Boxing Illustrated, February, 1963
Esquire, August 10, 1963
Ali, *The Greatest*, 1975
New York Times, July 22, 1963
New York Times, July 21, 1963
Schulberg, *Sparring With Hemingway*, 1995
Lem Banker interview
Time, August 2, 1963
Esquire, August 18, 1963
Denver Post, July 23, 1963
True Magazine Boxing Yearbook, 1964
Newsweek, August 5, 1963
Time, August 2, 1963
Denver Post, July 25, 1963
Sacramento Bee, July 25, 1963
Washington Post, July 19, 1963
Gay Talese, *The Overreachers*, 1965
New York Times, July 25, 1963
Sports Illustrated, July 29, 1963
Philadelphia Inquirer, July 24, 1963
Newsday.com
Mee, *Liston & Ali*, 2010
True Boxing Yearbook, 1964
Jim Murray, *An Autobiography*, 1993
U.S. Senate Hearings, April, 1964
Sports Illustrated, January, 1964
True Boxing Yearbook, 1964
Ayteo and Dennis, *The Holy Warrior*, 1975
Jose Torres, *Sting Like a Bee: The Muhammad Ali Story*, 1971
FBI Memo, August 20, 1963
Steen, *Sonny Liston*, 2003
Ring Magazine, November, 1963
The Sunday Herald, April 30, 2000
Boxing Illustrated, December, 1963
Associated Press, September 20, 1963
Denver Post, September 18, 1963
Steen, *Sonny Liston*, 2003

Sacramento Bee, September 19, 1963
Denver Post, September 18, 1963
FBI Memo, September 19, 1963
Associated Press, September 29, 1963
Denver Post, October 3, 1963
Remnick, *King of the World*, 1998
LA Times, November 3, 1963
Vanity Fair, January, 2007
Carl Fischer, Photo Shoot Notes, August, 22, 1963
Carol Polsgrove, *Esquire in the '60s*, 1995
George Lois with Bill Pitts, *George Be Careful*, 1972
Newsweek, December 16, 1963

CHAPTER SEVEN

Time, March 22, 1963
Kram, *Ghosts of Manila*, 2001
Jack Olsen, *Black is Best*, 1967
Playboy, October, 1964
Sports Illustrated, May 13, 1968
Gene Kilroy interview
Sports Illustrated, February 26, 1962
New York Daily News, January 1, 1997
Sports Illustrated, February 24, 1964
Time, August 2, 1963
LA Times, November 5, 1963
Newsweek, May 21, 1962
Sport Magazine, July, 1964
Boston Globe, September 14, 1964
Kram, *Ghosts of Manila*, 2001
The Sweet Science, July 9, 2008
Kram, *Ghosts of Manila*, 2001
Ali, *The Greatest*, 1975
Playboy, October, 1964
Miami Herald, February 20, 1964
Sports Illustrated, March 25, 1963
Ayteo and Dennis, *The Holy Warrior*, 1975

Boston Globe, September 13, 1964
Sport Magazine, July, 1964
New York Times, February 24, 1964
Denver Post, November 7, 1963
Torres, *Sting Like a Bee*, 1971
True Boxing Yearbook, 1964
Kram, *Ghosts of Manila*, 2001
Sports Illustrated, February 24, 1964
Miami Herald, February 16, 1964
Playboy, October, 1964
Eddie Futch interview
Boxing Illustrated, November, 1963
Liston-Clay, Fight of the Century, 1964
U.S. Senate Hearings, April, 1964
Ayteo and Dennis, *The Holy Warrior*, 1975
Kram, *Ghosts of Manila*, 2001
Playboy, October, 1964
Barney Baker interview
Ayteo and Dennis, *The Holy Warrior*, 1975
Denver Post, November 11, 1963
Denver Post, November 6, 1963
Miami Herald, November 6, 1963
New York Times, February 14, 1964
Philadelphia Inquirer, July 24, 1963
LA Herald Examiner, November 6, 1963
LA Times, November 8, 1963
Associated Press, July 23, 1963
Miami Herald, February 9, 1964
U.S. Senate Hearings, April, 1964
Washington Post, July 22, 1963
FBI Memo
Jet Magazine, January 21, 1971
Cannon, *Nobody Asked Me, But*, 1978
Barney Baker interview
Young, *The Champ Nobody Wanted*, 1963
Tommy Manning interview

Davey Pearl interview
Sports Illustrated, April 26, 1965
Cannon, *Nobody Asked Me But*, 1978
Miami Herald, January 30, 1964
Young, *The Champ Nobody Wanted*, 1963
Ash Resnick interview
Barney Baker interview
Look Magazine, February 25, 1964

CHAPTER EIGHT

Miami Herald, January 27, 1964
FBI Memo, August 26, 1963
Jack Olson Tapes, University of Oregon Library
Miami Herald, February 6, 1964
Portland Press Herald, May 25, 1965
Haley, *The Autobiography of Malcolm X*, 1965
Taylor Branch, *Pillar of Fire—America in the King Years*, 1999
Muhammad Ali, *The Greatest*, 1975
Honolulu Advertiser, February 14, 1964
Conrad, *Dear Muffo*, 1982
Elliott J. Gorn, *Muhammad Ali, The People's Champ*, 1998
Jack Olsen, *Black is Best—The Riddle of Cassius Clay*, 1967,
Miami Herald, January 30, 1964
Playboy, October, 1964
Miami Herald, January 27, 1964
Conrad, *Dear Muffo*, 1982
Boston Globe, May 24, 1965
Miami Herald, January 24, 1964
Jet Magazine, February 6, 1964
Mee, *Liston & Ali*, 2010
Miami Herald, January 30, 1964
Miami Herald, February 24, 1964

Steen, *Sonny Liston*, 2003
Kram, *Ghosts of Manila*, 2001
Gene Kilroy interview
Miami Herald, February 8, 1964
Playboy, October, 1964
U.S. Senate Hearings, April, 1964
Miami Herald, February 24, 1964
Ash Resnick interview
Lem Banker, *Lem Banker's Book of Sports Betting*, 1986
Miami Herald, February 20, 1964
Eddie Futch interview
Playboy, October, 1964
Gene Kilroy interview
Esquire, October, 1962
Philadelphia Inquirer, February 25, 1964
Kram, Ghosts of Manila, 2001
U.S. Senate Hearings, 1964
Miami Herald, February 24, 1964
Miami Herald, February 13, 1964
Sports Illustrated, February 24, 1964
New York Times, February 22, 1964
Time, March 6, 1964
Sports Illustrated, February 24, 1964
Boxing Illustrated, August, 1959
New York Times, September 20, 1962
Liston-Clay, Fight of the Century, 1964
Miami Herald, February 23, 1964
Olsen, *Black is Best*, 1967
Time, March 6, 1964
Olsen, *Black is Best*, 1967
Newsweek, March 9, 1964
Ali, *The Greatest*, 1975
Miami Herald, February 26, 1964
Conrad, *Dear Muffo*, 1982
San Francisco Examiner, February 25, 1979
Esquire, October, 1962
Remnick, *King of the World*, 1998

Ferdie Pacheco, *A View From the Corner*, 1992
The Independent, February 25, 1994
Sports Illustrated, August 21, 1967
Miami Herald, February 23, 1964
Newsweek, March 6, 1964
Associated Press, January 16, 2007
Lem Banker interview
Miami Herald, March 10, 1964
Ash Resnick interview
San Francisco Examiner, February, 25, 1979
Jack Olsen tapes, University of Oregon
Rob Steen, *Sonny Liston*, 2003
Miami Herald, February 27, 1964
Kram, *Ghosts of Manila*, 2001
Henry Winston interview
FBI Memo
Barney Baker interview
Ring Magazine, March, 1964
San Francisco Examiner, January 8, 1971
Encyclopedia Britannica
Don Chargin interview
Jimmy Jacobs interview
Ash Resnick interview
Playboy, October, 1964

CHAPTER NINE

Philadelphia Inquirer, February 26, 1964
Miami Herald, February 26, 1964
New York Times, February 24, 1964
New York Times, February 25, 1964
Newsweek, March 9, 1964
Steen, *Sonny Liston*, 2003
Time, March 6, 1964
Olsen, *Black is Best*, 1967

Pacheco, *A View From the Corner*, 1992
Gene Kilroy interview
Ali, *The Greatest*, 1975
Haley, *The Autobiography of Malcolm X*, 1965
Sports Illustrated, August 21, 1967
Kram, *Ghosts of Manila*, 2001
Associated Press, February 26, 1964
Ferdie Pacheco, *The Fight Doctor*, 1978
Playboy, October, 1964
Miami Herald, February 27, 1964
Peter Heller, *In This Corner!*, 1972
Roger Kahn, *A Flame of Pure Fire*, 1999
Sport Magazine, July, 1964
Playboy, October, 1964
Playboy, November, 1975
Time, March 6, 1964
Ernie Terrell interview
Cosell, *Cosell on Cosell*, 1973
Ash Resnick interview
Miami Herald, February 27, 1964
Sports Illustrated, August 21, 1967
Sports Illustrated Annual, 1964
Miami Herald, February 26, 1964
U.S. Senate Hearings, April, 1964
Boston Globe, May 19, 1965
Ali, *The Greatest*, 1975
Associated Press, February 27, 1964
Pacheco, *The Fight Doctor*, 1978
Playboy, October, 1964
San Francisco Examiner, February 25, 1979
Angelo Dundee, *I Only Talk Winning*, 1983
Liston-Clay fight telecast, February 25, 1964
Miami Herald, February 27, 1964
Miami Herald, February 26, 1964
Sports Illustrated, March 9, 1964
Associated Press, February 27, 1964
San Francisco Examiner, February 25, 1979
Remnick, *King of the World*, 1998
Branch, *Pillar of Fire*, 1999
FBI Memo, February 25, 1964
Ash Resnick interview
Dana Resnick Gentry interview
Marilyn Resnick interview
Miami Herald, March 10, 1964
Conrad, *Dear Muffo*, 1982
Mee, *Liston & Ali*, 2010
Ash Resnick interview
Associated Press, February 27, 1964
Miami Herald, February 26, 1964
Boston Globe, May 26, 1965
Miami Herald, February 27, 1964
Sports Illustrated, March 6, 1964
Newsweek, March 9, 1964
Philadelphia Inquirer, July 23, 1963
Denver Post, February 27, 1964

CHAPTER TEN

Willie Reddish Jr. interview
Denver Post, February 28, 1964
New York Times, February 28, 1964
Sports Illustrated, November 13, 1964
Miami Herald, February 27, 1964
Ring Magazine, August, 1964
Boston Globe, September 13, 1964
Miami Herald, February 26, 1964
Sports Illustrated, September 7, 1964
Newsweek, March 23, 1964
Miami Herald, March 5, 1964
Denver Post, February 28, 1964
Time, March 20, 1964
Sports Illustrated, March 23, 1964
Newsweek, March 23, 1964

262: NOTES

Denver Post, March 11, 1964
Miami Herald, March 24, 1964
Ash Resnick interview
Lem Banker interview
U.S. Senate Hearings, April, 1964
Time, April 10, 1964
Miami Herald, February 29, 1964
Sports Illustrated, September 7, 1964
Ash Resnick interview
ABC Wide World of Sports, April, 1964
Associated Press, April 7, 1964
Boston Globe, September 17, 1964
Ash Resnick interview
Boston Globe, September 15, 1964
Playboy, October, 1964
Sport Magazine, July, 1964
Sports Illustrated, April 26, 1965
Sports Illustrated, September 16, 1964
New York Times, November 8, 1964
Jack Olsen Tapes, University of Oregon
Sports Illustrated, November 16, 1964
Sports Illustrated, September 16, 1964
Boston Globe, November 10, 1964
Boston Globe, November 1, 1964
Ring Magazine, September, 1964
Sports Illustrated, November 2, 1964
Boston Globe, September 12, 1964
Sports Illustrated, November 16, 1964
Boston Globe, February 27, 1964
Boston Globe, November 14, 1964
Time, November 19, 1964
United Press International, November 13, 1964
Sports Illustrated, May 24, 1965
Boston Globe, March 23, 1965
Boston Globe, October 30, 1964
Boston Globe, November 12, 1964
Time, November 13, 1964
Mee, *Liston & Ali*, 2010

Boston Globe, October 11, 1964
Playboy, October, 1964
Sports Illustrated, November 16, 1964
Boston Globe, March 19, 1965
Sports Illustrated, May 24, 1965
Boston Globe, November 10, 1964
Boston Globe, November 12, 1964
Boston Globe, November 11, 1964
Boston Globe, November 16, 1964
Time, November 13, 1964
Boston Globe, October 29, 1964
Time, October 29, 1964
Sports Illustrated, November 14, 1964
New York Times, November 15, 1964
Sports Illustrated, November 23, 1964
Boston Globe, November 14, 1964
Denver Post, December 26, 1964
Denver Post, January 31, 1965
Sports Illustrated, April 26, 1965
Jack Olsen Tapes, University of Oregon
Sports Illustrated, February 14, 1991
Sports Illustrated, April 26, 1965

CHAPTER ELEVEN

Boston Globe, May 2, 1965
Boston Globe, May 3, 1965
Boston Globe, May 5, 1965
Boston Globe, May 4, 1965
Boston Globe, May 11, 1965
Boston Globe, May 6, 1965
Newsweek, June 7, 1965
Lewiston Review-Journal, May 10, 1965
SunJournal.com, May 22. 2005
New York Times, May 25, 1965
Yankee Magazine Archive
Boston Globe, May 12, 1965
Associated Press, May 11, 1965
Wikipedia

Boston Globe, May 10, 1965
New York Times, May 25, 1965
Ring Magazine, July, 1965
Sports Illustrated, May 24, 1965
Remnick, *King of the World*, 1998
Boston Globe, May 13, 1965
SunJournal.com, May 22, 2005
Lewiston Review-Journal, May 20, 1965
Lewiston Review-Journal, May 23, 1965
Boston Globe, May 23, 1965
Boston Globe, May 5, 1965
Philadelphia Inquirer, May 24, 1965
Boston Globe, May 6, 1965
Tony Davi interview
Ali, *The Greatest*, 1998
New York Times, May 23, 1965
Boston Globe, May 24, 1965
Boston Globe, May 23, 1965
Yankee Magazine Archive
Kram, *Ghosts of Manila*, 2001
SunJournal.com, May 22, 2005
Denver Post, May 22, 1965
New York Times, May 24, 1965
New York Times, May 25, 1965
New York Times, May 23, 1965
Ali, *The Greatest*, 2001
HBO Special, 1999
Boston Globe, October 27, 1964
Houston Post, March 18, 1960
New York Times, May 23, 1965
New York Times, May 25, 1965
Lem Banker interview
Yankee Magazine Archive
Boston Globe, May 23, 1965
Ash Resnick interview
Dana Resnick Gentry interview
New York Times, May 23, 1965
Ring Magazine, July, 1965
Ring Magazine, June 1965
New York Times, May 25, 1965

Lewiston Evening-Journal, May 28, 1965
Boston Globe, May 25, 1965
Tony Davi interview
Boston Globe, May 26, 1965
New York Times, May 25, 1965
Yankee Magazine Archive
Time, June 4, 1965
New York Times, May 21, 1965
Boston Globe, May 26, 1965
New York Times, May 26, 1965
New York Times, May 29, 1965
Ring Magazine, July, 1965
Ash Resnick interview
CBSSports.com, October 31, 2007
Marilyn Resnick interview
Ali, *The Greatest*, 1975
Sports Illustrated, June 4, 1965
Time, June 4, 1965
Yankee Magazine Archive
Cosell, *Cosell on Cosell*, 1973
New York Times, May 26, 1965
Ring Magazine, July, 1965
Jack Olsen Tapes, University of Oregon
Lewiston Evening-Journal, May 26, 1965
Lewiston Evening-Journal, May 28, 1965
Sports Illustrated, October 8, 1962
Floyd Patterson interview
Eddie Futch interview
Kram, *Ghosts of Manila*, 2001
Time, June 4, 1965
New York Times, May 27, 1965
Time, June 4, 1965
Mee, *Liston & Ali*, 2010
Boston Globe, May 28, 1965
Boston Globe, May 29, 1965
Lem Banker interview

264: NOTES

Ash Resnick interview
Barney Baker interview
Lewiston Evening Journal, May 28, 1965
Morris Shenker interview
Barney Baker interview
Ali, *The Greatest*, 1975
Sports Illustrated, February 14, 1991
Tosches, *The Devil and Sonny Liston*, 2000
Marilyn Resnick interview
Paul Abdoo Jr. interview
Tony Davi interview
Gary Bates interview
Marilyn Resnick interview
Kram, *Ghosts of Manila*, 2001
Helen Long interview
New York Times, May 27, 1965
Time, June 4, 1965
U.S. Senate Hearings, June, 1965
FBI Memo
Denver Post, May 27, 1965
Jack Olsen Tapes, University of Oregon
Sports Illustrated, May 13, 1968
Ring Magazine, July, 1965
New York Times, May 27, 1965
Boston Globe, May 27, 1965
Newsweek, June 7, 1965
Time, June 4, 1965
Yankee Magazine, May, 1979
Sports Illustrated, June 4, 1965
New York Times, May 26, 1965
Lewiston Review Journal, May 26, 1965
ABC's *Wide World of Sports*, June, 1965
Jack Olsen Tapes, University of Oregon
U.S. Senate Hearings, June, 1965
Liston/Intercontimental Promotions Lawsuit Documents
Kram, *Ghosts of Manila*, 2001

CHAPTER TWELVE

Reid/Demaris, *Green Felt Jungle*, 1963
Marilyn Resnick interview
Sports Illustrated, May 13, 1968
Jack Olsen Tapes, University of Oregon
Lem Banker interview
Ash Resnick interview
Gary Bates interview
Davey Pearl interview
Lem Banker interview
Sports Illustrated, May 13, 1968
Willie Reddish Jr. interview
Gary Bates interview
Marilyn Resnick interview
Ash Resnick interview
California State Athletic Commission files
Jack Olsen Tapes, University of Oregon
Wikipedia
Lem Banker interview
Gary Bates interview
Henry Winston interview
California State Athletic Commission files
New York State Athletic Commission files
Davey Pearl interview
Foreman, *By George*, 1995
Sports Illustrated, July 15, 1968
World Boxing, December, 1968
International Boxing, May, 1969
Henry Winston interview
Joe Frazier interview
Don Chargin interview
Lem Banker interview

Ash Resnick interview
Foreman, *By George*, 1995
Davey Pearl interview
Chicago Tribune, September 20, 1962
Banker, *Lem Banker's Book of Sports Betting*, 1986
LA Times, February 22, 1989
Lem Banker interview
Davey Pearl interview

CHAPTER THIRTEEN

Playboy, February, 1983
Conrad, *Dear Muffo*, 1982
Il Duce, *Eastside Boxing*
Sports Illustrated, May 13, 1968
Davey Pearl interview
Las Vegas Review Journal, January 7, 1971
Reid/Demaris, *Green Felt Jungle*, 1963
Lem Banker interview
Ash Resnick interview
Gary Bates interview
Esquire, January, 1974
Sports Illustrated, February 14, 1991
Barney Baker interview
Gary Bates interview
Lem Banker interview
Tony Davi interview
Dennis Caputo Interview
Conrad, *Dear Muffo*, 1982
Philadelphia Inquirer/Daily News, March 13, 1989
Esquire, January, 1974
Lem Banker interview
Eddie Futch interview
Davey Pearl interview
Tosches, *The Devil and Sonny Liston*, 2000
Philadelphia Inquirer/Daily News, February 22, 1989

Willie Reddish Jr. interview
LA Times, February 22, 1989
Henry Winston interview
Ash Resnick interview
HBO Special, 2000
Lem Banker interview
Davey Pearl interview
Ali, *The Greatest*, 1975
Willie Reddish Jr. interview
Tommy Manning interview
Philadelphia Inquirer/Daily News, March 13, 1989
Sports Illustrated, February 14, 1991
HBO Documentary
Dana Resnick Gentry interview
Banker, *Lem Banker Book of Sports Betting*, 1986
Las Vegas Review Journal, January 7, 1971
Las Vegas Sun, January 10, 1971
Sports Illustrated, February 14, 1991
Helen Long interview
Marilyn Resnick interview
AroundMaine.com, 2002
Las Vegas Sun, February 19, 2008

EPILOGUE

Helen Long interview
Sports Illustrated, February 14, 1991
Lee Page interview
Philadelphia Inquirer, January 8, 1971
Kruelwitch, *Now That You Mention It*, 1973
Cyber Boxing Zone Bulletin Board, March 27, 2006
Robert Lipsyte, *Sportsworld*, 1975
Life, January 19, 2010
Playboy, November, 1975

INDEX

Abdoo, Paul Jr., 214
Abdoo, Paul, 9, 214,
Akins, Virgil, 22, 34
Ali, Muhammad (see also Cassius Clay), ix, xi, 3, 6, 11, 23, 31, 36, 40, 85, 99, 101, 109, 118-126, 130, 137, 139-141, 143, 144, 146, 148, 149, 152, 153, 156, 157, 159-161, 166, 169, 174, 175, 177-188, 192-196, 198-200, 202-214, 216-218, 223-231, 233, 236, 242, 244, 246-250
Ali, Sonji, ix
Allah, 149, 160, 199
American Veteran Boxers' Association, 56
Anastasia, Albert, 21
Anderson, Tony, 15, 22
Anselmo, Vince, 100, 237
Arcel, Ray, 23
Armstrong, Henry, 149
Arum, Bob, 19, 239
Associated Press, 3, 57, 110, 128
Astor, Gerald, 136
Avena, Sal, 72, 175, 176
Baer, Max, 35, 150
Bailey, Dave, 165
Bailey, Milt, 136
Baker, Robert "Barney", 6, 22, 26, 29, 31, 34, 38, 81, 130, 135, 136, 150, 154, 155, 160, 165, 209, 212, 213, 233, 238
Baldwin, James, 51, 76, 81
Banker, Lem, 54, 62, 154, 174, 212, 222, 224, 227, 231, 234, 236-239, 241, 243-247
Barbee, Bobbie, 87
Barone, Pep, 31, 42, 58
Barr, Beverly, 183

Bates, Gary, 3, 6, 10, 214, 223, 227, 237, 238, 246
Beck, Dave, 27
Bennett, Dr., 154, 168, 169
Bentley, Ben, 53, 54, 109, 238
Bethea, Wayne, 5, 35, 37, 128
Big Brothers, 93, 94, 134
Big Red, 130, 144, 148, 192
Bimstein, Whitey, 149
Bingham, Howard, 130, 144, 246
Bingham, Worth, 140
Black, Charlie, 66
Black, Julian, 7
Bolan, Al, 202
Bolt, Usain, x
Boyle, Robert H., 79, 84, 97, 104, 179, 217
Braddock, Jimmy, 11, 84, 91
Braverman, Al, 9, 182
Brenner, Teddy, 151, 206
Breslin, Jimmy, 5, 31, 34, 87, 211
Brinkley, David, 125
Briscoe, Tommy, 24
Brooks, Fred, ix, 187, 193, 217
Brown, Drew "Bundini", 140, 151, 162, 164, 185, 202
Brown, Joe E., 160
Brown, Ned, 37
Brundage, Avery, 67
Buchalter, Louis "Lepke", 18
Buckley, William F., 81
Bunche, Dr. Ralph, 76
Burnes, Bob, 15, 24
Burns, Tommy, 42
Byrne, Garrett, 192, 193, 217
Cady, Steve, 200
Caesars Palace, 98, 99, 240
California State Athletic Commission, 48, 91

Calley, William Jr., 113
Cannon, Jimmy, 4, 135, 147, 148, 171, 200
Capote, Truman, 81
Caputo, Dennis, 240
Carbo, Frankie, 17-19, 21, 26, 29, 31, 33, 34, 42, 43, 45, 58, 66, 174, 176, 228
Carnera, Primo, 150
Carter, Rubin "Hurricane", 9, 10
Casciato, Dr. Nicholas, 82
Cassidy, Bobby, 51
Cayton, Bill, 164
CBS, 21
Certo, Al, 19
Chamberlain, Wilt, 55, 227, 245
Chapman, James, 30
Chargin, Don, 7, 10, 23, 30, 36, 77, 156, 231
Charles, Ezzard, 17
Charles, Ray, 75
Cherry, Garland, 95, 108, 128, 133, 175-177
Chicago Tribune, 232
Chuvalo, George, 109, 128, 236
Clark, Barbara, 223
Clark, Henry, 223, 230, 240
Clay, Cassius Sr., 117
Clay, Cassius, ix, 9, 45, 46, 81, 85, 90, 94-97, 99-101, 103-108, 117-132, 138-156, 158-167, 170, 172, 174, 175, 177, 179-186, 190, 191, 203, 207-210, 215, 217, 225, 227, 230, 235, 248, 249
Clay, Odessa, 117, 118
Clay, Rudolph, 117, 159
Clifford, Kent, 244
Cohen, Mickey, 18
Collins, Bud, 9, 216
Condon, David, 232
Congress on Racial Equality, 158
Conn, Billy, 23, 126, 127, 145
Conrad, Harold, 10, 14, 69, 71, 75, 77, 79, 85, 86, 140-142, 152, 168, 187, 190, 227, 235, 236, 241, Cooper, Bert, 56
Cooper, Henry, 105, 106, 109, 127, 145, 146, 184, 210
Cooper, Isaac, 60
Cosell, Howard, 36, 103, 155, 163, 184, 200, 208, 227, 232
Cox, Foneda, 61, 92, 110, 136
Currigan, Mayor Tom, 105
Curtis, Joey, 6, 56
D'Amato, Cus, 3, 45-47, 58, 63-66, 68, 77, 78, 82, 86, 90, 105, 150, 184
Daley, Arthur, 51, 147, 148, 151, 171, 216
Daley, Mayor Richard J., 71
Daniel, Dan, 50
Daniels, Billy, 184
Daniels, Terry, 109
Dardis, Martin, 244
Davi, Tony, 198, 214, 239
Davidson, Gordon, 48, 51, 60, 107, 108, 128, 129, 135, 167, 177
Davidson, Skinny, 48, 51, 60, 135
Davis, Sammy Jr., 221, 229, 245
DeJohn, Mike, 36, 39, 128
Dempsey, Jack, 19, 20, 67, 90, 96, 109, 125, 143, 156, 161, 211
Dempsey's Restaurant, 18, 19, 46
Denver Post, 6, 111, 171, 173
Dirksen, Senator Everett, 44
Doherty, Captain John, 28, 38
Duff, Mickey, ix, 55, 78, 109, 233
Dundee, Angelo, ix, 4, 5, 9, 10, 40, 45, 51, 81, 96, 98, 103, 106, 107, 122, 126, 127, 133, 139, 140, 147, 149, 152, 153, 159, 162-167, 177, 185,

187, 195, 196, 199, 201, 207, 230, 248
Dundee, Chris, 45, 133, 140, 177
Dunes Hotel, 29, 98, 100, 186
Durslag, Mel, 217
East St. Louis Journal, 155
Eisenhower, Dwight, 17, 44
Elbaum, Don, 10
Ellis, Delores, 60, 62
Ellis, Jimmy, 165, 200, 230
ESPN, 36, 56, 244, 249, 256, 262, 277
Esquire, 3, 53, 111-113, 152, 241
Evangelista, Alfredo, 109
Eveland, Sam, 15
Fabroski, Rick, 246
Fairmount Park, 60, 92
Falk, Harry, 67
Farr, Tommy, 109
Farrand, Joseph, 198, 205
Farrar, Harry, 171
Faversham, William, 106, 107, 128, 129, 151, 205
FBI, 18, 31, 58, 70, 108, 110, 134, 138, 139, 155, 158, 167, 174, 198, 215
Feldman, Saul, 196, 197
Feldman, Tudi, 197
Felix, Barney, 154, 160, 165-167, 209, 233
Fels, Jon, 15
Fenn, Al, 47
Fetchit, Stepin, 209
Fischer, Carl, 111, 112, 264
Fleischer, Nat, 41, 65, 68, 69, 93, 104, 105, 204, 206, 208, 231
Floyd, Pretty Boy, 13
Folley, Zora, 5, 6, 40, 46, 60, 90, 107, 140, 147, 165, 170, 218
Foreman, George, x, 4, 6-8, 23, 36, 52, 59, 63, 106, 109, 111, 112, 120, 121, 128, 131, 143, 157, 161, 172, 228-232, 236
Forrest City, Arkansas, 11
Foster, Mac, 234, 236
Fowler, Chris, 249
Fox, Billy, 19
Foxx, Redd, 237
Frazier, Joe, 109, 156, 230, 242
Friedman, Bruce Jay, 54, 241, 242
Futch, Eddie, 23, 34, 126, 127, 145, 210, 242
Galento, "Two Ton" Tony, 18
Gandy, Larry, 244
Gentry, Dana Resnick, 100, 112, 168, 202, 244
George, Gorgeous, 63, 120, 131
Gerstein, Richard, 172
Gibson, Truman, 19-21, 29, 34, 35, 42, 62, 81
Gillette, 21
Gleason, Jackie, 160, 185
Gold, Judge Joseph E., 62
Goldstein, Ruby, 97, 205, 209
Gonzales, Joe, 15
Goulet, Robert, 205-207, 224
Graham, Jim, 6, 58, 111
Graziano, Rocky, 6
Greb, Mel, 55, 120, 222, 237
Green, Detective Bob, 28
Green, Ed, 184
Greene, Shecky, 102
Gregory, Dick, 67
Gross, Milton, 151
Gutteridge, Reg, 50
Hamill, Pete, 174
Hamilton Court Hotel, 33
Harlow, 190
Harris, Ossie "Bulldog", 19
Harris, Roy, 19, 40, 47, 66, 235
Harrison, Monroe, 7, 15, 22, 24
Hart, Senator Philip, 174

Hauser, Thomas, 36
Hayes, Harold, 111
Heeney, Tom, 109
Heinz, W.C., 249
Henie, Sonia, 20
Hoffa, Jimmy, 27, 29
Holmes, Larry, xi, 109, 157
Hoover, J. Edgar, 42, 70, 108, 134, 174, 215
Hopkins, Fannie Mae, 25
Hunt, Jim, 211
Illinois Boxing Commission, 81
Inter-Continental Promotions (ICP), 94, 95, 107, 133, 176, 177, 218
International Boxing Club (IBC), 21, 34, 35, 42, 62, 65, 66, 132
Islam, 122, 138, 139, 141, 142, 148, 153, 175, 178, 198, 200, 213
Izenberg, Jerry, 105
Jackson, Tommy "Hurricane", 47, 109
Jacobs, Jimmy, 64, 124, 126, 156
Jamal, Ahmad, 92
Jefferson City Prison, 3, 13, 14, 134, 136, 196, 242, 247
Jeffries, James, 226
Jet Magazine, 43, 87, 91, 99, 134
Johansson, Ingemar, 39, 45, 47, 66, 67, 84, 94, 100, 105, 109
Johnson, Harold, 48, 94, 96, 140
Johnson, Jack, xi, 42, 50, 62, 76, 91, 94, 96, 108, 109, 129, 134, 140, 147, 209, 213
Joiner, Billy, 230
Jones, Leroi, 81
Jordan, Don, 34, 58
Kaplan, Hank, 154
Katz, George, 59, 64, 65, 106, 172
Kearns, Doc, 19
Keating, Senator, 174
Keenan, Peter Jr., 33, 57, 137, 213, 245

Keenan, Peter, 109
Kefauver, Senator Estes, 14, 44, 134
Kempton, Murray, 87, 152
Kennedy, President, 68, 93, 98, 170
Kennedy, Robert, 27, 51, 55, 56, 68, 82, 88, 91, 93, 98, 100, 111, 170, 213, 214, 248
Kerkorian, Kirk, 222, 248
Kilroy, Dan, 48
Kilroy, Gene, 119, 143, 146, 159
King, Don, 19, 239
King, Martin Luther Jr., 13, 76, 77, 109, 227
King, Teddy, 74, 92, 173, 181, 206
Klein, Alfred, 60, 68
Klein, Morris, 152, 169
Knox, Ernie, 128
Knuttsson, Bertel, 224
Kossman, Jacob, 43
Kram, Mark, 50, 81, 123, 143, 155, 181, 182, 199, 210, 214, 217, 218, 235
Kristofferson, Kris, 146
Kruelwitch, Melvin, 69, 248
L.A. Herald-Examiner, 217
L.A. Times, 106
LaFontaine, Barbara, 98, 190, 191
Lamb, Sheriff Ralph, 3, 241
LaMotta, Jake, 19, 147
Lansky, Meyer, 18, 26, 29, 174
Larson, Charles, 46
Las Vegas Convention Center, 102
Lassman, Ed, 52, 178
LaStarza, Roland, 109
Lauer, Matt, ix
Lavorante, Alejandro, 81, 128
Lawrence, Carol, 206
Lawrence, Ronald, 29
Laxalt, Senator Paul, 20
Leifer, Neil, x, 213, 249

Lennon, Jimmy, 229
Lennon, John, 142
Leonard, Benny, 23
Levinsky, Kingfish, 159
Lewiston, Maine, x, 185, 194, 198-200, 205, 210, 211, 214-217, 222, 224-226, 229, 242, 244, 249,
Liberator, 91, 92
Liebling, A.J., 79, 85
Life Magazine, 29, 82, 249
Lincoln, Amos, 28, 84, 93, 128, 184, 191, 192, 194, 202, 212
Lipsyte, Robert, 8, 160, 199, 205, 211, 249
Liston, Alcora, 25, 37, 56, 215
Liston, Arletha, 136
Liston, Eleanor "Choo Choo", 26, 136
Liston, Geraldine, x, 9, 28, 29, 33, 52-55, 57, 61, 68, 70, 72, 74, 78, 92, 98, 105, 110, 131, 133, 138, 152, 154, 168, 171, 177, 182, 187, 189, 191, 195, 211, 213, 214, 216, 222, 223, 225-227, 229, 232, 234, 236-241, 243, 245-247, 250
Liston, Helen, 3, 11-13, 85, 104, 156, 215, 245
Liston, Sonny Jr., 56
Liston, Tobe, 11, 12, 156
Lois, George, 111, 112, 264
London Evening Standard, 109
London, Brian, 47, 66, 109
Long, Helen, x, 25, 26, 28, 30, 54, 56, 247, 248
Look Magazine, 8, 136
Louis, Joe, ix, xi, 4-7, 11-13, 15, 17-20, 22-26, 28-32, 34, 35-40, 43, 44, 46, 55, 58, 60, 63, 73, 74, 76, 78-80, 84, 87, 90, 98-100, 102, 105, 109, 112, 117, 118, 121, 123, 125, 127, 130-132, 134, 136, 142, 144, 145, 153-157, 160, 163, 164, 166, 167, 170, 172, 182, 184, 185, 190, 197, 202, 203, 207-210, 213, 214, 222, 224, 225, 230, 231, 235-240, 242, 243, 245, 247
Louis, Martha Malone, 22, 26, 55, 98, 99, 213
Louisville Sponsoring Group (LSG), 106, 107, 122, 128, 175, 177, 179
Love American Style, 226, 231, 236
Lurie, Art, 5, 179
MacDonald, William B. Jr., 132, 133, 139, 140, 158, 177
Machen, Eddie, 8, 9, 40, 41, 46, 85, 90, 125, 140, 143, 147, 149, 162, 170, 178, 183
Madison Square Garden, 18, 20, 69, 90, 96, 127, 151, 248
Maguire, Monsignor Jack, 15
Mailer, Norman, 7, 9, 76, 81, 85, 151, 200
Manning, Tommy, 32, 33, 53, 54, 61, 78, 135, 243
Marciano, Rocky, xi, 4, 6, 11, 15, 17, 23, 35-37, 47, 58, 67, 82, 99, 100, 104, 107, 109, 111, 127, 150, 156, 163, 203, 211, 226, 231
Margolis, Sam, 15, 31, 33, 67, 72, 85, 176, 177, 179, 188, 193, 194, 197, 206, 211
Markson, Harry, 90, 127
Marshall, Marty, 6, 8, 24, 73, 151
Martin, Joe, 118
Martin, Leotis, 227, 231
McClellan Senate Committee, 27
McClellan, Senator, 176
McDonough, Frank, 208
McKinney, Jack, 32, 53, 75, 87, 88, 241, 243
McLaglen, Victor, 109
McMurray, Bill, 229

McNeeley, Tom, 7, 63
Mederos, Julio, 36
Mello, Patrolman, 28
Mello, Pete, 149
Mercante, Arthur, 209
Merchant, Larry, 87, 248
Miami Herald, 139, 159
Michael, John, 194
Michael, Sam, 194, 198, 206, 225
Mildenberger, Karl, 236
Miske, Billy, 109
Mitchell, Frank, 10, 12, 15, 16, 24, 29-31, 42, 54, 135
Moore, Archie, ix, 11, 15, 17, 19, 35, 40, 47, 81, 94, 95, 100, 101, 119, 120, 122, 123, 126-128, 157, 161, 179, 181, 229, 231, 245
Moore, Davey, 95, 128
Morefield, Bill, 74
Moynihan, Rev. James, 196
Muhammad, Elijah, 139, 148, 149, 180, 198, 199
Muhammad, Herbert, 227
Munson, Raymond, 136
Murder, Inc., 18
Murphy, C.J., 201
Murphy, Father Edward, 9, 51, 52, 60-62, 64, 82, 102, 181, 182, 196, 242, 245
Murray, Jim, 106, 147, 206
Muslims, 138, 139, 148, 166, 187, 198-200, 205, 213, 214, 242, 249
Myer, Georgianna, 55
Nack, William, 9, 238, 243
Nash, Warden E.V., 14, 28, 49
Nation of Islam, 122, 138, 142, 148, 198, 200, 213
National Boxing Association, 39, 45, 68, 179
National Golden Gloves Finals, 23

NBC, 21, 248
New York Boxing Writers' Association, 41
New York Mirror, 60, 258
New York Times, 51, 70, 85, 160, 199
Newfield, Jack, 88, 155
Newsweek, 7, 80, 87, 102, 112, 170, 217
Night Train, 73, 82, 181
Nilon, Bob, 34, 64, 94, 106, 128, 129, 132, 147, 176
Nilon, Jack, x, xi, 19, 20, 27, 32, 37, 42, 49, 50, 53, 55, 57, 58, 62, 64, 65, 67, 74-76, 87, 88, 90, 91, 94, 96, 98, 100, 105, 106, 108, 109, 125, 128, 129, 133, 141, 143-145, 147, 148, 154-156, 161, 164, 167, 169, 176, 177, 189, 196, 209-211, 213, 216, 217, 222, 236, 241, 243, 245
Nilon, Jim, 133
Norris, James, 20, 21, 34, 42
Oates, Joyce Carol, 8
Obama, President, 92
Olsen, Jack, x, 49, 50, 55, 141, 154, 189, 216, 217, 222, 236
On Boxing, 8, 42, 45, 107
Original Celtics, 98
Oswald, Lee Harvey, 27
Ozark AAU Title, 23
Pabst Blue Ribbon, 21
Pacheco, Ferdie, x, 153, 159, 160, 166, 195
Page, Henry, 26, 61, 247
Palermo, Blinky, 17, 19, 21, 29, 31, 33, 34, 38, 42, 43, 45, 58, 65, 66, 176, 228
Paret, Benny (Kid), 76, 128
Parker, Dan, 60, 67
Pastrano, Willie, 35, 127
Patterson, Floyd, ix, 3, 7, 11, 13, 34-

36, 39-42, 45-47, 57-59, 63-70, 76, 77, 80-87, 90, 92-95, 97, 98, 101-105, 109, 110, 121-123, 125, 126, 129, 132, 133, 154, 156, 170, 172, 181, 186, 198, 203, 210, 211, 218, 224, 230, 236
Patterson, Mrs. Annabelle, 81
Peabody, Governor Endicott, 179
Pearl, Davey, 7, 62, 74, 135, 223, 224, 229, 232, 234, 236, 237, 242, 243, 245, 247
Pearson, Drew, 93, 134
Pennsylvania State Athletic Commission, 50, 59, 132
Pep, Willie, 82, 161
Philadelphia Inquirer, 88, 248
Pian, Charles, 30
Pirolli, Archie, 74, 77, 181, 183
Playboy, 125, 249
Poiry, Bernard, 14
Poland Spring Inn, 196
Police Athletic League, 35
Polino, Joe, 74, 78, 79, 136, 164, 165, 182, 197, 202, 213, 225
Pope, Edwin, 159
Povich, Shirley, 8, 147
Powell, Adam Clayton, 67
Powell, Charlie, 127, 153
Quinn, Patsy, 33
Rademacher, Pete, 47
Ragni, Dr. Nick, 242
Ramos, Sugar, 95
Ray, James Earl, 13
Reagan, President Ronald, 20
Reddish, Willie, 5, 18, 19, 32, 35, 36, 41, 51, 53, 54, 63, 72-74, 77, 88, 92, 93, 101, 103, 135, 141, 150, 152, 160, 161, 166, 167, 171, 177, 181, 182, 187, 206, 208, 211, 225, 243
Reddish, Willie Jr., 19, 32, 51, 54, 72,

88, 92, 171, 243
Reed, Governor John, 194, 207, 217
Reid, Senator Harry, 223
Resnick, Ash, 7, 62, 78, 98-100, 112, 136, 145, 154, 156, 163, 168, 173, 174, 178, 179, 181, 202, 206, 212, 214, 222-224, 231, 232, 236, 237, 240, 243, 244
Resnick, Marilyn, 168, 206, 213, 214, 222, 246
Richardson, Nat, 225
Richardson, Willie, 184, 195
Rickey, Branch, 67
Riger, Robert, 3
Ring Magazine, 7, 18, 37, 41, 50, 65, 66, 93, 105, 171, 202, 204, 206, 216, 231, 236
Riviera Health Club, 154
Robbins, Dr. Alexander, 151, 152, 168, 169
Robinson, Jackie, 67
Robinson, Slim Jim, 210, 225
Robinson, Sugar Ray, 18, 58, 97, 99, 126, 147, 151, 156, 157, 199
Rockefeller, Governor Nelson, 70
Rogin, Gilbert, ix, 8, 163, 185, 217
Rolling Stone, 252
Roman, Jose, 109
Rome Olympics, 99
Rose, Murray, 203
Rosensohn Enterprises, 66
Rosensohn, Bill, 66
Rosenthal, Lefty, 223, 248
Ross, Barney, 150
Ruby, Jack, 27, 97, 205, 209
Russell, Carlos E., 91
Russell, Senator Richard, 175
Ruth, Babe, ix
S&W Foods, 54
Sanders, Ed, 23

Sarkis, Raymond, 25
Sarria, Luis, 159, 160
Saxton, Johnny, 136
Schaap, Dick, 248
Schlattman, Edward, 13
Schmeling, Max, 20, 26, 80, 91
Schoeninger, Ray, 4, 8, 111, 189
Schreiber, Mark, 13
Schulberg, Budd, 18, 50
Scotti, Alfred J., 18
Shabazz, Betty, 148
Shapiro, David, 245
Sharkey, Jack, 196, 210
Sharnik, Mort, 97, 152, 168
Shenker, Morris, 29, 212
Sheridan, Bob, 213
Siegel, Benjamin "Bugsy", 18, 26
Silverman, Sam, 179, 188, 193, 197, 211
Sinatra, Barbara, 99
Sinatra, Frank, 81, 83, 99
Skelton, Ben, 4, 6, 10
Smith, Donald, 189
Smith, Marshall, 8, 73, 80, 87, 93, 189
Smith, Red, 80, 87
Snider, James, 173
Spinks, Leon, 146, 157
Spinks, Michael, 198
Sport Magazine, ix
Sporting News, x
Sports Illustrated, x, 8, 9, 36, 41, 49, 67, 68, 73, 92, 96-98, 104, 112, 142, 152, 154, 163, 167, 168, 171, 179, 186, 189, 190, 217, 218, 238, 243, 244
St. Ignatius of Loyola Catholic Church, 61
St. Louis Post-Dispatch, 29
Steinhauser, W.P., 15, 52
Stevens, Father Alois, 3, 14-16, 38, 44, 52, 154, 196
Stevenson, Mildred, 238
Steward, Emanuel, 6
Sullivan, Ed, 111, 142, 245
Summerlin, Johnny, 23
Sutton, Percy, 76
Swift, Bill, 6
Talese, Gay, 9, 21, 104
Tate, Mayor James, 88
Taylor, Phil, 8
Teague, Robert, 85
Teamsters, 6, 26, 27, 29, 212
Terrell, Ernie, 10, 40, 51, 54, 107, 122, 123, 126, 128, 143, 162, 178, 218, 227
The Animals, 8
The Argus, 15
The Beatles, 142
The Bitter End, 96
The Champ Nobody Wanted, xi, 49, 72
The Ed Sullivan Show, 142
Time, 13, 37, 101, 184, 204, 210, 217
Thompson, Hunter S., 5
Thunderbird Hotel, 98, 111, 173
Tocco, Johnny 4-6, 22, 198, 214, 232-234, 238, 239, 241-243
Tolson, Clyde, 174
Tomato Red, 96
Torres, Jose, ix, 53
Trampler, Bruce, 239
Tulane, Mike, 154
Tunney, Gene, 109, 156, 196, 211
Turley, Bob, 228
Turner, Gil, 59
Twombly, Wells, 155
Tyson, Mike 6, 10, 23, 63, 76, 80, 156, 157, 164
Udall, Congressman Stuart, 47
Urch, Jack, 91
Urtain, Jose, 236

Vachon, John, 136
Valdes, Nino, 6, 23, 36, 37
Veterans of Foreign Wars, 158
Vitale, John, 24, 25, 31, 38, 39, 42, 43, 45, 214
Walcott, Jersey Joe, 11, 17, 35, 36, 90, 203, 207-210, 224
Warhol, Andy, 226
Washington Post, 70
Weissman, Bernie, 7, 37
Wepner, Chuck, 4, 232, 242
Westphal, Albert, 63, 210
Whitehurst, Bert, 6
Wilkins, Gloria, 55
Willard, Jess, xi, 20, 129, 213
Williams, Cleveland, 4-6, 8, 36, 37, 39, 40, 44, 46, 90, 107, 128, 140, 147, 165, 184, 201, 210, 218
Williams, Lee, 184
Wilson, Jimmy, 35
Wilson, Peter, 87
Wilson, Thurman, 15
Wingate, William, 9, 56, 81, 85, 106, 113, 128, 132, 151, 196, 205, 238, 243
Winston, Henry, 9, 53, 78, 79, 155, 227–229, 231, 243
Wirtz, Willard, 20
Witkin, Mort, 43, 51, 52, 54
Woods, Tiger, x
World Boxing Association (WBA), 46, 52, 60, 178-180, 218
X, Malcolm, 75, 138-141, 148, 153, 160, 167, 198, 199
Young, A.S. "Doc", xi, 49
Young, Jimmy, 157
Zephyr, Richard, 188
Zimmering, Stanley, 181-184
Zwerner, Jack, 57
Zwerner, Mike, 57, 97

PAUL GALLENDER

People who know Paul Gallender say they've never met anyone with a deeper commitment to truth, a bigger heart, or a greater love of dogs and cats. A native Chicagoan who now lives in Denver, Paul spent 35 years in central and northern California raising money for a variety of non-profit organizations. This is his first book. He wrote it for Sonny Liston. *Author photo by Josie Roase.*